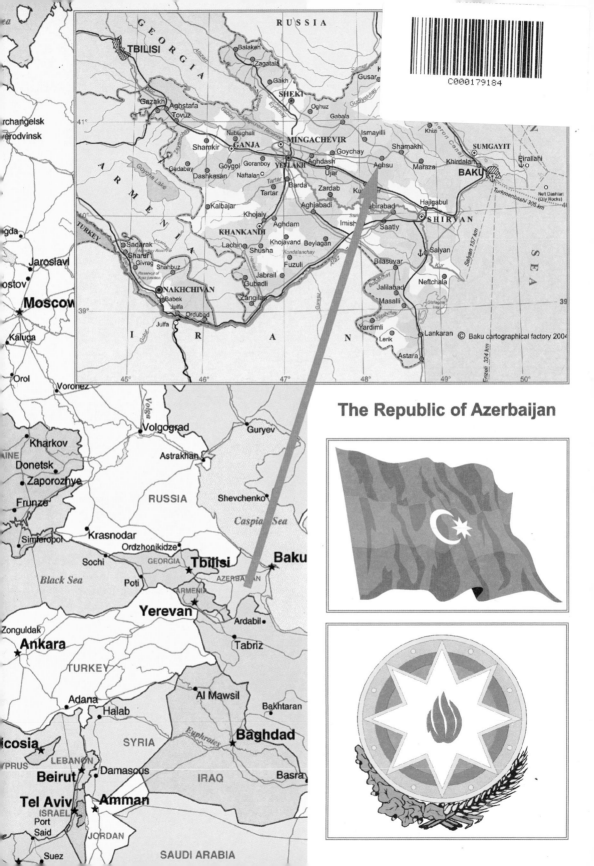

The Republic of Azerbaijan

© Baku cartographical factory 2004

...The Azerbaijanis have always tried to introduce their achievements, their culture, traditions and art to the world. It's essential that we always value intellectual work in Azerbaijan.

...Very few people knew about our country prior to our independence. But even this legal, political act has not made Azerbaijan known around the world as much as we would have desired. For this to happen, we must work consistently and tirelessly. We must work in all spheres. Our statesmen, public and private organizations, cultural workers, scientists - all of us - must make Azerbaijan known to the world. We must speak about the just cause of Azerbaijan in every corner of the globe. It is especially important these days because Armenia has encroached on our territory.

Heydar Aliyev
President of the Republic of Azerbaijan
22 November, 1997

AZERBAIJAN

100 Questions Answered

BAKU - 2008

The project's authors: The European Azerbaijan Society
The Anglo - Azerbaijani Youth Society

Editors: Tale Heydarov and Taleh Bagiyev

Researched and written by:

Tale Heydarov
Taleh Bagiyev
Jeyhun Novruzov
Vusala Zahirova
Akif Maharramzadeh
Rovshan Didavari

The authors are grateful to the Ministry of Foreign Affaires and National Academy of Sciences of Azerbaijan (ANAS) for their recommendations and advice about the book.

The authors are grateful for the help of the following individuals and organisations in providing information and support for this publication:

Anne Thompson, editor and writer on Caucasian affairs
Thomas Goltz, professor, University of Montana
The late Susan Crouch MBE, chairman of the Caspian Events Limited
Robin Bennett OBE, ex-chairman of the British Business Group
Sevinc Asadova, Public and Press Affairs Officer of the British Embassy in Baku
Subi Kagramanzadeh, head of Information Analytic Department of AzEuroTel
Ilyas Babayev, Correspondent Member of ANAS
Dr. Sanubar Baghirova, UNESCO expert on non-material heritage of humanity
Dr. Mejnun Kerimov, Baku Musical Academy
Fiona Maclachlan, independent researcher
Aydin Kazimzadeh, specialist in cinema study
Alexandre, bishop of Baku and Caspian Eparchy
Semyon Ikhilov, head of Religious Community of Mountain Jews
Ministry of Culture and Tourism
Ministry of Ecology and Natural Resources
Ministry of Youth and Sport
The National Board of Archives
National Olympic Committee
State Committee for the Work with the Religious Associations
State Statistics Committee

Photographers: Babek Quliyev, Husein Huseinzadeh, Ilqar Jafarov, Islam Atakishiyev, Kamal Babayev, Maqsad Guliyev, Oqtay Aydinoghlu, Rafiq Baghirov, Agdes Bagirzadeh

Designed by Fuad Aliyev and Eldar Farzaliyev
Printed in Azerbaijan by CBS

First edition: 2005, second edition: 2006, this expanded and full updated edition: 2008
Russian edition: 2008

Please send any comments you have to: azerbaijan_100@yahoo.com

ISBN 978 9952 806 80 9

WE ARE GRATEFUL TO OUR SPONSORS:

GILAN HOLDING
Financial and Industrial Group

AZERBAIJAN

100 questions answered

If you've ever wondered where Azerbaijan is or why it's called the Land of Fire, or if you're looking for a colourful and ancient culture or a country linking Europe and Asia, you need look no further than this book.

Azerbaijan: 100 Questions Answered is the result of a survey undertaken by The European Azerbaijan Society and the Anglo-Azerbaijani Youth Society to find out the most common and interesting questions asked about Azerbaijan.

As the publisher, we hope this book will be useful not only to visitors to Azerbaijan, who want information about the country from the practical to the obscure, but also to anyone who has an interest in Azerbaijan, whether they are a student or specialist, a journalist looking for an interesting topic or a business executive wanting a different insight into the country.

It's very important that people from many countries read this book, especially people in government, business, diplomatic and financial circles...

Contents

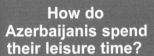

How do Azerbaijanis spend their leisure time?

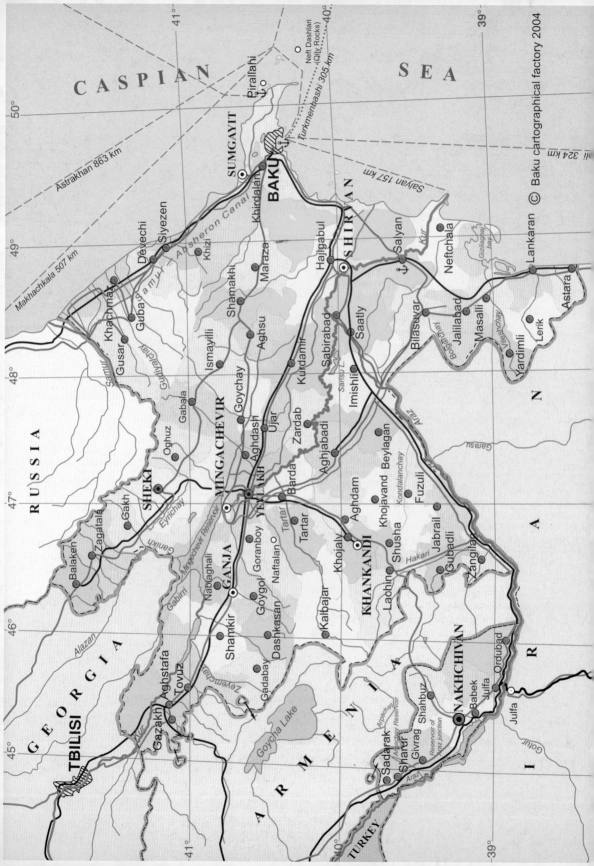

Facts & Figures

1 Where is Azerbaijan?

The Republic of Azerbaijan is located in the south-east of the Caucasian region with an 825-km coastline along the Caspian Sea. Much of the country is mountainous. The Greater Caucasian range rises to the north, where Bazarduzu (4,466 metres) is the highest peak. Below the mountains lies the Kur-Araz lowland. Azerbaijan has a total area of 86,600 square kilometres (33,400 square miles) including the Nakhchivan Autonomous Republic. Of the total area of the country 12 per cent is forested, 1.6 per cent is water and 54.9 per cent is agricultural land, of which 31.1 per cent is pasture and 31 per cent other land. The country lies between 44 and 52 degrees longitude east and 38 and 42 degrees latitude north. The capital, Baku is situated on the 40th parallel.

Azerbaijan's northern border with the Russian Federation is 390 kilometres long. The longest border is with Armenia to the west, 1,007 kilometres. To the north-west the border with Georgia stretches 480 kilometres. To the south-west, in Nakhchivan, the border with the Turkish Republic is only 15 kilometres long. To the south, Azerbaijan, including Nakhchivan, has a 765-km border with the Islamic Republic of Iran.

Azerbaijan consists of the following administrative entities: one autonomous republic (Nakhchivan with a total area of 5,500 square kilometres), 66 districts, 70 towns, 13 urban districts (11 in Baku and 2 in Ganja), 239 urban type settlements and 4,279 rural settlements. The representatives of local authorities (villages and settlements) are appointed by the heads of districts and cities who, in turn, are directly appointed by the president. On 12 December 1999 municipal elections were held for the first time.

The territory of Azerbaijan also includes the islands of Sari, Kurdili, Pirallahi, Chilof, Khara-Zira and Big Zira in the Azerbaijani sector of the Caspian.

2 Why is Azerbaijan called the Land of Fire?

There are several theories as to why Azerbaijan is called the Land of Fire. One of the earliest names for oil-rich Azerbaijan, mentioned in Persian sources, is Aturpatakan. This means "a place where sacred fire is preserved". Oil extraction in the Absheron peninsula, which is one of the world's oldest oil regions, dates back to the 7th-6th centuries BC and is mentioned in the works of ancient and medieval historians. Roman historian Ammianus Marcellinus (4th century AD) wrote in his *History* that the ancient states of Azerbaijan used "Midian oil" which was called *nafta* in the local language.

The South Caucasus is considered one of the first regions where fire was used. At various sites in the South Caucasus gas ignites on escaping from the ground, creating the effect of a burning hillside. Fire-worship was strong in Azerbaijan and Zoroastrianism spread. This can be seen in monuments and superstitions which consider fire to be sacred. Moreover, in ancient Greek mythology Prometheus was bound by a chain to the Caucasus Mountains by order of Zeus, because he had stolen fire from the gods and brought it to mankind.

3 What do Azerbaijan's state symbols stand for?

Under the Constitution Azerbaijan's state symbols are the *state flag, state emblem* and *national anthem.*

On 9 November 1918, the government of the Azerbaijani Democratic Republic adopted the tricolour national flag. The flag was rejected by the Soviet regime, which took over after the collapse of the Azerbaijani Republic on 28 April 1920. The tricolour was restored on 17 November 1990, when the Supreme Majlis of the Nakhchivan Autonomous Republic decided to approve it as its national flag. At the same time the Supreme Soviet of the Nakhchivan AR asked the Supreme Soviet of the Azerbaijani SSR to recognize the tricolour flag as the national symbol of Azerbaijan. On 5 February 1991 the Supreme Soviet of the Azerbaijani SSR duly adopted the tricolour as the national flag of Azerbaijan.

Blue signifies Turkic origin
Red signifies modernity and democracy
Green signifies Islam
The crescent and octagonal star
represent the Moon and the Sun, eternity and secularity

The state emblem was adopted by law and charter, signed by the Azerbaijani president on 19 January 1993.

The shield on the emblem stands for defence
The tricolour circular lines stand for the flag
The octagonal star on the circular lines stands for the Sun
The tongues of flame in the middle of the octagonal star stand for the Land of Fire
The wheat ears signifiy abundance
The branches of the oak tree signify eternity

The Azerbaijani National Anthem, written by Uzeyir Hajibayov with lyrics by Ahmad Javad, was adopted as the national anthem under a law signed by the Azerbaijani president on 27 May 1993.

Music by Uzeyir Hajibayov
Words by Ahmad Javad

Azerbaijan, Azerbaijan!
You are a country of heroes!
We will die that you might live!
We will shed our blood to defend you!
Long live your tricolour banner!
Thousands of people have sacrificed their lives
You have become a battlefield.
Every soldier fighting for you
Has become a hero.
We pray for your prosperity,
We sacrifice our lives to you.
Our sincere love for you
Comes from the bottom of our hearts.
To defend your honour,
To raise your banner,
All the young people are ready.
Glorious motherland,
Azerbaijan, Azerbaijan!

11

4 What is the population of Azerbaijan and its major cities?

Baku

Azerbaijan is the most populous of the republics of the Caucasus. More than 8.5 million people live here, of whom over 379,500 live in the Nakhchivan Autonomous Republic. In 2007 152,000 children were born in Azerbaijan, that is, 416 per day. The birth rate was 18 per 1,000 of the population, while the ratio of live births was 11 per 1,000.

Average life expectancy is 72; 69 for men and 75 for women. Children under 15 constitute one-quarter of the whole population while those of working age make up about 60 per cent. Of the population, 49.3 per cent are men while 50.7 per cent are women. Some 80 per cent of the population is concentrated in valleys and low lands that are irrigated and suitable for farming and where the large industrial centres lie. The average population density of Azerbaijan is 97 persons per square

Guba

Ganja

kilometre. The urban population makes up 51.7 per cent (4,501,000). After Baku (1,893,300), the largest towns are Ganja (308,000 inhabitants) Sumgayit (296,900), Mingachevir (95,500), Nakhchivan (76,000), Shirvan (74,600), Sheki (56,000) and Khankandi (54,800 in 1989).

The capital of Azerbaijan is Baku. The city covers 192,000 hectares.

5 What is Azerbaijan's ethnic make-up?

The geographical position of Azerbaijan and its people's cosmopolitan traditions have attracted various ethnic groups to live here. Most of them are ancient Caucasian peoples. From the ethnic, physiological and cultural point of view they are kindred nations to the Azerbaijanis. From 1828 Armenians and in the mid-19th century Russians were resettled to the territory of Azerbaijan.

According to the last census in 1999, the ethnic make-up of the country is as follows:

Azerbaijanis - 7,205,500 (90.6 per cent), *Lezgins* - 178,000 (2.2 per cent), *Russians* - 141,700 (1.8 per cent), *Armenians* - 120,700 (1.5 per cent), *Talish* - 76,800 (1 per cent), *Avars* - 50,900 (0.6 per cent), *Akhiska (Meskheti) Turks* - 43,400 (0.5 per cent), *Tatars* - 30,000 (0.4 per cent), *Ukrainians* - 29,000 (0.4 per cent), *Tzakhurs* - 15,900 (0.2 per cent), *Georgians* - 14,900 (0.2 per cent), *Kurds* - 13,100 (0.2 per cent), *Tats* - 10,900 (0.13 per cent), *Jews* - 8,900 (0.1 per cent), *Udins* - 4,200 (0.05 per cent), and other peoples 9,600 (0.12 per cent).

The official language of the Azerbaijani Republic is Azerbaijani. Azerbaijani is the first language of 99.2 per cent of the population and of 99.8 per cent of ethnic Azerbaijanis.

6 What religions are represented in Azerbaijan?

Religious freedom is stipulated in the Azerbaijani Constitution. Under the Constitution religion is separate from the state and all religions

Sheikh ul-Islam Haji Allahshukur Pashazada, Alexander, Bishop of Baku and the Caspian Eparchy, and Simon Ikhilov, head of the community of Mountain Jews in Azerbaijan

are equal before the law. There is no official religion in the country. The majority of the population in Azerbaijan is Muslim. Here the Shi'a and Sunni faiths do not differ from one other, but formally two-thirds of Muslims consider themselves to be Shi'a and one-third Sunni. There are five Russian Orthodox, three Georgian Orthodox, one Armenian Gregorian, one Catholic and 13 Old Believers' churches (some of which are Molokan churches), as well as three Jewish synagogues, one Lutheran church, six Baptist churches and one place of worship for the Baha'i and Hare Krishna faiths respectively.

Muslims - 93.4 per cent
Russian Orthodox - 2.5 per cent
Armenian Apostolic - 2.3 per cent
Other - 1.3 per cent
Note: religious affiliation is still nominal in Azerbaijan; percentages for actual practising adherents are much lower

7 Where are Azerbaijan's parks and nature reserves?

Villa Petrolea, the first park in Azerbaijan, was laid in 1882 in Baku on the initiative of Ludwig Nobel (1831-88), an oil baron and philanthropist. There are now eight National Parks in Azerbaijan - the Seaside National Park[1], known as the Boulevard (Sabail and Nasimi districts in central Baku), the Absheron[II] (Azizbeyov district), Shirvan[III] (Salyan, Neftchala and Garadagh district of Baku), Agh-Gol[IV] (Aghjabedi and Beylaqan districts), Altiaghaj[V] (Khizi and Siyazan districts), Hirkan[VI] (Lankaran and Astara districts), Hasan Aliyev[VII] (Ordubad District, Nakhchivan) and Goygol[VIII] (Goygol, Dashkasan and Goranboy districts).

There are 14 National Nature Reserves in Azerbaijan: Shahbuz[1] (Shahbuz District, Nakhchivan), Turyanchay[2] (Aghdash, Yevlakh and Gabala districts), Pirgulu[3] (Shamakhi District), Garayazi[4] (Aghstafa and Gazakh districts), Shirvan[5] (Salyan District), Ismayilli[6] (Ismayilli District), Ilisu[7] (Gakh District), Goygol[8] (Goygol District), Basitchay[9] (Zengilan District), Eldar Shami[10] (Samukh District), Gara-Gol[11] (Lachin District), Gizilaghaj[12] (Lankaran and Masalli districts), Zagatala[13] (Zagatala and Balakan districts) and Korchay[14] (Goranboy District).

Q&A

15

8 What are Azerbaijan's main exports and imports?

Oil and oil products are Azerbaijan's main exports. The Contract of the Century, signed between the State Oil Company of Azerbaijan (SOCAR) and leading world oil companies, led to an increase in oil exports from 1998. This rapid growth was the result of the exploration of new oil deposits and the high oil price on the world market. Other leading exports are foodstuffs (vegetables, fruits, meat etc.), technology and equipment, textiles (mainly seedless raw cotton), chemicals, metals and plastics.

Imports are more diversified, though they still indirectly reflect the needs of the oil industry. Technology, transport components and other equipment for the oil industry make up the lion's share of total imports. Mineral products (including oil products), metals, chemicals, plastics and food products also constitute an important share of imports. Other imports include wood, paper, products for the printing industry and textiles.

According to recent statistics, Azerbaijan has import and export operations with 135 countries around the world. Exports make up 50.8 per cent of foreign trade, while imports account for 49.2 per cent.

History

9 Why is Azerbaijan considered an ancient centre of civilization?

Azerbaijani archeologist Mammadali Huseynov with the jawbone of prehistoric Azikh Woman, which he discovered in 1968. It is 350,000-400,000 years old

The territory of Azerbaijan is rich in archaeological sites that show it was one of the most ancient settled areas in the region. With continuous human habitation, Azerbaijan has a wealth of monuments from every evolutionary period. The history of human life on Azerbaijani territory goes back about two million years.

Azikh, Taghlar (Khojavand District, Karabakh), Damjili, Dashsalahli (Gazakh District) and Gazma (Nakhchivan) are amongst the world's most ancient archeological sites. Azikh Cave (*azikh* in ancient Turkish means *bear*) is the biggest cave in Azerbaijan. It is located in south-western Azerbaijan, close to the Iranian border, near the town of Fuzuli in the Quruchay Valley. The Cave is 230 metres long and has six interconnecting chambers. In 1968, Azerbaijani palaeontologist Mammadali Huseynov (1922-94) discovered the lower jawbone of a Neanderthal in Azikh Cave. It has since been analysed independently in the West and confirmed to be between 350,000 and 400,000 years old. The jawbone, with one molar totally intact and another partially broken, is believed to have belonged to a female about 18 years old. It was named after the place where it was found - Azikhantrop (Azikh Man).

Azikh Man, one of Earth's earliest inhabitants, once lived in the region now known as Azerbaijan

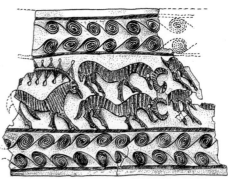

Cultural artefacts from Khojali-Goranboy, late Bronze and early Iron Age (1300-700 BC)

18

According to French palaeontologist Dr Henry de Lumley, the Azikh jawbone is the fourth oldest human relic ever found. The first was discovered by Louis Leakey, his wife Mary and son Richard in Olduvai Gorge, Tanzania; the second, in Kenya; and the third, in France. Azikhantrop is the oldest ever relic found in the former Soviet Union.

Stone tools were also found in Azikh Cave. They date back to the Palaeolithic period, which makes them between one and 1.5 million years old.

Sadly, it is not possible to see Azikh Cave today because the region that the Cave is located was captured in 1993 by Armenians and remains under military occupation. Armenian forces at present occupy a large chunk of Azerbaijani territory in the western part of the country.

First fireplace in human history

One of the most important finds in Azikh Cave concerns the history of fire-making. Five fireplaces were discovered in different stratigraphic levels. One was surrounded by a crescent-like stone wall, 30 centimetres thick, built to protect the living area from sparks. It is the first known construction in human history and the first known fireplace. Archaeologists date it to a period 700,000 to 500,000 years ago. Of particular interest is the fact that the fireplaces existed during different periods at the same site, providing important evidence of the continuity of tradition and settlement. This find shows that Azerbaijan is a place where human life emerged. Because of the find, the territory of Azerbaijan has been included in the map of Europe's oldest inhabited areas.

The Stone Age has yielded a rich archaeological heritage. Excavations in Gemiqaya, Nakhchivan and Gobustan have revealed

Red pottery drinking horn (200-100 BC)

Dagger with tracery (900-800 BC), bracelets (700-500 BC). Bronze

Sulphur-clay vessel (900 BC)

Sulphur-clay, boot-like vessels with white encrustation (1100-900 BC)

Sulphur-clay vessel (1000-900 BC)

Sulphur baking vessel with polished surface (500-300 BC)

carved pictures of fauna and flora and scenes from daily life.

Archaeological finds in Kultepe, Nakhchivan, Ganjachay Valley, the plains of Mil and Mughan and Gazakh and Aghdam districts have provided evidence of agriculture and cattle-breeding between 6,000 and 4,000 BC in Azerbaijan.

In the early Bronze Age, the Kur-Araz culture, situated between the two rivers of the same name, spread beyond the territory of Azerbaijan. Black ceramics, unique in the region, are characteristic of this culture. Fascinating weapons survive from the period, as do bronze axes.

The cultures of Khojali-Gadabay, Talish-Mughan and Nakhchivan emerged in the late Bronze and early Iron Ages in Azerbaijan. Many vessels, luxurious garments and decorative items made out of bronze, copper and agate have been discovered in burial mounds or *kurgans.* The civilization that emerged in 1,000 BC during the Iron Age in Azerbaijan lasted until 300 BC, the period of Caucasian Albania. The gold and silver items found in the graves of this period are especially fine.

The abundance, variety and quality of archaeological finds in Azerbaijan testify to its special role in the evolution of world civilization.

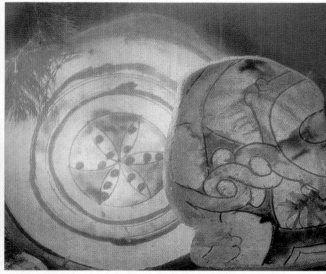

Details of glazed cups with geometrical and vegetable patterns, 12th-13th century

10 When was the first state formed in Azerbaijan?

The Azerbaijani people have one of the oldest histories of state building. The first states and ethnic entities (Aratta, Kuti, Lullu, Turukki and Su) emerged on the territory of Azerbaijan in 3000-2000 BC. At that time Azerbaijan had close relations with Sumeria, Akkadia and Assyria, states in Mesopotamia that have left their mark on world history, and with states in Asia Minor.

State structures in Azerbaijan later began to enlarge and the state became much more developed. In the first millennium BC and the early centuries AD, powerful states such as Manna, the Scythian kingdom of Iskit or Skif, Atropatena and Albania emerged on the territory of Azerbaijan.

The Kingdom of Manna emerged in about 900 BC. The name of the state is first encountered in the form Munna in 843 BC in an inscription of Assyrian King Salmanasar III (859-823 BC). Later on, this name is reflected in various sources as Manna, Mannash, Mana and Mini. The state's borders stretched to the Diyala and Little Zab rivers in the south, the Caspian Sea in the east, the Araz River in the north and Lake Urmia in the west. The capital of the state was Izirtu (Zirtu), situated on Lake Urmia.

Gold fillet (1st millennium BC), Jafarabad (Khalkhal, Western Azerbaijan, Iran), Azerbaijan Museum, Tabriz, Iran

21

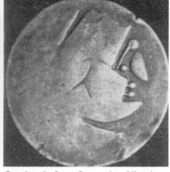

Fortress walls (4th-early 3rd century BC),
Gabala, village of Chukhur Gabala

Greek coin from Caucasian Albania

Manna, which was repeatedly attacked by Urartu and Assyria, flourished during the reign of Iranzu (740-719 BC). The last kings of Manna were in alliance with Assyria. The people of Manna are last mentioned in the Chronicle of Gedd in connection with events in 616 BC. Manna is thought to have been invaded by neighbouring Media in 590 BC.

Atropatena and Albania emerged after the death of Alexander the Great (326-323 BC). These states played a big part in nation and state-building on the territory of Azerbaijan in ancient times. Historical annals are good sources of information about Caucasian Albania, which covered Northern Azerbaijan (now the Azerbaijani Republic) and the southern part of Dagestan. The Albanians are mentioned in the work of second century historian Arrian (Flavius Arrianus) in connection with events in the 4th century BC. Yet before the establishment of their independent state the Albanians took part in the battle of Gavgamel against Alexander the Great as part of the army of Achaemenid ruler Dara III (336-23 BC). In the 1st century BC the Albanians are known to have had an army of 60,000 infantry and 22,000 cavalry. The first capital of Albania, from the 4th century BC, was Kabalaka (now the town of Gabala), and from the 5th century AD the capital moved to Partav (now the town of Barda). Albania was primarily ruled by a local dynasty. From the 6th to 8th centuries the country was ruled by the Mehranis dynasty.

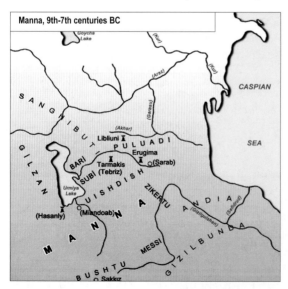

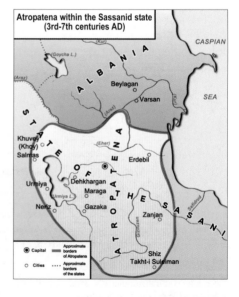

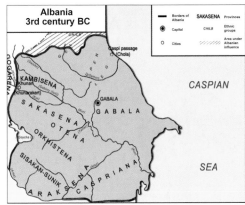

**Albania
3rd century BC**

Stone with inscription in the Albanian language found in
Mingachevir, Azerbaijan, 5th-6th centuries AD,
History Museum of Azerbaijan, Baku

The name Atropatena was applied to the area of Azerbaijan south of the Araz River (now in Iranian Azerbaijan) and originated from the name Atropat, the first satrap or vice-regent of the Achaemenids who later became the first ruler of Lesser Media and general of Alexander the Great. The capital of Atropatena was Gazaka, now the city of Maragha in Iran on the south-eastern shore of Lake Urmia. Historical records mention five rulers of Atropatena after Atropat. In the 1st century BC the army of Atropatena consisted of 40,000 infantry and 10,000 cavalry. The Roman Empire was in conflict with Parthia over Albania and Atropatena from the 2nd century BC to the 3rd century AD. The Romans and the Parthians regularly attacked Albania and Atropatena. Prominent Roman generals Lucius Licinius Lucullus (69-67 BC), Pompey or Gnaeus Pompeius Magnus (66-65 BC) and Publius Canidius Crassus (37-36 BC) all marched on the region. Between 72 and 74 AD the nomadic Alan tribes attacked Albania and Atropatena several times.

Atropatena was included in the Sassanid Empire (226-650 AD), while Albania became an independent country.

Latin inscription, 1st century AD, Gobustan, Baku

ıMPDOMITIANO
CAESARE·AVC
CERMANIC
ɩIVLIVS
MAXIMVS ⊃
LEC XII·FVL

"Imp (eratore) Domitiano Caesare
Aug (usto) Germanic (o) L. Julius
Maximus > leg (ionis) XII Ful (minata)"

During the reign of the emperor Domitian Caesar
Augustus Germanicus, Lucius Julius Maximus,
Legion XII Fulminata

11 What is Azerbaijan's medieval history?

Javanshir (638-680), ruler of Caucasian Albania

The medieval period in Azerbaijani history encompasses the 3rd-17th centuries AD. Caucasian Albania was the first state on Azerbaijani territory during this period, lasting until 705 AD. The first centuries AD were tough times for Azerbaijan: in the 3rd century, Azerbaijan was invaded by the Sassanid Empire and in the 7th century by the Arab Caliphate. After the demise of the Caliphate in the 9th century, old state-building customs began to grow in Azerbaijan. States such as the Shirvanshahs (9th to 16th century), the Sajids (879-941), the Salarids (941-981), the Ravvadids (980-1054) and the Shaddadids (971-1088) began to form in Azerbaijan. The Shirvanshahs' state lasted the longest in Azerbaijani history, existing for seven centuries. In the mid-11th century the territory of Azerbaijan became part of the Seljuk Empire. As the Seljuk Empire decayed, the Shirvanshahs became more powerful and the Atabaylar (1136-1225) established a new independent state on the territory of Azerbaijan.

The territory of Azerbaijan was ruled by the Mongols from 1239 to 1358-59 and was part of the state of Hulaki-Elkhani (1258-1357). After the Mongol regime local states emerged: the Jalaris (1358-59 -1410), the Qaraqoyunlu or Black Sheep (1410-1468) and Aghqoyunlu or White Sheep (1468-1501). During the reign of Uzun Hasan or Hasan the Tall, founder of the Aghqoyunlu state, Azerbaijan was involved in international affairs and maintained diplomatic relations with some European states, as

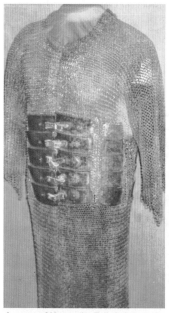

Armour of Hasan the Tall, Aghqoyunlu ruler, 15th century, Military Museum, Istanbul, Turkey

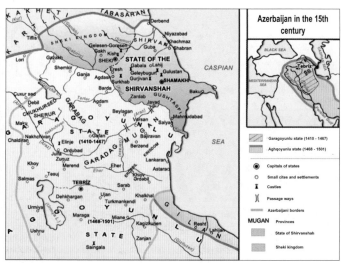

24

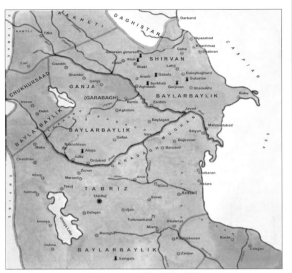
Azerbaijan in the 16th century. The Safavid State

Shah Ismail Khatai (1486-1524)

Venice, Hungary, Poland, Rodos and others. The state of the Safavids (1501-1736), founded by Shah Ismail Khatai I (1501-1524), a prominent poet and statesman, was a powerful empire which competed with the Ottomans (1299-1922). Between 1736 and 1747 the territory of Azerbaijan was under the rule of Nadir Shah, who seized power from the Safavids. In 1747 after Nadir Shah's death, the state was divided into 20 khanates, five sultanates and one jamaat, which existed as small feudal entities until the early 19th century, when they were invaded and divided between Tsarist Russia and Persia.

Q&A

History

Well-known statesman, founder of the Safavid state, and poet. In 1501 at the age of 14 he declared himself shah, thus establishing the state of the Safavids. The Safavids were considered a hegemonic state in the Near East. During his reign the Azerbaijani language became a state language and was used in diplomatic correspondence.

He was also a talented poet and wrote classical, epic and lyric poetry mainly in Azerbaijani, Persian and Arabic. His prominent *Dahname* and *Nasihatname* are brilliant examples of the Azerbaijani epic genre of poems. The *Dahname* deals mainly with human love and has Sufi influences.

Coins of Azerbaijani feudal states. Shirvanshahs, Sajids, Atabaylar, Safavids

The battle between Shah Ismail I and Shirvanshah Farrukh Yasar, 1541, British Museum, London

12 How did the terms Southern and Northern Azerbaijan emerge?

These terms emerged in the 19th century after Russia and Iran divided Azerbaijan between them. Following the Russo-Persian wars, Tsarist Russia and Iran signed the Gulustan Treaty on 12 October 1813 and the Turkmenchay Treaty on 10 February 1828. Under these treaties, Azerbaijani land north of the River Araz was incorporated into Russia, while land south of the river was annexed by Iran.

The Azerbaijanis later dubbed these territories Northern and Southern Azerbaijan or sometimes "this side" and "the other side" of Azerbaijan. The Azerbaijani Republic now covers the territory of Northern Azerbaijan. Southern Azerbaijan is the northern part of Iran and includes the *ostans* (provinces) of Western Azerbaijan (with Urmiya as its centre), Eastern Azerbaijan (with Tabriz as its centre), Ardabil (with Ardabil as its centre), Zanjan (with Zanjan as its centre), Qazvin (with Qazvin as its centre) and the northern part of Gilan (with Rasht as its centre) and Hamadan. The size of these territories is estimated at around 170,000 sq. km (106,000 sq. miles), although larger estimates are prevalent.

According to unofficial sources, up to 30 million ethnic Azerbaijanis live in Southern Azerbaijan.

The native language of the ethnic Azerbaijanis belongs to the Turkic language family, whilst the language family of Persian and other Iranian groups' is Indo-Iranian. Despite all the dissimilarities and very distinct ethnic, linguistic and cultural differences, Azerbaijanis have played a key role in all aspects of the history of the Iranian peoples and their many states and empires.

The signing of the Turkmenchay Treaty, as depicted by Russian painter V. Moshkov, 1828

13 Where is Western Azerbaijan?

Western Azerbaijan covers the area of the modern-day Republic of Armenia, which historically belonged to Azerbaijan. All historical monuments, toponyms and homonyms prove that the Azerbaijanis were the aborigines in that land.

In 782 BC Argishti I, king of Urartu, founded the fortress of Erebuni, since 1936 known as Yerevan. The name Irevan was first mentioned in manuscripts in the 6th century AD. Irevan, which was an important economic and trading centre since early medieval times, was a prominent part of Azerbaijan during the reign of the Qaraqoyunlu (1410-67) and Aghqoyunlu (1468-1501) because of its geographical situation and mild climate. The Safavid shahs (1501-1736) paid special attention to reconstruction and rebuilding in the city. During the wars between the Safavids and Ottoman Empire in 1514-83 the city changed hands frequently. Finally Safavid Shah Abbas I (1587-1629) seized Irevan in 1604. It was the centre of Chukhur S'ad *baylarbaylik* or province. The land of Nakhchivan and Zangazur were part of the Ganja-Karabakh and Tabriz *baylarbayliks*. During his reign Nadir Shah (1736-47) preserved the administrative divisions.

In the mid-18th century khanates in Western Azerbaijan, centred on Irevan and Nakhchivan, were founded in the same way as in other parts of Azerbaijan. The Irevan khanate consisted of 12 *mahals* (districts) and was ruled by monarchical dynasties until 1828. The khanate was conquered by Russia during the Russo-Persian war of 1826-28. This occupation was made official by the Treaty of Turkmenchay (10 February 1828). On 21 March 1828 by the order of Russian Tsar Nikolay I, an Armenian Region was formed on the territory of the Nakhchivan and Irevan khanates which had been occupied by Russia. The region was divided into the provinces of Nakhchivan and Irevan and the *okrug* or district of Ordubad. Later various provinces were created there - the Irevan governorate covering Echmiadzin, Yeni Bayazid and Surmeli districts and the Ganja governorate covering Zangezur and Gazakh.

After the occupation of Tsarist Russia, Armenians were resettled to this region. Russian author N.I. Shavrov, in his book *A New Threat to Russian Affairs in the Trans-Caucasus: The Forthcoming sale of Mugan to Foreigners*, said that between 1828 and 1830 40,000 Persian Armenians and 86,400 Armenians from Ottoman Turkey migrated to the South Caucasus, now the territory of Armenia, and settled in the best

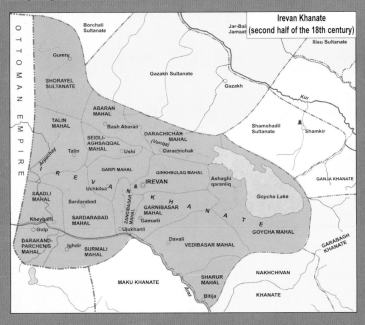

land in the Irevan and Ganja governorates. His records said that more than one million out of 1.3 million Armenians living in the South Caucasus in the early 20th century were not local inhabitants. They had been resettled here by the Russian authorities. As a result of the migration, the ethno-demographic balance in the region changed dramatically in a short time.

In spite of this migration, local people outnumbered the Armenian settlers. This is obvious from official statistics, particularly those printed in the *Caucasian Calendar*, a book published for more than 50 years; publication of the first Russia-wide census in 1897 showed that Azerbaijanis were in the majority in the territory of the modern-day Armenian Republic, even after Russia's migration policy. In 1897 in Zangezur *uezd* or district Azerbaijanis made up 53.2 per cent of the population, while Armenians made up 45.8 per cent; in Irevan Azerbaijanis were 66 per cent and Armenians 34 per cent of the population, while Azerbaijanis were one-third of the total population in Echmiadzin, Yeni Bayazid and Surmeli.

Intending to create a "Greater Armenia", 20th century Armenians three times committed mass deportation, slaughter and genocide against Azerbaijanis in 1905-06, 1918-20 and finally in 1988-91.

Western Azerbaijan did not escape the first Armenian-Muslim slaughter either. In this period Armenians, relying on the support of Tsarist Russia, committed unprecedented atrocities against

	Azerbaijanis		Armenians	
	1823-27	1828-30	1823-27	1828-30
Nakhchivan region (previous Nakhchivan khanate)	86 per cent	51 per cent	13 per cent	49 per cent
Armenian region (previous Irevan khanate)	76 per cent	46 per cent	24 per cent	54 per cent

Azerbaijanis in the provinces of Irevan, Zangezur and Echmiadzin (Uch kilse). Just a few facts are enough to show the Armenian atrocity: in August 1906 the village of Gatar in Zangezur *uezd*, where 3,500 Azerbaijanis lived, was completely destroyed and the survivors had to move to the village of Giretag, which was 10 kilometres away.

Between 1918 and 1920, as a result of the slaughter committed by Armenian chauvinists such as Andranik and Nejdeh against Azerbaijanis living in the territory of modern-day Armenia, out of 575,000 Azerbaijanis 565,000 were murdered or deported. The Karabakh general-governorate formed on 25 January 1919 by the Azerbaijani Democratic Republic to repulse Armenian aggression included the Zangezur *uezd* too. It is worth noting that this administrative entity existed until the Soviet invasion. Parts of Western Azerbaijan, such as Irevan environs and Surmeli adjacent to Nakhchivan, first belonged to the Araz-Turkic Republic that existed here, but later passed to the South-West Azerbaijan general governorate which, in turn, existed until the Soviet occupation.

After the disintegration of the Trans-Caucasus *Seim* (Assembly) in 1918, the Armenians managed to form the Republic of Ararat (1918-20) which was the first independent state of the Armenian people in the Caucasus. The republic covered 10,000 square kilometres. The top officials of the Azerbaijani Democratic Republic granted the city of Irevan to the Armenian people, hoping that would put an end to their aggression. However, later events showed that Armenian nationalists instead fuelled their hostility against Azerbaijan. On 30 November 1920 the Bolsheviks "granted" the region of Basarkechar in Yeni Beyazid *uezd* and Vedibasar region of the Irevan governorate, as well as the western part of Zangezur region (a total area of 9,800 square kilometres) of the Ganja governorate to the Armenians, as a result of which Nakhchivan became an exclave separated from the main body of Azerbaijan. In 1921 the Soviet government legalized Armenia's hold on Zangezur, thus driving a wedge between the Azerbaijani SSR mainland and its province of Nakhchivan.

The following year, in 1922, Dilijan and Geycha were also transferred from Azerbaijan to the

28

Armenian SSR. A number of villages were also transferred to Armenia without reciprocity from Nakhchivan in 1929, from Gadabay in 1969 and, as late as 1984, from Gazakh District. During the Soviet period, as a result of land transfers from Azerbaijan to Armenia, the territory of Azerbaijan shrank from 97,300 sq. km in 1920 (while still independent) to 86,600 sq. km in 1988 under the Soviet Union.

At the instigation of the Armenian lobby in Moscow, Soviet leader Stalin signed decrees dated 23 December 1947 and 10 March 1948 under which up to 100,000 Azerbaijanis who lived on the territory of the Armenian SSR were forcibly deported to the Kur-Araz lowlands of the Azerbaijani SSR. The majority of the displaced people, who lost almost all their property, died because of the climatic change and the lack of normal living standards in the new areas. Armenians from foreign countries were resettled in their lands.

In the late 1980s the Armenians, taking advantage of processes under way in the USSR, started a new stage of aggression in Western Azerbaijan. The ethnic cleansing policy carried out by the Republic of Armenia against its Azerbaijani population, was patronized by Mikhail Gorbachev, the last Soviet leader. In 1918 there were 1,200 Azerbaijani-populated villages in 33 of the 36 regions of the present-day Republic of Armenia, but in 1988 there remained only 185 Azerbaijani-populated villages in 22 regions.

In 1986 the Azerbaijanis were deported from Mehri and Gafan regions of Armenia. However, large-scale aggression under the slogan "sweep the Turks out of Armenia" and "Armenia is only for Armenians" began on 19 February 1988, when a nationalist and anti-Azerbaijani rally was held. In those few days Armenians destroyed the last Muslim mosque in the capital Yerevan. On 8 August 1991 200 Azerbaijani inhabitants of Nuvadi, the last Azerbaijani-populated village in Armenia, were ousted in a day. Overall, as a result of bloody aggression in 1988-91 about 230,000 Azerbaijanis were deported from 185 villages and settlements; 225 were killed and 1,154 wounded and their property plundered.

Migration of Armenians from Iran to Northern Azerbaijan (Nakhchivan, Irevan, Karabakh), by Russian painter V. Moshkov, 1828

14 What was the first parliamentary republic in the East?

In February 1917 the tsarist regime in Russia was overthrown. A provisional government took power and formed the Special Committee for the Administration of the Trans-Caucasus. But the provisional government's rule did not last long. After the October 1917 Revolution, the deputies elected in the South Caucasus to represent Caucasian people in Russia's Assembly were no longer able to go to Petrograd or Moscow. They assembled on 14 February 1918 in Tiflis (Tbilisi) and formed the Parliament of the Trans-Caucasus, the Supreme Executive Body of the Caucasus. The Muslim faction of 44 deputies who had been elected to Russia's Assembly represented the Muslim people in the Caucasian Assembly. On 9-22 April 1918 the Caucasian Assembly declared independence, thus forming the Trans-Caucasian Republic. However, because of sharp differences of opinion on internal and foreign policy the Republic could not act. As a result, the Georgian representatives left the parliament on 26 May, declaring the independence of Georgia.

On 27 May members of the Muslim faction in the parliament had a meeting and decided to declare the independence of Azerbaijan. The Muslim Council of the Trans-Caucasus declared itself to be Azerbaijan's National Council, thereby forming the first parliamentary republic in Azerbaijan.

On 28 May the National Council held its first meeting, adopting the Declaration of Independence, which proclaimed the independence of Azerbaijan. The Declaration announced that a parliamentary republic, the first secular and democratic administrative model in the East, as well

Mammad Amin Rasulzada (1884-1955) Chairman of Azerbaijan's National Council (1918)

Alimardan bay Topchibashov (1862-1934) Chairman of Azerbaijan's Parliament (1918-1920)

Map of the Azerbaijani Democratic Republic

Drawn up by the Information Department of the Ministry of Foreign Affairs in 1920.

By L.Qumich

Legend

Borders of:

┠┼┨	The Azerbaijani Democratic Republic
━╫━	The Republic of Georgia
┿╋┿	Turkey and Iran
───	*Gubernia* (governorate) and regions
••••••	*Uezd* (district)
▨▨▨	Areas disputed with Armenia
▭▭▭	Areas disputed with Georgia
⊛●○	*Gubernia, uezd* towns and villages

30

as in the Muslim world, had been established in Azerbaijan. On 11 January 1920 the independence of Azerbaijan was de facto recognized by the Supreme Council of the Paris Peace Conference. The area of the Azerbaijani Democratic Republic (ADR) was 113,897 square kilometres with a population of 2,861,862. However, as a result of frequent territorial claims by Armenia the area of the modern-day Azerbaijani Republic has shrunk to 86,600 square kilometres. These territories were bestowed to Armenia by the USSR leadership and the indigenous Azerbaijanis were deported. The ADR collapsed on 27-28 April 1920 as a result of occupation by Soviet Russia.

Fatali Khan Khoyski
(1875-1920)
Prime Minister of the
ADR (1918-1919)

The ADR did not lag behind traditional European democracies in terms of political structure, democratic rights and freedoms. It formed a parliament and government from different ethnic groups, founded the first secular educational institution, Baku State University, and introduced votes for women.

15 How was the Azerbaijani Soviet Socialist Republic formed?

The policy of Soviet Russia, which emerged after the October 1917 Revolution, was in fact to restore control over the former empire. The territory of Azerbaijan, which was rich in natural resources and enjoyed a good geographical position, was essential to the Soviet state. The Azerbaijani Democratic Republic, which was in a difficult internal and international situation, was invaded by the 11th Red Army on the night of 27-28 April 1920. Later the Azerbaijani Soviet Socialist Republic (SSR) was declared.

The independence of Azerbaijan, which had de facto been internationally recognized, was partly preserved between 1920 and 1922 because it was in Russia's national interests. Azerbaijan's independent domestic and foreign policy can be seen in the treaty on equal military and economic relations with Soviet Russia (1920), the adoption of the Constitution of the Azerbaijani SSR in March 1921, the Moscow Treaty (1921), signed between Soviet Russia and Turkey and the Kars Treaty (1921), signed between Russia, Armenia, Azerbaijan and Georgia on one side and Turkey on the other side as well as representation at the Genoa international conference (1922) and the exchange of diplomatic missions with Russia and Turkey. Its admission to the Federative Soviet Socialist Republics of the Trans-Caucasus (a confederative state uniting all three Caucasian Republics) in March 1922 was a step towards the loss of independence. With the establishment of the USSR on 30 December of that year the independence of Azerbaijan came to an end. Though it preserved some state symbols, such as a flag and constitution, in other areas it lost the right of a subject under international law.

Red Army and Bolshevik leaders shortly after the takeover of Baku, May 1920

16 What's the history of Nakhchivan?

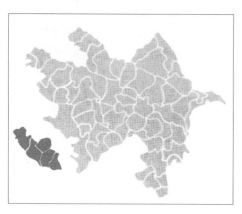

Nakhchivan occupies the south-western end of the Dereleyez and Zangezur chain of mountains of the Lesser Caucasian Range. It is wedged between Armenia (which cuts it off entirely from the Azerbaijan mainland to which it belongs), and has a long, continuous border with Iran and a few kilometres of border with Turkey in the south-west. Most traffic is airborne, which is very limiting. For any goods or passengers to reach Nakhchivan overland from the rest of Azerbaijan, they have to travel an uncertain route inside Iran and enter Nakhchivan from there. Without the free flow of transport through Armenia, the autonomous republic is in a virtual blockade and so they, more than anyone; desire a peaceful resolution to the dispute with Armenia, so that the embargo against them can be lifted.

Q&A

Nakhchivan is rich in natural resources: rock salt, rare metals, arsenic, gypsum, marble, dolomite and medicinal mineral waters. Its flora and fauna are also remarkable and some of its landscapes are exceptionally beautiful. There are also sites of historic interest which testify to a long history of human habitation since the beginning of time.

Nakhchivan was an important transit route and part of the Silk Road. There were at least 150,000 inhabitants at the time and local art and trade developed in parallel. Politically it had a lively history too. The Hurrami movement (778-838 AD) in the early 9th century when Azerbaijanis resisted Arab rulers had a significant presence in Nakhchivan. Towards the end of the 10th century and following the feudal states of the Sajids and Salarids, the Nakhchivan Shahlighi was created, which succumbed only in 1064 to the Seljuk Turks. The importance of Nakhchivan city continued to grow until 1175 when the capital of the local Atabaylar-Eldanizlar state was transferred to Tabriz further south.

The Mongol or Golden Horde invasion, the fighting between Safavid and Ottoman troops on its territory and later the invasions of Shah Abbas I all eroded the prosperity which Nakhchivan had

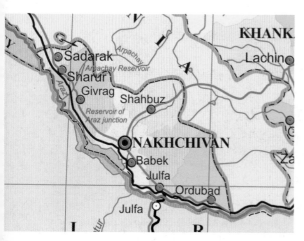

once enjoyed. Shah Abbas actually resettled some of the local population in Mazandaran, Isfahan and other places.

Under the treaty of Kirmanshah (1732), signed between Tahmasib II, the Safavid shah, and the Turkish sultan, Nakhchivan was incorporated into Ottoman Turkey. Later, Nadir Shah reconquered Nakhchivan and other land previously occupied by Ottoman Turkey. In 1747 after the collapse of Nadir Shah's state in Iran, Heydarqulu Khan, head of the Kangarli tribe, formed the khanate of Nakhchivan. Thus Nakhchivan became one of the 20 khanates formed on the territory of Azerbaijan in the 18th century.

Furthermore, some of the neighbouring feudal lords - of Kartli-Kakheti and the khans of Karabakh and Irevan - also made attempts to incorporate Nakhchivan into their lands. As a result of the Russo-Persian wars in the early 19th century, Nakhchivan was also occupied by Russia, together with other territories of Azerbaijan and, under the Treaty of Turkmenchay in 1828, was annexed to Russia together with the Irevan khanate. On the order of Tsar Nikolay I the khanates of Nakhchivan and Irevan were abolished and the Armenian Region was established. One of the conditions of the Turkmenchay Treaty worthy of attention was, as mentioned earlier, a provision for the relocation of Armenians who had been living in Iran and Turkey to the territory of Azerbaijan, including the Nakhchivan and Irevan khanates. The ethnic balance, however, did not change significantly until the establishment of the Soviet Union in the region. Nevertheless, despite retaining an Azerbaijani majority, the imperial Russian government skilfully used the mixed population to create unrest in order to quell demands for political

Mominakhatun tomb, 1186

independence. During the 19th century, however, a number of secular schools were opened in Nakhchivan and a prominent intelligentsia emerged which made a significant contribution to Azerbaijan culture.

When the tsarist government fell, fighting broke out as Armenians, led by Andranik, attempted to take Nakhchivan. In November 1918, a state structure called the Araz-Turkish Republic was established here and it lasted until March 1919. It included the following regions: Sharur, Dereleyez, Ordubad, Sardarabad, Ulukhanli, Gemerli and Mehri. The capital of the republic was Nakhchivan.

Karabakhlar monument, 12th-14th centuries

After the First World War, Nakhchivan was included in the area of influence of the United Kingdom. When the British recognized the independence of the Azerbaijani Democratic Republic, the new Azerbaijani government established a Nakhchivan general governorship and appointed Bahram Khan Nakhchivanski governor-general. The Armenian side tried to establish a similar "Armenian administration" but were unsuccessful, even when they attempted, after the British left Nakhchivan in late 1919 and were replaced by the USA, to establish a pro-Armenian American general governorship.

The 11th Russian Army overthrew the independence of Azerbaijan in 1920, then in July that year Nakhchivan was also occupied by the invading Bolshevik army and on 28 July the Nakhchivan Soviet Socialist Republic was proclaimed. It was declared an inseparable part of the Azerbaijani

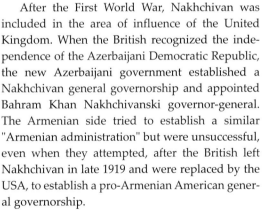

Ilandagh, Nakhchivan

SSR. As with Karabakh, the Armenians did not relinquish their claims to Nakhchivan, even after Soviet power had been established in Armenia.

In the early days of Bolshevik rule in the Caucasus an agreement between the Dashnaks (members of Armenian Dashnaksutyun party) and Bolsheviks emerged during the March massacre in 1918. They began to devastate the borders of the Azerbaijani Democratic Republic. First, on 20 November 1920 ancient Azerbaijani land, such as Zangezur region and other territories (9,800 square kilometres in total), were incorporated into the Armenian SSR. But in fact the plans of the Armenians were more extensive and the main target was Nakhchivan. They considered the annexation of Zangezur to Armenia a step towards this. The annexation of Zangezur, which linked Nakhchivan with the main part of Azerbaijan, turned Nakhchivan into an exclave and made autonomy inevitable.

The efforts of the Armenians to incorporate Nakhchivan into Armenia failed because of the resolute attitude of the people of Nakhchivan. More than 90 per cent of the population of Nakhchivan voted to be part of Azerbaijan in a referendum held at the initiative of delegations from Russia, Azerbaijan and Armenia in early 1921.

The autonomous status of Nakhchivan within Azerbaijan was further confirmed in the Moscow Treaty, signed by Russia and Turkey on 16 March 1921 and in the Kars Treaty, signed by Russia, Azerbaijan, Georgia, Armenia and Turkey in October 1921. The confirmation of the autonomous status of Nakhchivan within Azerbaijan in the international treaty was politically important both then and now.

In December 1922 the first congress of the Soviets of the Trans-Caucasus confirmed by special decree the autonomous status of Nakhchivan as an integral part of the Azerbaijani SSR. In December 1923 the Central Revolutionary Committee asked the Trans-Caucasus Revolutionary Committee to confirm the decision concerning the formation of the Autonomous Nakhchivan SSR within Azerbaijan. Later in January 1924, the Committee ratified this decision. By decree of the Azerbaijani Central Executive Committee, issued on 9 February 1924, the Autonomous SSR of

34

Nakhchivan was formed on the basis of the autonomous region of Nakhchivan.

Although Armenia should have officially accepted Nakhchivan as an integral part of Azerbaijan, it could not agree with this at all and put in a territorial claim for Nakhchivan. The Armenian authorities, supported by their protectors in Moscow, could have seized some portions of Nakhchivan. In 1929-30 according to a decree of the Trans-Caucasian Central Revolutionary Committee, a further 657 square kilometres of Nakhchivani land were granted to Armenia. And in 1930 Aldara, Lehvaz, Astazur, Nuvedi and other settlements were given to Armenia, as a result of which the district of Mehri was formed. Armenia's claims on Nakhchivan have continued to this day.

The next phase of Nakhchivan's history was typically Soviet: the late 1920s and early 1930s saw the establishment of several industrial enterprises and during the Second World War a strong contribution to the war effort. After the war more industrial enterprises were built and agrarian activity was transformed into a thriving agrarian-industrial sector.

On 19 January 1990 the village of Kerki in Sharur District of Nakhchivan was invaded by Armenians under the auspices of the 7th Army of the Ministry of Defence of the USSR. The destruction of historical monuments around the village of Kerki, dating back to the 2nd millennium BC, was a barbarous act against the cultural heritage of mankind. By 19 January 1990, the governing body of the time, the Supreme Soviet of the Autonomous Republic of Nakhchivan, had voted to withdraw from the USSR. This was one of the reasons that prompted the Soviet government to order the army into Baku where they committed atrocities. This period has been referred to ever since as Black January. By the summer of 1990, Heydar Aliyev, later to play an important role as president of the whole country, returned to his native Nakhchivan and became chairman of the local parliament. Nakhchivan took further defiant action, removing by act of the local parliament on 17 November 1991 the words "Soviet Socialist" from their emblem and flying the former national flag of independent Azerbaijan. By the end of 1991 the Soviet Union ceased to exist and independence became reality, with Nakhchivan an integral part of the new Azerbaijani Republic.

The first Constitution of independent Azerbaijan, adopted on 12 November 1995, declared Nakhchivan an autonomous republic and on 28 April 1998 it obtained its own constitution.

Nakhchivani khan's house (17th century) which is now a carpet museum

17 What's the history of Mountainous Karabakh?

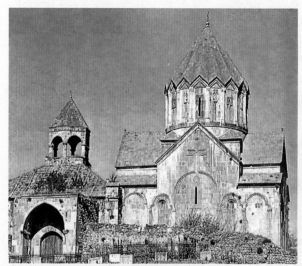

Karabakh (Qarabagh) is one of the ancient regions of Azerbaijan. The name of this integral part of Azerbaijan consists of two different Azerbaijani words: *qara (black)* and *bagh (garden)*. The word *qara* has other meanings too in Azerbaijani and other Turkic languages, such as *dense, thick, big* and *strong*. The name Karabakh may, therefore, mean *black garden, large garden, dense garden, thick garden* or *picturesque garden*.

The name Karabakh first occurred in the 7th century. Initially Karabakh was the name of a smaller historical and geographical area, but it was later applied to a wider geographical area. This is typical of Azerbaijan: Nakhchivan is the name both of the town of Nakhchivan and of the region as a whole; Shaki is the name of the town of Shaki and the region as a whole; Ganja is the name of the city of Ganja and the region as a whole; Lankaran of the town of Lankaran and the region as a whole, etc.

Silver coin of the Karabakh khanate, 1785, Panahabad, Karabakh

When Karabakh is discussed, one of the first questions to arise concerns the location of Karabakh. What part of Azerbaijan includes Karabakh?

Mirza Jamal Javanshir, ruler of Karabakh, wrote in his *History of Karabakh*: "According to ancient historical texts, the borders of Karabakh are: in the south the River Araz - from Hudafarin Bridge to Sinig Bridge. At present the population of Gazakh, Shamsaddin and Damarchi-Hasanly lives near this bridge, for which the Russian Tatars use the Russian name, Krasniy Most, that is the Red Bridge. In the east the border is the Kur River, which flows into the Araz River at Javad village and on to the Caspian Sea. In the north the border is the Goran River, which flows from the Yelizavetpol (Ganja) border of Karabakh to the Kur River, down to the Araz River. In the west the border is the high mountains of Karabakh called Kusbak, Salvarti and Erikli."

The name Karabakh did not apply only to the Mountainous (Nagornyy in Russian) part of Karabakh, but also to the lowland part. In other words, the name Daghlig Karabakh (Mountainous Karabakh) is a product of later periods and a name given to one part of Karabakh as a result of separatist intentions. There is both Daghlig (mountainous) and Aran (lowland) Karabakh in Azerbaijan.

Karabakh has always been an integral part of all state formations of Azerbaijan. For a long period, the territory of Karabakh was part of a state in northern Azerbaijan - the kingdom of Caucasian Albania (not to be confused with Albania in the Balkans) which emerged in the 4th century BC and ceased to exist in the 8th century AD. Later it was

Gandzasar, general view of the complex, 13th century, Karabakh, Aghdara District

Gandzasar, decorative design on the cupola's drum

continuously part of other state formations ruled by Azerbaijani dynasties: the Sajids (9th to 10th centuries), the Salarids (10th century), the Shaddadids (10th-11th centuries), the Atabay-Eldanizids (12th-13th centuries), the Jalarilar (14th-15th centuries), the Qaraqoyunlu (15th century), the Aghqoyunlu (15th-16th centuries) the Safavids (16th-17th centuries) and foreign empires which included Azerbaijani territory such as the Arabian Caliphate (8th-9th centuries), Seljuk Empire (11th-12th centuries), Mongol Hulakis (13th-14th centuries) and the Qajars (18th to 19th centuries).

After the fall of the Arabian Caliphate, the princedoms of Sunik and Artsakh-Khachen were established in Karabakh in the 12th-13th centuries. In the late 12th century the Sunik princedom fell and dynastic rule ceased there after the deaths of Gregor and Smbat in 1166. The Khachen princedom that flourished on the territory of Artsakh was part of ancient Albania.

From the 9th to the early 13th century Azerbaijan grew stronger under the rule of the Sajids, Atabays and Shirvanshahs. The Sajids and Atabays unified the historical lands of Azerbaijan. The Khachen princedom, established on former Albanian territory, reached its highest level of development during the reign of Hasan Jalal (1215-1261) of the Mehranis dynasty. Epigraphs found in monuments of the period describe him as the prince of the Khachen states, the mighty prince of the Khachen and Artsakh states and the ruler of Albania. One of the pearls of Albanian architecture - Gandzasar monastery - was built during this period. It is worth mentioning here, as an instance of the subordinate relationship between local rulers and their sovereigns, that in the 15th century Jahan, shah of the Qaraqoyunlu dynasty, granted the title of *melik* (from the Arabic for owner, lord, possessor or ruler) to Hasan Jalal, the ruler of Karabakh, and his Jalalid dynasty. The land of the Jalalids was later divided into five Albanian feudal princedoms (Gulustan, Jeravert, Khachen, Varanda and Dizaq).

Different faiths and different political powers competed in the formation of the Azerbaijani nation. At the time of the adoption of Christianity in Azerbaijan in the 4th century AD, Azerbaijan was a multi-ethnic and multi-confessional environment. Until the 4th century the population of Caucasian Albania, being ethnically Azerbaijani, professed the religion of fire-worship, which consequently spread to Iran and developed into Zoroastrianism. Over the course of the historical development of Azerbaijan, Christianity and Islam prevailed at different times and, consequently, there were several splits within the Azerbaijani ethnos. When Caucasian Albania adopted Christianity (AD 313) as the state religion, some of the Azerbaijanis who refused to become Christians continued to worship fire. The chasm deepened when a considerable part of the population began to practise Islam. However, the autocephalic Albanian Church, founded in the 6th to 7th centuries AD, continued to exist until its abolition in 1836 by the Russian Tsarist government.

The Russian Empire, acting in its own interests, used religion to gain influence in the region. To this end the independent Albanian Church was abolished on the Synod's decision and the Albanian

Panah Khan, founder of the
Karabakh khanate

Shusha, fortress walls

Patriarchate was subordinated to the Armenian Gregorian Church. The Armenian Church had grown from 1441 onwards after the Azerbaijani Qaraqoyunlu dynasty allowed the seat of the Armenian Patriarchate to be moved from Cilicia to Echmiadzin, near Irevan. The Christian population of Albania was gradually forced to join the Armenian Church.

Even when the local Caucasian Albanians of Karabakh embraced the Armenian Gregorian Church, some remained defiant and migrated to the left bank of the Kur River - their descendants still live in the Oghuz and Gabala districts of Azerbaijan.

The Safavid state began the centralization of all the lands of Azerbaijan in 1501. The Safavids established four *baylarbays* or provinces in Azerbaijan including the Karabakh or Ganja province. In 1593 the Ganja-Karabakh province consisted of seven regions and 36 districts. Almost all the 1,300 placenames were of Azerbaijani origin. None were Armenian in origin.

After the Safavids weakened, Azerbaijan became the subject of wars between Iran, the Russian Empire and the Ottoman Empire.

During this period the land of Ganja-Karabakh was part of the Ottoman Empire. Ottoman records show the domination of Azerbaijanis among the region's population. According to census figures, the population of the Ganja-Karabakh province was 122,000 people in 1727. Azerbaijanis accounted for 80,300 people (66 per cent), Armenians (or to be more exact Armenianized Albanians who had converted to Gregorianism) for 37,800 people (31 per cent) and Kurds for 3,700 people (3.1 per cent).

In 1909 and 1910 the Russian authorities connived with the Armenian Church to destroy local Albanian archives, including samples of Caucasian Albanian literature. The Russian historian V.L. Velichko deplored these actions in both Caucasian Albania and Georgia, which had something of a similar experience.

The history of Armenia also needs to be considered in order to understand better the appearance of the first ethnic Armenians in Azerbaijan in general and in Karabakh in particular.

From the Middle Ages to the end of May 1918, Armenia was an assumed territory, only a concept, since there was no corresponding administrative entity. The territory known today as the Republic of Armenia was shaped through international agreements in 1920 and 1921 on the territory of Western Azerbaijan.

According to Armenian historians, the Armenian state was established in the 6th century BC in Asia Minor, albeit within the political control of Persian and then Roman overlords, until its demise in the 4th century AD. Then an Armenian kingdom was brought into existence in the 9th to 14th centuries AD. These developments all took place outside the Caucasus.

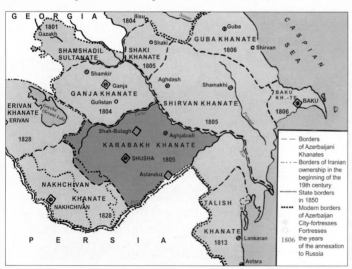

The occupation of Northern Azerbaijan by the Russian Empire (1801-28)

With the emergence of the Ottoman Empire, which resulted in the loss of hope for a sovereign state, some Armenians moved northwards into the Caucasian heartland, which included such Azerbaijani strongholds as Ganja and Zangezur.

From the 18th century onwards the Armenians gained an ally, Russia, which used them in its rivalry with the Ottoman and Persian empires. To ensure the success of its policy in the region, paying scant regard to the indigenous population's right to their own lands, Russia endeavoured to remove the indigenous inhabitants from their homes, particularly in the Azerbaijani provinces of Karabakh and Zangezur. By 1805 Russia was engaged in negotiations with the war-weary local rulers, particularly Ibrahim Khalil-Khan, the khan (lord) of the Azerbaijani independent Karabakh khanate (where the fortress in the capital Shusha was named Panahabad), and also with the lords of the Sheki and Shamakhi khanates. Through military conquest, Russia annexed the rest of the local Azerbaijani principalities of Lankaran, Baku, Guba, Ganja, Derbent and, in 1826, the Azerbaijani khanates of Nakhchivan and Irevan.

After the abolition of the khanate, military rule was established in Karabakh, as in other regions of North Azerbaijan, and it was annexed to the Military-Muslim District which had its centre in Shusha. The tsarist government was influenced by the 1830s revolts and conducted administrative and political reform in the South Caucasus. On 10 April 1840 Karabakh was turned into the Shusha Region and placed under the supervision of the Caspian Province which had its centre in Shamakhi. Thus, the concept of Karabakh lost its political meaning and was preserved merely as a geographic area.

During the administrative division of 1846, the Shusha Region was subordinated to the newly established Shamakhi Province and from 1859 to Baku. In 1867, with the creation of the Yelizavetpol (Ganja) Province, the Shusha Region was put under its administration and

Govhar Agha's two-minaret mosque, Shusha, early 19th century, painted by V.V. Vereshchagin

three more districts - Zangezur, Javanshir and Jabrayil - were created there. In this way the Shusha Region also lost its unique administrative-political meaning.

Russia had an interest in establishing a fellow Christian population of Armenians on the border of its empire, as a buffer against the local Azerbaijani khanates struggling to maintain their independence.

Under the Edirne Treaty of 1829 Armenians started to move from the Ottoman Empire to the newly occupied lands of North Azerbaijan. Armenians mainly moved to Karabakh.

The ethnic composition of the Karabakh khanate at the time of its abolition was recorded on the instructions of A.P. Yermolov, the commander-in-chief of Russian troops in the Caucasus. In spite of the policy of Armenianization, carried out before the record was drawn up (1805-22), most of the Karabakh population had remained Azerbaijanis since 1593.

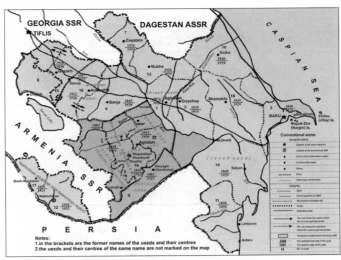

Karabakh in the administrative-territorial division of the Azerbaijani SSR (1920-29)

RESULTS OF ARMENIAN AGGRESSION

Occupied territories of Azerbaijan

Nagorny-Karabakh region

Territory	- 4 388 sq. km
Population (1989)	- 189 085
Armenians	- 145 450 (76,9%)
Azerbaijanis	- 40 688 (21,5%)
Russians	- 1922 (1%)
Others	- 1025 (0,6%)

Shusha district

Territory	- 289 sq. km
Population (1989)	- 20 579
Azerbaijanis	- 19 036 (92,5%)
Armenians	- 1 377 (6,7%)
Occupied	- May 8, 1992

Districts outside Nagorny-Karabakh region

	Occupation	Expulsion
Lachin	- May 18, 1992	- 71 000
Kelbajar	- April 2, 1993	- 74 000
Aghdam	- July 23, 1993	- 165 600
Fizuli	- August 23, 1993	- 146 000
Jabrayil	- August 23, 1993	- 66 000
Gubadly	- August 31, 1993	- 37 900
Zangilan	- October 29, 1993	- 39 500

Victims of aggresion

Killed - 20 000   Disabled - 50 000   Missing - 4 866

Destructions and damage

Settlements	- 890
Houses	- 150 000
Public Buildings	- 7 000
Schools	- 693
Kindergartens	- 855
Health Care Facilities	- 695
Libraries	- 927
Temples	- 44
Mosques	- 9
Historical Places	- 9
Historical Monuments and Museum	- 464
Museum Exhibits	- 40 000
Industrial and Agricultural Enterprises	- 6 000
Motor Ways	- 800 km
Bridges	- 160
Water Pipelines	- 2 300 km
Gas Pipelines	- 2 000 km
Electricity Lines	- 15 000 km
Forests	- 280 000 ha
Sowing Area	- 1 000 000 ha
Irrigation Systems	- 1 200 km

The total damage is estimated up to 60 billions US $

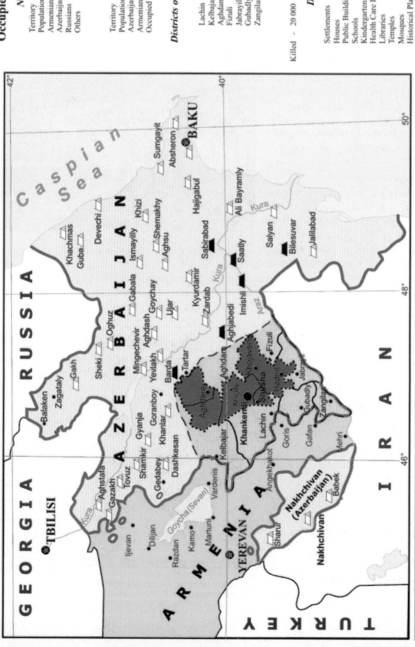

Refugees and IDP

Refugees from Armenia	- 250 000
Internally displaced persons from the occupied territories	- 660 000
Internally displaced persons from regions along the border with Armenia and line of occupation	- 100 000
Total	**- 1 010 000**

Armenian Armed Forces in the occupied territories

Tanks - 316	Artillery - 322		
ACV - 324	Personnel - 40 000		

Settlers illegally transferred to occupied territories

Nagorny-Karabakh	- 8 500
Lachin	- 13 000
Kelbajar	- 700
Zangilan	- 520
Jabrayil	- 280
Total	**- 23 000**

Legend:

- Temporary Refugee/IDP settlements
- IDP tent camps
- Occupied territories
- – – – Line of occupation
- ·········· Admin. line of the former NKAO of Az.SSR

In Yermolov's *Description*, 15,729 of 20,095 families in Karabakh were Azerbaijani (1,111 urban and 14,618 rural), while 4,366 families were Armenian, including Albanian (421 urban and 3,945 rural). Most of these Armenians were Gregoriyanized and Armenianized Albanians. New Armenian villages such as Maragali and Janyatag began to appear in Karabakh as the result of the mass resettlement of Armenians to the province. (Some time later Armenians erected monuments recording their resettlement to Karabakh, but destroyed them during their territorial claims against Azerbaijan in the 1980s.)

In 1828-30 alone, in accordance with the Treaty of Turkmenchay, the Russian imperial government settled about 130,000 Armenians from Iran and Turkey in the territories of the Azerbaijani khanates, including more than 50,000 in Karabakh. When Russia conquered the South Caucasus, the notion of "Armenia" was not linked with a political, integral entity. Armenians were simply known as a Christian community among the Muslim majority within Azerbaijani states. Following the Treaty of Turkmenchay, however, Russia created a new administrative unit and called it the Armenian Region (*Oblast*), despite the Armenians constituting the minority. It included the Irevan, Nakhchivan and Ordubad districts of

The treaty of 14 May 1805, signed by Ibrahim Khan of Karabakh and Russian General Tsitsianov, on the transfer of the Khanate to Russian rule, Kurakchay

Azerbaijan. The Armenian Region was abolished in 1849 and replaced with the Irevan Governorate, in accordance with the structure of the administrative-territorial divisions within the Russian Empire.

From the 19th century onwards the Armenians, despite their military and political weakness, tried to set a political agenda of their own (with the ultimate goal of creating an independent Armenian state) and to gain the utmost from the rivalry of the Great Powers in Anatolia and the South Caucasus. Between the Congress of Berlin and the San Stefano Conference in 1878 and the outbreak of the First World War in

Memorial erected in 1978 in the villlage of Maragha, Aghdara District, in Mountainous Karabakh (previously Mardakert) on the occasion of the 150th anniversary of the migration of the Armenian people from the Maragha region of Iran to this region. There is an inscription *Maragha-150* on the monument. In 1988 after Armenian territorial claims on Mountainous Karabakh the inscription on the monument disappeared. Later, the monument itself was completely destroyed. However, it is a fact that the Armenian people are not indigenous inhabitants of this region, but migrated there from Maragha region in Iran.

1914, the emergence of the "Armenian Question" gave rise to conflict. During that time, 500,000 Armenians were resettled with Russian acquiescence from Iran and Turkey to the historical lands of Azerbaijan.

The ambitions of Armenian ultra-nationalists, intent on creating their own states at the expense of Azerbaijan, played into the hands of the Russian overlords, creating a coincidence of interests. These shared policies continued into the Soviet period.

The February and October Revolutions of 1917 in Russia marked a new stage in the "Armenian Question". In October 1917 the Armenian Congress convened in Tiflis (now Tbilisi, the capital of Georgia) and demanded the annexation by Russia of Eastern Turkey, occupied by the Russian Army during the First World War. On 31 December of the same year, the Council of People's Commissars adopted a decree, signed by Lenin and Stalin, on the right to self-determination of "Turkish Armenia".

On 28 May 1918, the first democratic state in the Muslim world, namely the Azerbaijani Democratic Republic, was established. One of the first steps taken by the government of the new country was to yield on the following day, 29 May 1918, the city of Irevan (as stated earlier, the capital of the former Azerbaijani Irevan khanate) to the Republic of Armenia, which had declared its independence one day prior to Azerbaijan, on 27 May 1918, but which as yet had no political centre. The territory of the Republic of Armenia at the time was limited to Echmiadzin, Alexandropol and parts of the New Bayazid and Irevan districts, both with 50 per cent Azerbaijani populations.

Following the entry of British forces into Baku in 1918, General Thompson, who represented the Allied Powers, recognized Mountainous Karabakh together with the neighbouring Zangezur district under the administration of Azerbaijan. He confirmed the Azerbaijani government's appointment of Khosrov Sultanov as governor of the Karabakh General-Governorship, of which these two regions were part. In 1919 the Armenian Assembly of Mountainous Karabakh recognized officially the authority of Azerbaijan.

Nevertheless, the Armenian government, led by the Dashnak party (the Dashnaktsutyun), claimed from Azerbaijan the territories of Nakhchivan, Zangezur and Karabakh, and this led to war between Azerbaijan and Armenia in 1918-20. Thousands of Azerbaijanis were killed on the battlefield and in mas-

sacres committed by Dashnak-led Armenians and Bolsheviks in nearly all the main towns of Azerbaijan. This conflict seriously undermined the struggle of Azerbaijan and the other states of the region to maintain their independence and sovereignty.

The Armenian Dashnak government continued to wage war in the same areas of Karabakh, Nakhchivan and Zangezur until November 1920, when the entire Dashnak government was overthrown by Soviet Russia. This did not, however, lead to a solution of the territorial dispute.

The Armenian Soviet Socialist Republic continued to press the same territorial claims as its predecessors. Responding to these demands, the Caucasus Bureau of the Central Committee of the Russian Communist Party decided at its meeting of 5 July 1921 that:*"Taking into consideration the necessity of national peace between the Muslims and the Armenians, the importance of the economic relations between Upper and Lower Karabakh and the permanent relations of Upper Karabakh with Azerbaijan, Mountainous Karabakh shall be retained within the boundaries of the Soviet Socialist Republic of Azerbaijan and broad autonomy shall be given to Mountainous Karabakh with the city of Shusha as its administrative centre."*

In 1922 the Azerbaijani Soviet Socialist Republic was absorbed into the USSR and by a decision of July 1923, the Soviet Azerbaijan Central Executive Committee created for Mountainous Karabakh the status of autonomous region (the NKAO or Mountainous Karabakh Autonomous Oblast), a legal entity within the Azerbaijani SSR. The administrative centre of the NKAO was moved from Shusha to Khankandi (whose name was changed to Stepanakert later in the same year by Armenians to honour Stepan Shaumian, a well-known Armenian Bolshevik). The administrative divisions of Mountainous Karabakh were drawn artificially so as to ensure an Armenian majority in this ethnically mixed region. Official tsarist population records indicate that the population of Karabakh was overwhelmingly Muslim prior to the mass migration of Armenians (numbering more than 50,000) from Iran under the Treaty of Turkmenchay which ended the Russo-Persian War of 1826-28. Those who retained their

Chingiz Mustafayev (1960-1992)
He was one of Azerbaijan's most noted journalists, even though most of his work spans less than a year. With no formal journalistic training, he created a video anthology of the Karabakh war between Armenia and Azerbaijan - an incalculable contribution documenting the brutality of a war that ultimately claimed his own life. He was killed on 15 June 1992 during the war. He was declared a National Hero of Azerbaijan.

Christian faith were not ethnic Armenians, but descendants of ancient Albanians who had not accepted Islam. The Armenian majority that emerged in this way was used as the basis for the artificial creation of an Armenian entity.

The policy of the Soviet Union was far from even-handed. Several points have to be made here. For example, in contrast with the NKAO and its 138,600 Armenian and 47,500 Azerbaijani population (1989), neither the central government of the USSR nor the Armenian SSR had ever considered the possibility of granting even some status of cultural autonomy to the 300,000 Azerbaijanis residing compactly in Armenia (given the fact that Azerbaijan's population at the time was seven million in comparison to Armenia's three million). Moreover, many of them were forcibly deported from Armenia, particularly in 1948-50. Ethnic cleansing of all Azerbaijanis from Armenia was finalized in 1988-89.

Armenian expansionist ambitions, so skilfully exploited by the central authorities in Moscow to create havoc in the regions, eventually led in the late 1980s to the terrible aggression and calamity, which has blighted the whole area for more than a decade. On 1 December 1989, the Supreme Soviet of Armenia adopted a resolution on the unification of Mountainous Karabakh with Armenia. This resolution has never been rejected by the authorities of independent Armenia and can be interpreted as Armenia's official claim to Azerbaijani territory. On 26 November 1991 the Supreme Soviet of Azerbaijan adopted a law abolishing the resolution.

One-eighth of Azerbaijanis are now refugees or displaced persons, driven from Mountainous Karabakh or their homes in the surrounding areas or from Armenia. When Armenians had occupied Mountainous Karabakh (the former Mountainous Karabakh Autonomous Oblast) and seven surrounding Azerbaijani districts, in 1992-93 they committed unprecedented atrocities in these territories and ethnic cleansing. On 12 May 1994 a cease-fire agreement between the conflicting sides entered into force. Since 1992 the OSCE's Minsk Group has been tasked with helping to resolve the conflict. In 1993 the UN Security Council adopted four resolutions (822, 853, 874 and 884) condemning the occupation of Azerbaijani territories by Armenian forces and demanding their immediate and unconditional withdrawal from the occupied territories. In March 2008 the UN General Assembly adopted another resolution on the situation in the occupied territories of Azerbaijan. The resolution reaffirms the territorial integrity of Azerbaijan and demands the withdrawal of all Armenian forces from the occupied territories.

Neither history nor oppression can justify the Armenian territorial claims, which led to the conflict. The government of Azerbaijan is, therefore, committed to seeking a peaceful solution to the tragic conflict and to the elimination of all its consequences including, first of all, the withdrawal of troops from all the occupied territories and the return of the Azerbaijani population to their homes.

18 Why is 31 March the Day of Genocide of the Azerbaijanis?

By decree of Azerbaijani President Heydar Aliyev of 26 March 1998, the date 31 March was declared the Day of Genocide of Azerbaijanis in order to commemorate all the tragedies of genocide suffered by the Azerbaijani people.

Since the early 20th century Armenian nationalists, who were supported first by the Russian tsar and then the Soviet Union, aimed to clear the South Caucasus of local people in the hope of creating a "Greater Armenia". As a result of frequent crimes of genocide by the Armenians, two million Azerbaijanis were deported, 1.5 million were killed and ancient settlements, including historic monuments, were destroyed.

Under the terms of the Gulustan Treaty (1813) and Turkmenchay Treaty (1828) concluded between Russia and Iran, and the Edirne Treaty (1829) between Russia and the Ottoman Empire, 125,000 Armenians migrated from Turkey and Iran to Azerbaijani territories.

Although the Armenians settled in Azerbaijani khanates such as Irevan (the modern-day Armenian capital Yerevan and nearby territories), Nakhchivan and Karabakh and were in the minority compared with Azerbaijanis, they succeeded in creating an administrative

The Ismailiyye building ruined during the March slaughter in Baku, March 1918

Bazarnaya Street (now Azerbaijan Avenue) after the tragedy in Baku, March 1918

entity called the Armenian Region on the territories of the Irevan and Nakhchivan khanates. This was stipulated by decree of the Russian tsar on 21 March 1828. At that time there was no Armenian state or administrative entity in what is now modern-day Armenia. This artificial territorial division established the policy of ousting Azerbaijanis from their homelands and slaughtering them.

In 1905-07 Armenians overtly carried out massive bloody attacks against Azerbaijanis. The atrocities, begun by Armenians in Baku, spread to Azerbaijani villages and Azerbaijani-populated villages in what is now Armenia. Hundreds of settlements were destroyed and thousands of Azerbaijanis were ruthlessly killed.

The Armenians took advantage of the First World War and the February 1917 Revolution in Russia and managed to implement their claims under Bolshevism. From March 1918 a plan was worked out under the guise of a struggle against anti-revolutionary forces to sweep the Azerbaijanis away from the Baku governorate. Crimes perpetrated by Armenians at that time are engraved forever in the memory of the Azerbaijani people. Thousands of Azerbaijanis were murdered because of their ethnicity. Thousands of Azerbaijanis were tor-

Ambushed and murdered family in Khojali, 1992

tured and killed in Baku in just three days in March. The genocide of the Azerbaijani people was carried out in a targeted, brutal manner in Baku, Shamakhi, Guba, Karabakh, Zangezur, Nakhchivan, Lankaran, Goychay and other areas.

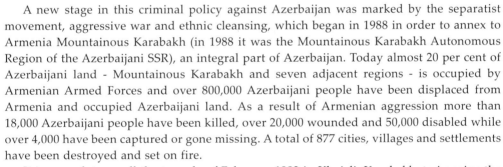

A son finds his dead mother after the massacre in Khojali, 1992

The Armenians skillfully took advantage of the sovietization of the South Caucasus and declared Azerbaijan's Zangezur district a part of the Armenian SSR in 1920. Later, in 1948-53, they achieved the mass deportation of the Azerbaijani population from their homeland. The policy of deportation of the Azerbaijanis was set out in a decree dated 23 December 1947 of the USSR Soviet of Ministers and entitled "A special decision on the migration of collective farmers and other Azerbaijani people from the Armenian SSR to the Kur-Araz plain of the Azerbaijani SSR ". Under this decree more than 150,000 Azerbaijanis were forcibly exiled from Armenia.

A new stage in this criminal policy against Azerbaijan was marked by the separatist movement, aggressive war and ethnic cleansing, which began in 1988 in order to annex to Armenia Mountainous Karabakh (in 1988 it was the Mountainous Karabakh Autonomous Region of the Azerbaijani SSR), an integral part of Azerbaijan. Today almost 20 per cent of Azerbaijani land - Mountainous Karabakh and seven adjacent regions - is occupied by Armenian Armed Forces and over 800,000 Azerbaijani people have been displaced from Armenia and occupied Azerbaijani land. As a result of Armenian aggression more than 18,000 Azerbaijani people have been killed, over 20,000 wounded and 50,000 disabled while over 4,000 have been captured or gone missing. A total of 877 cities, villages and settlements have been destroyed and set on fire.

It is enough to recall the tragedy of February 1992 in Khojali, Karabakh, to imagine the scale and brutality of the genocide against Azerbaijanis perpetrated by the Armenian Armed Forces. The town of Khojali was destroyed and 613 civilians, including 18 children and 106 women were brutally killed, 487 disabled and 1,275 inhabitants captured and cruelly tortured.

All the tragedies of the Azerbaijani people in the 19th-20th centuries, including the occupation of their territory, have been various stages in a genocidal policy systematically worked out by Armenians.

19 When did Azerbaijan restore its independence?

The independent Azerbaijani state collapsed in April 1920 as a result of the invasion of Soviet Russia. It was restored 70 years later in 1991. On 30 August 1991 the declaration on "the restoration of the state independence of the Republic of Azerbaijan" was adopted. On 18 October the same year a new era of independent development began with the adoption of the Constitutional Act on "the restoration of the state independence of the Republic of Azerbaijan".

The emergence of independent Azerbaijan was the inevitable result of socio-political processes under way in the USSR and all over the world. These processes resulted in the disintegration of the Soviet Union, the dismantling of the Communist Party and the independence of all the union states of the USSR.

Today the Republic of Azerbaijan, as a politically and economically stable state in the region, plays a specific role in the world community. Azerbaijan has established diplomatic relations with more than 145 states and joined 14 international organizations, including the UN, OSCE and Council of Europe. Azerbaijan collaborates with the European Union within the framework of a Partnership and Co-operation Agreement on the economy, legislation and culture as well as in combating illegal immigration and human trafficking.

46

Who is the most prominent Azerbaijani statesman?

Azerbaijan's most famous statesman is Heydar Aliyev. He was born on 10 May 1923 in the city of Nakhchivan in Azerbaijan. In 1939, after graduating from the Nakhchivan Pedagogical School, he studied at the architectural department of the Azerbaijani Industrial Institute (now the Azerbaijani State Oil Academy). The incipient war stopped him completing his education.

In 1941, Heydar Aliyev headed a department at the People's Commissariat of Internal Affairs in the Nakhchivani ASSR and in 1944 was sent to work in the state security bodies. Heydar Aliyev continued to work for the security apparatus and in 1964 became deputy chairman, and in 1967 chairman of the State Security Committee under the Cabinet of Ministers of the Azerbaijani Republic, with the rank of lieutenant-general. In these years, he received special higher education in Leningrad (now St Petersburg), and in 1957 he graduated from the history department of the Azerbaijani State University.

In July 1969 the Plenum of the Central Committee of the Communist Party of Azerbaijan elected Heydar Aliyev first secretary of the Central Committee of the Communist Party of Azerbaijan. This meant that he was the leader of the republic. In December 1982, Heydar Aliyev was elected a candidate member of the Politburo of the Central Committee of the Communist Party of the Soviet Union, and appointed first deputy chairman of the Cabinet of Ministers of the USSR, thereby becoming one of the leaders of the Soviet Union. For 20 years Heydar Aliyev was a deputy of the USSR Supreme Soviet and for five years deputy chairman of the Supreme Soviet. In October 1987, Heydar Aliyev, as a sign of protest against the policy pursued by the Politburo of the Central Committee of the Communist Party of the Soviet Union and personally by the secretary general, Mikhail Gorbachev, resigned from his post.

On 20 January 1990 over 100 people were killed by Soviet troops on the streets of Baku. Heydar Aliyev appeared the next day at the Azerbaijani Representation in Moscow and made a statement, demanding punishment for the organizers and perpetrators of this crime against the people of Azerbaijan. As a sign of protest against the hypocritical policy of the leadership of the USSR and in connection with the critical conflict brewing in Mountainous Karabakh, Heydar Aliyev left the Communist Party of the Soviet Union in July 1991.

In July 1990 Heydar Aliyev returned to Azerbaijan, living first in Baku, then in Nakhchivan. The same year he was elected a deputy to the Supreme Soviet of Azerbaijan. In 1991-93, he held the posts of chairman of the Supreme Majlis of the Nakhchivan Autonomous Republic and deputy chairman of the Supreme Soviet of the Republic of Azerbaijan. In 1992, at the constituent congress of the Yeni Azerbaijan (New Azerbaijan) Party in Nakhchivan, Heydar Aliyev, was elected chairman of the party.

In May-June 1993, as the result of extreme tension in the government, the country was on the

verge of civil war and of losing its independence. The people of Azerbaijan called for Heydar Aliyev to return to power. The then leaders of Azerbaijan were obliged officially to invite Heydar Aliyev to Baku. On 15 June 1993, Heydar Aliyev was elected chairman of the Supreme Soviet (or parliament) of Azerbaijan, and on 24 July, by resolution of the parliament, he took on the powers of president of the Azerbaijani Republic.

On 3 October 1993, in a nationwide poll, Heydar Aliyev was elected president of the Azerbaijani Republic. On 11 October 1998 he gained 76.1 per cent of votes in an election with a high turnout and was, therefore, re-elected president of the Azerbaijani Republic. Heydar Aliyev gave his consent to be nominated as a candidate in the 15 October 2003 presidential elections, but had to withdraw because of health problems.

The historic destiny of Azerbaijan over the last 30 years is inseparably linked with the name of Heydar Aliyev. The revival of the people during this period in all spheres of socio-political, economic and cultural life is connected with his name. During this period of his leadership Heydar Aliyev helped his native land, Azerbaijan. He persistently strove towards progress and was proud of Azerbaijan's rich culture and great history. He was concerned for future generations and helped the state to overcome harsh ordeals.

In June 1993, when the people of Azerbaijan believed that national statehood was on the edge of destruction, when the hardest times began, they insisted on a change in the authorities and since that time entrusted their destiny to Heydar Aliyev. Heydar Aliyev, seeing the misfortune of his nation, accepted the invitation and returned to national politics in Azerbaijan. The day of his return, 15 June, is now celebrated as the Day of National Salvation by his grateful people.

Heydar Aliyev died at the age of 80 on 12 December 2003, and was mourned deeply by the Azerbaijani nation.

There are Heydar Aliyev monuments in Baku, Bucharest, Cairo, Kiev, Tbilisi and other cities worldwide.

21 What is the Azerbaijani landscape like?

The most remarkable geographical feature of Azerbaijan is its variety. The country has nine of the world's 13 climatic zones. From dry and humid subtropics to mountainous tundra, temperatures range from +45°C in the plains to -45°C in the mountains.

Some of the plains are markedly dry, while other humid regions are green and lush. The passage from the hot house of the lowlands and humid subtropics to permanent snow and glaciers in the mountains is striking. The medium altitude and subalpine zones with maximum humidity have allowed splendid natural mountain forests and subalpine meadows to flourish.

Caucasus Mountains in Khizi

Most of the flat territory of Azerbaijan consists of a semi-desert, arid steppe type of landscape. This covers the following areas: the southern part of the Samur-Davachi lowland, the Absheron Peninsula, most of Gobustan, all the Kur-Araz lowland and part of the right bank of the Kur River from Ganja to Aghstafa. The same landscape can be traced from the northern shores of Mingachevir Reservoir to Gobustan and down to the plain of Nakhchivan.

Gabala

This area is flat, relieved only by small clusters of low foothills (in Gobustan and in the Ganja-Gazakh plain) damaged by soil erosion and so arid that locally they are called "badlands". The predominant soil in this landscape is grey earth, with saline and fragmentary meadow. Vegetation cover is poor. Yet the economic importance for Azerbaijan of this landscape is considerable. For centuries, indigenous cultivation and irrigation have turned this region into one of intensive agricultural production.

Hills range from altitudes of 400-500 metres to 1,400-1,600 metres, from the Jeyranchel-Ajinur foothills in the south-east of the Greater Caucasus range down to the mountains of Nakhchivan. Mountainous grey-brown, dark-chestnut, chestnut and light chestnut soils are all found here. Lowland meadow-forest and moderately dry landscapes are typical of the Shollar Plain, the north of the Samur-Davachi lowlands and the lower area of the Alazan-Agrichay Plain. These areas typically have river deposits and meadow and forest soils.

A forest landscape is widespread at the high altitudes from 800 metres to 2,000-2,200 metres, within the low and middle mountainous zones. Here broadleaf forests of the Iberian type (oak, hornbeam, beech and chestnut) are widespread. The eastern slopes of the Talysh Mountains are mainly covered by forests of this type (locally called *Girkan*). Meadows and shrubs appear in large clearings. In the mountains soils are mostly red and brown and in the less mountainous areas meadows are chalky. Within the Talysh region, poorer quality mountain yellow earth can be observed.

An Alpine meadow landscape is to be found at heights of 2,000-3,000 metres on the narrow slopes of both the Greater and Lesser Caucasus ranges and on the gently sloping areas of the Karabakh volcanic plateau. Subalpine and alpine meadows serve as summer pastures.

Glacial landscapes can be seen on the high mountains above 3,000 metres. Here exposed rocks, screes and moraines predominate, with some permanent snow and a few individual glaciers. Ancient glacial forms of landscape are widely developed. Economic activity throughout the ages reflected all these variations of the complex landscape of the country.

Fauna and flora

Azerbaijan is rich in fauna and flora. There are 4,200 species of plant in Azerbaijan, 66 per cent of the flora of the Caucasus. Of the 6,000 plant species in the Caucasus Azerbaijan possesses 4,100. Azerbaijan's landscape is filled with an incredible variety of plants. Mountain grass and forest and mountain xerophyte are common in the republic. Olive, mulberry, pomegranate, cornelian cherry and

Gazelles and deer in the Shirvan National Park

plane trees grow in Azerbaijan. The plant species in Azerbaijan belong to 125 families, which is 80 per cent of all Caucasian varieties. There are up to 370 plant species endemic in Azerbaijan. The regions of Nakhchivan and Zuvand in Azerbaijan are rich in plants and make up 9 per cent of the total flora of the republic. Though forest covers a small part of the country (11.5 per cent of the total area), it boasts many plant species. There are 435 kinds of wild trees and bushes in the forests.

Azerbaijan has 607 animal species (mammals, reptiles and amphibians), 5.3 per cent of the world's fauna. There are 97 mammal species, including the mountain goat, leopard, marked deer, gazelle, roe deer, wild boar, bear, hyena, squirrel, wild cat, seal, wolf, fox, jackal and lynx.

Geographical Features & Natural Resources

Zagatala

Gakh

Lerik

Ismayilli

There are 58 species of reptile, 23 of them are snakes, of which five are poisonous. The most important ones are the Caucasian viper, the shield-faced snake and the Asia Minor viper.

Azerbaijan is also rich in amphibians and birds. There are hundreds of species of birds that nest in the lakes of Gizilaghach, Agh Gol, Shahdili, Davachi and Mingachevir. In Azerbaijan there are 358 species of birds, of which the most famous are partridges, pheasants, nightingales, sultan hens, herons, storks, sandpipers, hawks, bustards, swallows, woodpeckers, quail, starlings, blackbirds and different species of geese, ducks and eagles.

A couple of Bactrian camels, Absheron National Park

Azerbaijan is rich in fish too. There are 95 species of fish in the Caspian Sea and other water basins of the country. Most notable are the sturgeon, omul, bream and lamprey.

Rivers and lakes

Q&A

Of the more than 1,000 rivers in Azerbaijan, only 21 are longer than 97 kilometres (60 miles). The Kur, the largest river in the Caucasus, flows through Azerbaijan from north-west to south-east and empties into the Caspian Sea. The main tributary of the Kur is the Araz River. Most of Azerbaijan's rivers are in the Kur basin. In the plains the rivers are used for crop irrigation. The large Mingachevir Hydroelectric Power Plant and the Mingachevir Reservoir, 605 square kilometres in area (234 square miles), are located on the Kur. Most of the 250 lakes in Azerbaijan are small. Lake Hacigabul is the largest, with an area of 16 square kilometres (six square miles), and Lake Boyukshor with an area of 10 square kilometres (four square miles) is the next largest while Goygol is the deepest.

Aghdara

22 What are Azerbaijan's natural resources?

Azerbaijan is very rich in natural resources, the most important being oil. Most of the famous oil-fields are situated around the Absheron Peninsula, offshore and onshore. Gas too has been discovered and there are also unique sources of medicinal oil, called Naftalan, located near the city of Ganja.

Mud volcano, Absheron

Minerals include iron ore, alunite, sulphuric pyrites, molybdenum and arsenic. Other metal ores have been found in Filizchay.

There is iron ore in Dashkasan in the Lesser Caucasus, and in nearby Zaglik is one of the largest known reserves of alunite, from which aluminium is made. Cobalt and sulphuric pyrites can be mined in the same region. Rock salt, arsenic ores and molybdenum can be mined in Paragachay in Nakhchivan.

There is also marble and granite in the Lesser Caucasus, and gravel, limestone and fire-resistant brick clay in Absheron. Well-known mineral waters, which arise from volcanic and limestone rocks, come from Istisu, Turshsu and Badamli.

Azerbaijan consists of a flat plain surrounded by steep mountains which slope towards the Caspian Sea and isolated plains. The mountains provide barriers from the northern winds and rain from the west. They also moderate the humidity from the Caspian Sea. Only from the north-east and east is Azerbaijan open to the intrusion of air masses from the Urals, Siberia and Central Asia.

These major features and Azerbaijan's geographical location determine its natural habitat, which differs from that of other countries located on the same latitudes.

Although there are some pockets of desert and steppe which resemble those of Central Asia they can be crossed in less than three hours driving and there is dense forest in the surrounding mountains. Vegetation is more tolerant of dry conditions on the edges of the Greater and Lesser Caucasus. On the mountain slopes, where there are few trees, some cultivation is possible.

A great number of rivers flow from the mountains to the plains and fan out to create "dry deltas" in the foothills, in a line of oases. Most of the cities and villages of Azerbaijan are situated in this zone. Here is much water for gardens, plantations, vegetable plots, vineyards, and trees such as poplars, walnut trees, plane trees and others.

23 Where did industrial production of oil start?

Oil is one of the main strategic, natural assets to have played a significant role in the history of Azerbaijan and its economic development.

Azerbaijan is often referred to as the Land of Fire, since ancient religions based on fire-worship originated here. Oil extracted in Azerbaijan in the 4th to 3rd centuries BC was called Median oil. Among the first written sources referring to Baku oil are those of Marco Polo, who travelled along the ancient Silk Road. The fame of Baku's oil riches spread around the world and later attracted a flow of foreign investors as the industrial revolution gained momentum.

At Bibi Heybat on the Caspian coast near Baku an oil well was drilled mechanically for the first time by 1848, 11 years before a similar well was drilled in the USA. But in oil literature it is accepted that an oil well was first drilled mechanically in 1859 in Pennsylvania, USA. This date is widely accepted as the beginning of the oil industry. In 1871 the country witnessed the first use of steam-engine oil production. At the turn of the century Azerbaijan was producing over half of the world's oil. Baku was, therefore, widely recognized as the cradle of the oil industry.

In 1872 with the abolition of the state monopoly on the oil industry the economy began to develop dynamically and foreign companies and commercial entities broadened their activity. In the second half of the 19th century oil production in Baku exceeded the USA. As a result of changes in the oil industry, Baku ranked first in the world in this field. During this period foreign investments played an important role in the development of the oil industry. In 1879 the Nobel brothers founded their company in Baku. Baku oil played a big part in the establishment of the Nobel fund, which is behind the Nobel Prize. When this fund was set up about 12.4 per cent of the capital belonged to Alfred Nobel, one of the stock holders in the Nobel Brothers Company in Baku. Businessmen, such as Rothschild, also invested in the Azerbaijani economy. In 1901 Baku provided more than 50 per cent of the oil produced worldwide, which in turn was 95 per cent of the oil extracted in the Russian Empire.

The development of the oil industry stimulated other industrial sectors too and, in 1907, the construction of the Baku - Batumi kerosene pipeline promoted oil export. It was one of the first industrial pipelines connecting the Caspian and Black Seas.

During the First World War Baku oil was at the centre of attention, because of the need for fuel for new military hardware. In 1918-20 this interest resulted in political struggles between various states (Russia, Turkey, Germany and Britain) and in 1920 Bolshevik Russia occupied Azerbaijan.

Geographical Features & Natural Resources

The dynamic development of the oil industry, as well as the ever growing world demand for oil and the need to transport it to international markets, led to technological innovation. The world's first oil tanker served Baku and in 1924 the first offshore well was drilled, thus pioneering offshore exploration.

Baku oil played a crucial role in defeating German fascism, fuelling one in two Soviet combat tanks and one in three war planes. Baku was a prime target in Hitler's plan to defeat the Soviet Union.

Keeping up with the innovative tradition, in 1949 offshore developments expanded further into the open seas, resulting in the erection of the world's first and largest "town" built on stilts at sea, known as Neft Dashlari (Oily Rocks). For the rest of the Soviet period the Azerbaijani oil industry was neglected in favour of further oil exploration and development, as new oilfields were discovered in Western Siberia. However, Azerbaijani oil engineers and specialists played an important role in discovering and developing new oilfields in Russia, in other republics of the former Soviet Union, in the Middle East, North Africa and East Asia.

Haji Zeynalabdin Taghiyev (1823-1924)
A well-known Azerbaijani entrepreneur and the first patron of science and the arts in the East. Haji Zeynalabdin Taghiyev was a stonemason, but thanks to his hard work and shrewd investments he rose to become one of the richest men in tsarist Russia. He was the only Azerbaijani entrepreneur to invest in almost all areas of the economy. He was progressive in his charitable work, supporting talented Azerbaijani young people studying abroad. Haji Zeynalabdin Taghiyev supported cultural and educational organizations, including schools and newspapers. He opened Azerbaijan's first school of agriculture (1894), first theatre (1883) and the first girls' school (1901). He also built a water pipeline to Baku (1917). Because of his philanthropic work, Azerbaijanis called him the Father of the Nation.

According to experts' rough estimates, over six billion barrels (about one billion tonnes) of oil have been extracted so far from Azerbaijani onshore fields. Despite the crude and neglectful exploitation of local oilfields, most reserves still remain untapped.

Proven recoverable oil reserves in Azerbaijan are about six-seven billion barrels. Estimated total reserves are over thirty billion barrels. There are 67 discovered oilfields in Azerbaijan of which only 44 are currently operating. More than 75 per cent of oil resources are offshore.

A new era in the country's oil industry started in the early 1990s with the independence of Azerbaijan. Resisting all internal and external pressure, the leadership of Azerbaijan opened the riches of the Caspian Sea to the international community by inviting oil majors to take part in developing its reserves.

Geographical Features & Natural Resources

On 20 September 1994 the Contract of the Century was signed between the government of Azerbaijan and a number of multi-national oil companies for the development of the Azari, Chiraq and Gunashli oilfields. Under this contract over half a billion tonnes of oil will be extracted. The extraction and export of oil are now well under way.

Since this first international contract, many production-sharing agreements (PSAs) worth over 40 billion US dollars have been signed with leading multinational oil companies to develop offshore and onshore fields. Oil majors such as Agip, BP, Chevron, Exxon-Mobil and LUKoil and many others, representing over 14 nations, are now established in Baku, turning the capital of Azerbaijan into a true United Nations of the oil industry.

Peak oil production is expected to be reached by 2010 at a level of 65-70 million tonnes a year (currently just over 50 million tonnes). Baku again, as a century ago, is on track to revive itself as a major oil centre in the new global province around the Caspian Sea.

Extensive oil exploration led to the creation of a huge industrial complex to serve the developments around the Caspian and parts of the former USSR. Over 20 large enterprises, employing 20,000 people, satisfied up to 70 per cent of the needs of the whole USSR for special equipment and machinery. Product ranges included industrial pumping units, submersible oil pumps, drilling rigs, offshore platforms, well installations, water and gas taps, derricks and so on. The largest offshore

platform production plant in Europe was put into operation in the early 1980s. Nowadays, the industry aims to serve the massive developments in the energy sector in the Caspian region as well as in other oil regions. At present, industry is in desperate need of restructuring and modernization so that it can switch production to internationally acceptable engineering standards.

As well as oil, Azerbaijan has become a significant gas exporter too. Azerbaijan has proven gas reserves of 2,000 billion cubic metres (bcm). Projected production, however, will increase up to 45 bcm by 2015 . Azerbaijan's natural gas production is based on the reserves of offshore fields and associated gas from offshore oilfields. The newly developed Shah Daniz gas field in the Caspian provides Azerbaijan with 25 million cubic metres of gas per day. Shah Daniz is estimated to have reserves of more than 1,000 bcm. In the past term 6 bcm of gas were extracted from Shah Daniz, 2.5 bcm of which were exported via the Baku - Tbilisi - Erzurum gas pipeline to Turkey. So gas is becoming increasingly important in Azerbaijan's energy sector.

24   What is medicinal oil?

One of the unique riches of Azerbaijan is a rare type of oil - Naftalan. It is famous worldwide for its healing properties. This rare kind of oil does not burn and is used both internally and externally for medicinal purposes. The word Naftalan comes from the Azerbaijani *neft alan* ("an oil buyer"). The town of Nafatalan, where Naftalan oilfield is situated, is 320 km from Baku in Goranboy District.

The first use of Naftalan oil is lost in the mists of time. According to one story, a medieval herder decided to leave behind a particularly sick, mangy camel. The beast rolled over into an oil pool and was left for dead. But when the herder returned some weeks later, he found the camel miraculously cured. He credited the oil with healing the camel.

According to medieval annals, most ailments were cured some days after treatment. The medical significance of Naftalan was known not only among the local population but also far beyond Azerbaijan. When patients left Naftalan after treatment, they took some oil to continue the procedure at home. This was the first, unorganized "export" of Naftalan oil. A group of merchants later formed who sold Naftalan oil in Iran, Asia Minor and elsewhere in the east.

Azerbaijani poet Nizami (1141-1209) mentions Naftalan oil in his poem *Khamsa*. He describes Naftalan oil being taken from the village of Seficurd by caravan. Traveller Marco Polo, who visited Azerbaijan in the 13th century, also refers to Naftalan oil in his writings about *Great Tatarstan*.

Prospecting, exploitation and processing of Naftalan oil on an industrial scale began in the 19th century. During this period Naftalan oil gained popularity in the west. An area of 48 hectares in Naftalan oilfield was given to eight Germans (four of them were German or Austrian and the others Russian citizens) by the local governor in 1868. One of them, German chemist and engineer

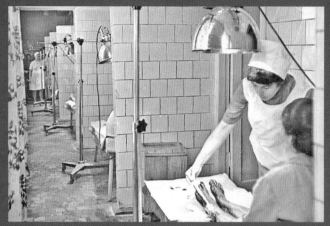

K. Yeguer, investigated the chemical properties of the oil He was very disappointed not to discover petroleum fractions in the oil, as the oil did not burn. When he heard later about the medicinal properties of the oil, Yeguer developed a small factory to produce ointment in 1892, with the permission of the Russian tsarist government, and sold it as an effective medicine. Yeguer's company enjoyed rapid success. He sent samples of Naftalan ointment to prominent doctors worldwide. Professor List from Magdeburg took great interest in the oil and bought up the product for Germany. Interestingly, Yeguer's ointment was banned in Russia and was imported there from Germany under patent and sold at a high price. Yeguer produced another ointment based on Naftalan, Kojelan, and this product was also commercially successful. Kojelan oil keeps the body's skin smooth and protects leather goods and metals.

In 1911-12 another German businessman, Kuel, founded the German-Naftalan Stock Company and launched production of some medicines. Two more stock companies were established - Naftalan in Magdeburg and Naftalan in Dresden - and produced a variety of ointments, pills, pastes, liniments, soaps for soft skin and cosmetic products and exported them to various countries including Russia.

Demand for Naftalan oil and its products increased in a short time in Germany, Britain, France, Japan, Austria and elsewhere. During the Russo-Japanese war every Japanese soldier had Naftalan ointment in his kitbag to treat skin diseases and frostbite. As medicines based on Naftalan oil became famous worldwide, the German producers presented their goods as German medicine rather than Naftalan oil. During the Second World War Naftomastica medicine, prepared from Naftalan oil, was widely used in hospitals to treat injuries, traumatic arthritis, burns and frostbite.

The first studies of Naftalan were made by the Russian doctors Rosenbaum, Malishev, Mendeleyev and Burozovich. Azerbaijani scientist Yusif Mammadaliyev was the first to identify that the healing properties of Naftalan are related to the polycyclic naften hydrocarbons that are the main active ingredients in Naftalan. Academician Ali Quliyev defined the biological specifications and

their effects on the organism. This research led to the technique of separating naften hydrocarbons.

Physical and chemical analysis reveals that Naftalan differs from other kinds of oil. The density of purified Naftalan ranges from 0.923 to 0.974 grams per cubic centimetre. Naftalan boils at 200-250°C and freezes at -20 to -30°C. Sulphur and nitrogen are the main ingredients of Naftalan crude, but it also contains a wide variety of micro elements. Naftalan oil does not include light fractions and methane hydrocarbons and does not burn.

Medicine made from Naftalan is used in various external and internal treatments. It is used against inflammation as an anaesthetic and disinfectant. As it penetrates the skin, Naftalan accelerates the metabolic process, thereby boosting cell regeneration. It has a calming, cooling and antiseptic effect, relieves joint pain, cures psoriasis, calms nerves and beautifies the skin. The type of application depends on the specific disease and the doctor's recommendations. For diseases such as eczema and psoriasis, for instance, Naftalan-based medicine is rubbed on the skin. The oil also helps ultrasound to penetrate more effectively, so is rubbed on the skin before ultrasound is applied. Naftalan is used in tampons and suppositories to reduce internal inflammation and to treat gynaecological problems.

Patients who suffer chronic arthritis have to have ongoing drug treatment. Yet in Azerbaijan patients who undergo 10 days of Naftalan treatment often find that their pain is alleviated for an entire year, meaning that they don't have to take additional medicine. Patients take baths of Naftalan oil which has been heated to 38°C.

The field is currently exploited by SOCAR's (State Oil Company of the Azerbaijan Republic's) Azneft production unit. Naftalan crude is a unique resource in Azerbaijan. It holds great promise for international medicine at a time when Azerbaijan's offshore oil is in great demand on the world fuel market.

25 What is the world's biggest lake?

The Caspian Sea is the largest salt lake in the world. But its size, hydrologic characteristics and origin mean that it can also be called a sea. In the past, the Caspian was linked to larger seas in the west and the north. The past connection with northern seas can be seen through the palaeontological data of some types of animal forms preserved in the Caspian (up to 15 types of crustaceans and fish and other representatives of cold water fauna).

The total area of the Caspian is 376,000 square kilometres and it is, therefore, larger than some seas. The volume of water is 76,000 cubic kilometres. The length of the coastline is approximately 7,350 kilometres of which 800 are in Azerbaijan. The northern coast of Azerbaijan borders the Middle Caspian and the Southern Caspian in the south-east. These two areas are divided by a marine ridge which is a continuation of both the Caucasian mountain range and the Absheron Peninsula. The deepest part of the Derbent trough of the Middle Caspian is 760 metres, whereas the Lankaran trough is 1,020 metres deep.

Surface and underground outflows and atmospheric precipitation fill the Caspian Sea with water at an annual rate of approximately 417 cubic kilometres. The same amount evaporates from the surface. The sea level changes when this balance is not achieved. The present level of the sea is 28 metres lower than mean sea level, but this has fluctuated greatly in the past. There is evidence for this from historical documents, archaeological ruins and coastal terraces.

The temperature of the water also changes significantly according to season and the area of the sea. The average temperature in summer varies from 22ºC along the north coast of Azerbaijan to 26ºC in the south. In winter the water can fall to 5ºC in the north and to 8ºC in the south. Salt levels in the Middle and Southern Caspian vary between 11 and 13 per cent and drop to nearly 0 per cent near river estuaries.

Only the northern part of the Caspian Sea freezes in winter and this does not affect Azerbaijan, except sporadically at the end of winter (February). But in abnormally cold years, ice is driven from the north by winds and currents up to Absheron and they threaten the offshore oilfields and platforms. Local ice, 20-25 cm thick, has also been observed here.

Azerbaijan's north-eastern sea coast is almost straight, with hardly any indentations at all. Only

the Absheron Peninsula stands out into the sea. It is approximately 70 kilometres long and 35 kilometres wide. Further south the coast is more indented. Capes, bights, bays and archipelagos were formed, because the coastline was susceptible to tectonic changes. Mud volcanoes are active here too. The coast sinks into the water, and islands and even ruined human settlements rise up again when the waters recede.

There are ancient legends of sunken cities in the Caspian Sea and of a neck of land that once connected the western and eastern sea coasts. Yunan Sheher (City of the Greeks) was the name given to a supposed city close to Baku and now popularly presumed to be submerged under the Caspian waters. Arab geographer Istakhri (951-1000 AD) mentioned another city on an island in the Kur River estuary, the Devil's Settlement. The name also appeared on an 1825 map for a nearby island.

In May 1861 an island appeared near an eruption. It had disappeared by the beginning of 1862 and research indicated it rose again as a shoal in 1869. It has risen and disappeared again, even in the past 10 years. Could this have been the legendary sunken island? Even today fishermen and navigators call this area Kharaba Sheher (Ruins of the City). The Caspian Sea is crucial to Azerbaijan as a transport route, a source of different minerals and, of course, of oil and gas from the seabed.

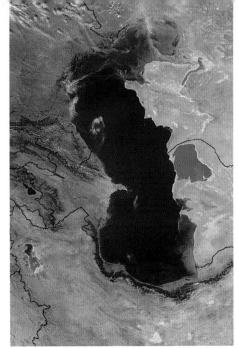

The world's largest inland lake, the salty Caspian Sea separates Europe from Asia. Around the Sea, the snow has largely disappeared, except in the snow-capped Caucasus Mountains, and the land is turning green with the first flush of spring. Five countries border the Sea. Starting in the top right corner and moving clockwise, they include: Kazakhstan, Turkmenistan, Iran, Azerbaijan, and Russia.
Credit Jeff Schmaltz, MODIS Rapid Response Team, NASA/GSFC

26   What is the Azerbaijani weather like?

In Azerbaijan summer is hot and dry, autumn is warm and rainy, winter is cool and spring is irregular. The mountains can be windy. These are the general climatic characteristics of Azerbaijan, which is basically transient to subtropical and attracts tourists. There are nine of the 13 climatic types in Azerbaijan and most of the country is either dry or humid and subtropical. This in turn means that some subtropical crops are grown here.

The highest temperature observed during the year is +44°C (Julfa District, Nakhchivan) and the hottest months are July and August. In general the average temperature in the summer varies between 26°C and 35°C and the weather is hot and humid.

In January, which is the coldest month, the temperature can drop to zero and sometimes reaches -13°C to -17°C and elsewhere even -20°C. It's interesting that the lowest temperature (-32°C) is observed in Nakhchivan too. The lowest rainfall (200 mm) is observed on the Absheron Peninsula while the highest is in the south (Lankaran lowland).

Climate	
Annual average temperature	+ 12.9°C
Average temperature in January	+ 0.1°C
Average temperature in July	+ 23.6°C
Annual average precipitation	484.1 mm

Baku boulevard

questions

27 to

32

Constitution & System of Government

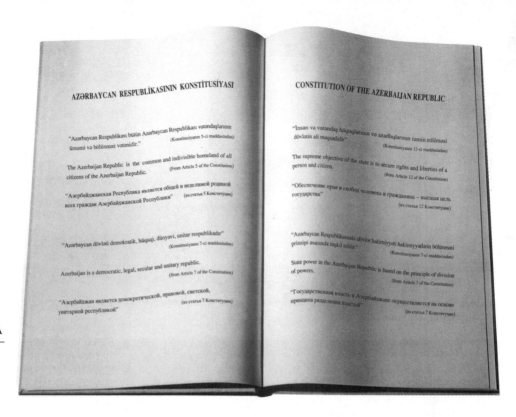

27 Does Azerbaijan have a constitution?

The Constitution of the Republic of Azerbaijan, which was adopted on 12 November 1995 by referendum, is the first constitution of independent Azerbaijan. Until this Constitution came into force the country operated on the basis of an amended version of the last constitution of the Azerbaijani SSR, adopted in 1978. The very first Constitution of the Azerbaijani SSR was adopted in 1921. The current Constitution was drawn up by a commission led by the Azerbaijani president, which included representatives of legislative, executive and judicial bodies and prominent lawyers. It was submitted for popular discussion. The Constitution consists of five divisions, 12 chapters and 158 provisions and is considered in terms of its content and principles to be one of the most democratic in the world.

According to the Constitution, Azerbaijan is a democratic, law-governed and secular state, which gives priority to human rights and the division of powers. The Constitution says that the Azerbaijani president holds executive authority, the parliament of the Republic of Azerbaijan holds legislative authority and the independent courts hold judicial authority.

On 24 August 2002 a referendum was held on constitutional amendments needed to reflect new provisions deriving from Azerbaijan's accession to the European Convention on the Protection of Human Rights and Basic Freedoms, court reforms and the development of the election system. For more details on the Constitution of Azerbaijan, go to:

www.constitutional-court-az.org/constitution.htm

28 Who is the head of state and what power do they have?

The Presidential Palace, Baku

The head of state is the president of Azerbaijan who represents the country in its external and internal affairs. The president symbolizes the unity of the Azerbaijani people and ensures the state legacy. He or she guarantees the independence and territorial integrity of Azerbaijan, the observation of international treaties that Azerbaijan has joined and the independence of the judiciary.

The president is granted broad authority in accordance with the Constitution. The president:

- appoints and dismisses the prime minister with the consent of the Milli Majlis (parliament);
- forms central and local authorities;
- establishes central and local executive authorities;
- presents the state budget to the Milli Majlis for confirmation;
- makes recommendations to the Milli Majlis on the appointment of court judges;
- makes representations to the Milli Majlis on electing an ombudsman;
- submits recommendations to the Milli Majlis on the establishment of diplomatic representations, appoints and dismisses diplomatic representatives;
- receives credentials and letters of recall from diplomatic representatives;
- concludes inter-governmental and international treaties;
- appoints and dismisses the General Staff of the Armed Forces;
- has the authority to submit legislative initiatives to the Milli Majlis.

Constitution & System of Government

29 How is the president elected?

Q&A

**Ilham Aliyev,
President of the Republic of Azerbaijan**

The president is elected for a five-year term by general, direct and equal elections, with a free, personal and secret ballot. The candidate who has gained more than half of votes cast is elected president. Under the Constitution, any Azerbaijani citizen over the age of 35 who has resided permanently on the territory of the Azerbaijani Republic for more than 10 years, who has the right to vote, who has no previous convictions or liabilities in other states, who has a university degree and who does not have dual citizenship may be elected president of Azerbaijan. No-one may be elected president for more than two consecutive terms. The results of presidential elections are officially announced by the Constitutional Court within 14 days of voting day. Within three days of the announcement of the results, the president elect takes an oath in the presence of the judges of the Constitutional Court: "Assuming the authority of the president of the Azerbaijani Republic, I swear to follow the Constitution of the Azerbaijani Republic, to protect the sovereignty and territorial integrity of the state and to serve the people." The Azerbaijani president begins to carry out his or her official powers from the day the oath is sworn.

30 How is the Cabinet of Ministers formed?

The Azerbaijani president establishes the Cabinet of Ministers to carry out executive authority. The Cabinet of Ministers is the president's supreme executive and subordinate body. The Cabinet of Ministers includes the prime minister, the deputy prime ministers, ministers and heads of other central bodies of executive power. The prime minister is appointed by the president with the consent of the Milli Majlis. If the Milli Majlis rejects three times the prime ministerial candidatures proposed by the president, then the president may appoint the prime minister without the consent of the Milli Majlis.

The Cabinet of Ministers

The prime minister, as the head of the president's supreme executive body, is the second most important person in the state. If the president has to leave office prematurely, then the prime minister assumes the presidential functions until new, extraordinary presidential elections can be held.

The Milli Majlis chamber

31 How is the Milli Majlis formed?

The Milli Majlis is the legislative body of the Republic of Azerbaijan. The Azerbaijani Milli Majlis has one chamber consisting of 125 deputies. Any citizen of the Azerbaijani Republic who is over the age of 25 may stand for election as a deputy of the Milli Majlis. Persons who hold dual citizenship or have obligations to other states, those who work in the bodies of executive or judicial power, those involved in paid employment other than scientific, educational and creative work, clergy, those whose incapacity has been confirmed by a court of law, those condemned for grave crimes or who are serving a sentence imposed by a court of law may not be elected a member of parliament. The Milli Majlis is elected for five years on the basis of a majority election system and free vote. Elections to the Milli Majlis are held every five years on the first Sunday in November. The Milli Majlis is deemed to have authority once 83 of its deputies have been approved by the Constitutional Court. A deputy of the Milli Majlis enjoys immunity throughout their term of office. The Milli Majlis defines the working process, forms the necessary bodies, chooses its chairman and vice-chairmen, establishes permanent and other commissions and forms the counting chamber.

Apart from legislation, the Milli Majlis approves the state budget and monitors its implementation, gives its consent to the appointment of the prime minister, appoints judges of the constitutional and supreme courts and the Court of Appeal and grants authority to the Cabinet of Ministers. The Milli Majlis also has the authority to dismiss the president via impeachment based on the recommendation of the Constitutional Court.

The Milli Majlis has permanent commissions on legal policy and state-building, security and defence policy, economic policy, natural resources, energy and the environment, agricultural policy, social policy, science and education, culture, international and inter-parliamentary relations, regional problems, human rights, and internal discipline.

Constitution & System of Government

32 What are the main political parties?

When Azerbaijan was part of the Soviet Union, there was only one political party, the Communist Party. After independence Azerbaijan chose democracy and a multi-party system was established. The Constitution gives every citizen the right to establish any association, including a political party, trade union or other public organization. The unrestricted activity of all associations is ensured under the Constitution. But the Constitution prohibits the activity of any association that seeks the forcible overthrow of the legal order in Azerbaijan. Activity of associations which violates the Constitution and law can be stopped by decision of the courts.

Political parties participate in political life through representatives in the Milli Majlis and local authorities.

Today 42 political parties have been officially registered in Azerbaijan. The main political parties are: *Yeni Azerbaijan* (New Azerbaijan), *Milli Istiqlal* (the Azerbaijan National Independence Party), the Azerbaijani People's Front Party, *Musavat*, the Azerbaijan Democratic Party, the *Ana Vatan* Party, the Social Democrats and others.

Constitution & System of Government

Economy

33 What are Azerbaijan's headline economic figures?

Before 1991, Azerbaijan's economy was part of the Soviet economic system. It was geared to meeting the demands of the other Soviet republics under what was known as the principle of "Union-wide division of labour". As a result, very large enterprises in the oil exploration and extraction industry, agribusiness and the industrial sector dominated the economy. Azerbaijan used to supply nearly 70 per cent of the Soviet Union's oil exploration and extraction machinery, 30 per cent of its fresh fruits and 20 per cent of its fossil fuels. Moreover, a large part of Azerbaijan's industrial and agricultural production was exported to other republics in the form of raw materials, semi-finished goods and component parts, resulting in a significant under-utilization of Azerbaijan's economic potential and creating a high dependency on the rest of the Soviet Union.

The collapse of the Soviet Union had a harsh impact on Azerbaijan. The country's economy suffered from the sudden separation from Soviet markets and the drop in demand. This problem was compounded by the breaking of transport links to Azerbaijan's traditional markets as a result of fighting in Chechnya, war with Armenia over Mountainous Karabakh and low oil prices.

The unstable internal political situation made it impossible to embark on radical economic reforms. Following President Aliyev's return to power in August 1993, the internal political situation stabilized and a cease-fire was arranged in Mountainous Karabakh in May 1994. The government adopted an economic programme supported by the International Monetary Fund (IMF) and the World Bank and started implementing widespread economic reforms. Since 1995 three government

Map of the economic-geographical regions of the Republic of Azerbaijan

Economic-geographical regions:

1 Absheron
A variety of industries including oil, petrochemicals and machine-building dominate here. Many subtropical plants grow in the region, a consequence of the development of suburban horticulture.

2 Guba-Khachmaz
Fruit and vegetable canning, livestock rearing and fishing are developed in the region. It is an area of natural beauty.

3 Mountainous Shirvan
Viticulture, wine-making, arable farming and livestock rearing are highly developed in the region.

4 Sheki-Zagatala
This region grows fruit and nuts, including walnuts and hazelnuts, and tobacco. Silk is produced and there is a food processing industry based on livestock rearing and arable farming.

5 Aran
A major cotton growing region with highly developed, irrigated agricultural areas. Electric power generation, the oil and gas industry, fishing, livestock rearing and arable farming also dominate in the region.

6 Ganja-Gazakh
A major region for the mining of ore and manufacture of non-ferrous metals. The region has light industry and food processing based on its mixed agriculture.

7 Mountainous Karabakh
This region has highly developed irrigated agriculture, including viticulture, cotton-growing, livestock rearing, the silk industry and wine making. It is an area of natural beauty.

8 Kalbajar-Lachin
An agricultural area irrigated for arable and tobacco farming. Viticulture and livestock rearing are developed in the region, which is an area of natural beauty.

9 Lankaran
The humid climate allows the growth of subtropical fruits (tea, citrus), early ripening vegetables, arable farming and viticulture. Vegetable canning and fishing are also developed in the region.

10 Nakhchivan
Arable farming, viticulture, fruit-growing, mineral water bottling and the mining industry are developed in the region.

The borders of the economic-geographical regions

programmes aimed at ensuring macro-economic stabilization, structural adjustments and stimulating economic growth have been implemented. Government reforms consisted of several major components: macro-economic stabilization through responsible fiscal and monetary management; economic liberalization through the removal of production controls and the liberalization of domestic and foreign trade regimes; and small-scale privatization. In 2004 the Azerbaijani government adopted the State Programme on the Socio-Economic Development of the

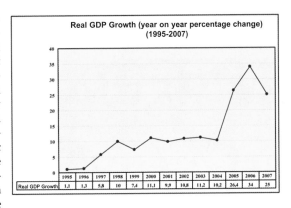

Real GDP Growth (year on year percentage change) (1995-2007)

	1995	1996	1997	1998	1999	2000	2001	2002	2003	2004	2005	2006	2007
Real GDP Growth	1,1	1,3	5,8	10	7,4	11,1	9,9	10,8	11,2	10,2	26,4	34	25

Regions (2004-08). The programme aims to boost productivity, create a proper infrastructure, attract investors, cut unemployment and provide credits to businesses in the country's regions.

Azerbaijan's performance in achieving macro-economic stability and restarting growth since 1995 has been "impressive", according to the World Bank and the European Bank for Reconstruction and Development. Azerbaijan was the lead country in terms of real GDP growth rate in 2006 and 2007. Azerbaijan is fifth amongst CIS countries in terms of GDP. According to the 2007 statistics, Azerbaijan accounts for more than 66 per cent of the region's GDP.

Azerbaijan's responsible fiscal and monetary management, accompanied by favourable global economic trends, have significantly improved the country's macro-economic situation. Price stability and currency convertibility have been restored and maintained in a manner unparalleled in the countries of the CIS. As a result of the Central Bank's tight monetary policy, the dramatic hyperinflation characteristic of 1991-95, which reached approximately 1,660 per cent in 1994, has been eliminated. Inflation decreased to 3.6 per cent in 1997 and remained negative throughout 1998 and 1999. Inflation stayed low in 2000 at 1.8 per cent, 1.5 per cent in 2001, 2.8 per cent in 2002, 2.2 per cent in 2003 and 6.7 per cent in 2004. But due to global price increases and a rise in living standards inflation has risen gradually and was 9.6 per cent in 2005, 8.3 per cent in 2006 and 16 per cent in 2007.

FOREIGN DIRECT INVESTMENT. Azerbaijan made a relatively late start among the former Soviet republics in attracting foreign direct investment (FDI). Nevertheless, as a result of the country's abundant natural resources and recent political stability, Azerbaijan has the third highest cumulative inflow of FDI in value terms amongst CIS countries. Total inflows of FDI are not markedly less than those of Turkey. Relative to its population size and GDP, Azerbaijan has far outstripped many countries in the region as a destination of choice for FDI.

After the signing of the Contract of the Century on oil extraction in 1994, Azerbaijan started to experience a dramatic rise in FDI inflows. Since 1994 the influx of foreign investments to Azerbaijan has increased every year. In the last 10 years US$20 billion have been invested in the Azerbaijani economy via joint ventures and foreign enterprises. In 2003-07, foreign capital accounted for 63.3 per cent ($20,389,800,000) of total investments of $32bn in the country's economy. In 2007 investment in the non-oil sector increased 28.8 per cent, accounting for 49.9 per cent of total investments.

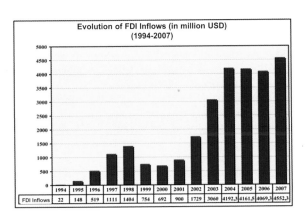

Evolution of FDI Inflows (in million USD) (1994-2007)

	1994	1995	1996	1997	1998	1999	2000	2001	2002	2003	2004	2005	2006	2007
FDI Inflows	22	148	519	1111	1404	754	692	900	1729	3060	4192,3	4161,5	4069,3	4552,3

34 What are Azerbaijan's main industries?

Signing of the Contract of the Century, 20 September 1994

Azerbaijan's industrial sector is well diversified with a production capacity able to sustain a steady export programme. Before independence, industrial enterprises produced a wide range of products, including oil and gas related products (equipment for the oil and gas sector and petro-chemicals), machines, textiles and light manufacturing products and ferrous and non-ferrous metal goods. However, the break-up of the Soviet Union brought a number of challenges to the entire industrial sector. The severance of links to foreign sources of raw material and markets and the drop in export demand presented enterprises with unprecedented difficulties that resulted in a lack of investment in new equipment. The country's overall productivity and competitiveness on international markets suffered due to this unfavourable macro-economic situation. But the gradual stabilization of the economy in the country in the late 90s and the huge oil revenues stimulated economic development as a whole and especially industrial development. Industry accounted for 60.6 per cent of GDP in 2007, worth $20bn.

OIL AND GAS EQUIPMENT. As Baku has been a booming oil city since the beginning of the 20th century, the main manufacturing sector is clearly oil and gas-related. Azerbaijan was once the Soviet Union's main supplier of oil equipment. Today, this sector and related machine-building sectors still account for a large part of the country's industrial base, and prospects are good for further expanding these areas. Additional oil exploration, oil production and the construction of infrastructure for transporting oil and gas to international markets are currently planned, creating the opportunity to develop a thriving supply chain to the oil and gas sector.

Major opportunities exist for oil and gas equipment producers, resulting from the expansion of BP's offshore oil and gas production operations. These have promised over $10bn in procurement opportunities. The construction of the Baku - Ceyhan pipeline provided further opportunities, as the pipeline operator committed to spending $4bn on equipment, materials and service contracts.

The pipeline has supervisory control and data acquisition systems, including leak detection, operations control centres, pump stations, mainline block valves and tank farms.

CHEMICAL AND PETROCHEMICAL INDUSTRY. One of the government's priorities is to support the development of the oil and gas downstream sector, which will add value to Azerbaijan's natural resources through further processing. Currently, few products are finished; most come in the form of raw materials or in a semi-finished state and are then sent abroad for further processing.

Azerbaijan's chemical and petrochemical industry is in need of modernization. The sector consists of two oil refineries, Azarneftyag and Azarneftyanajag, with a total technical capacity of 22 million tonnes of crude oil per annum. Five big petrochemical plants are located in Sumgayit. Synthetic rubber, detergents and polymeric building materials are the most common petrochemical products. Azarkimya is the state-owned holding company that oversees most chemical plants. Some of the plants are slated for privatization, including plants producing sulphuric acid, aluminium sulphate, perlite, pharmaceutical products, rubber goods, technical rubber tubes (pipes), glass fibre, electro-insulating materials, polyethylene tubes (pipes), polyethylene covers and plastics.

MACHINE-BUILDING.

The machine-building sector initially focused on oil equipment manufacturing. It developed continuously during the 1970s and 1980s and expanded in a number of new areas, producing equipment for agriculture, road construction, light industry and the food-processing sector. However, due to a lack of investment in new technologies and equipment, the machine-building

Azeri-Chirag platform

Oily Rocks (Neft Dashlari)

Sangachal terminal

sector is now producing at only a fraction of its capacity. Recent reforms, including privatization on the basis of specific investment programmes, have created new prospects for the sector's development.

MINING AND METALLURGY. Several types of metals (aluminium, lead, zinc, cobalt, mercury, silver and gold) have been discovered and mined for quite some time in Azerbaijan. During the past decades this area has become more highly developed, resulting in the creation and development of a metallurgic industry in Azerbaijan.

The ferrous metallurgy sector is one of Azerbaijan's more important industries. The sector's major players are the Dashkasan Ore Mining and Processing Plant Joint-Stock Company, the Azarboru Tube-Rolling Plant JSC and the Dash Salahli Iron Ore Mining Plant JSC. The biggest iron ore field in the Caucasus is located in Azerbaijan. As such, ore-mining and ore-processing can be further developed. Introducing new processes, such as blasting, would add significant value to the sector's products. Eighty per cent of Azerbaijan's ferrous metallurgy production comes from the Azarboru Tube-Rolling Plant.

The Baku Steel Company won a tender and created Azerbaijan's first major steel manufacturing facility. A total of $50 million was invested in the construction of the plant, which now provides competition in this market sector.

Azerbaijan was one of four aluminium producers in the former USSR. The raw material is mined from fields around Dashkasan. Alumina is produced at a plant in Ganja, where annual production used to reach 500,000 tonnes. The alumina is then transported to Sumgayit near Baku and converted into aluminium.

In April 2000 the Azerbaijani president signed a decree to revive the aluminium industry in Azerbaijan by integrating processing facilities. This brought together Sumgayitelvanmetal, Giltorpaq (Ganja) and the Zeilik mining department in a single enterprise Azerbaijan Aluminium (Azaraluminium).

CONSTRUCTION. Construction in Azerbaijan has experienced a recent boom thanks to the development of the oil and gas sector. Many new architecture, design and construction firms have been created which demand the latest Western technology and building materials.

Renovation of residential and commercial buildings, construction related to the oil and gas sector and

demand for modern construction equipment and materials are key elements of future market growth. Residential construction, whether multi-storey, multiple dwelling units or detached houses, is under way in Baku and the surrounding area, creating a growing demand for high-quality building materials. These materials include wood for parquet floors, bricks, ceramic products and heating, ventilation and air conditioning systems. Pre-fabricated housing and warehousing are also needed for large oil and gas industry projects.

Investment in commercial and hotel development has been growing quickly in recent years.

TEXTILES AND LIGHT INDUSTRY.
Azerbaijan's light industry developed rapidly during the 20th century. A large number of factories producing consumer goods were established and Azerbaijan developed into an important producer of cotton yarn, silk thread, wool yarn, leather products, shoes, furniture and carpets. The textile industry was one of Azerbaijan's most important industries during the Soviet period. There are four major textile plants in the country, which use domestically produced cotton.

Today, the light industry sector with its outdated equipment needs new technology and additional capital investments to reach modern standards. (The government estimates that the industry requires approximately $200 million in investment.) The sector's potential could be realized by building on its existing industrial base and seizing privatization opportunities. The skilled labour force, existing know-how and natural resources create favourable conditions for the sector's revival.

The textile sector is a good illustration of the country's potential for economic development. Indeed, livestock rearing (the number of cattle has reached 2.4 million head, and the number of sheep and goats 7.8 million head) ensures an abundant supply of leather and wool that could boost the textile sector. The government has declared the development of the textile industry, in part through the construction of spinning mills, as one of the priorities of its industrial development policy.

35 Which agricultural sectors are the most developed in Azerbaijan?

Agriculture is the second largest sector in the Azerbaijani economy after oil and gas. Approximately 40 per cent of the population is involved in this sector. This fact alone makes farming vital to Azerbaijan's future. Azerbaijan has nine climatic zones and over one million hectares of arable land irrigated by over 40,000 km of canals and pipelines. The combination of climatic conditions and fertile farmland allows a wide variety of crops to be cultivated. These include fruits (apples, cherries, grapes, olives, lemons, persimmons, melons, watermelons, raspberries, strawberries, currants, plums, peaches, pears, quince, pomegranates and tomatoes), vegetables (potatoes, carrots, beets, cabbage, cucumbers and onions), grains (wheat, maize, barley), tea and nuts.

Azerbaijan exports cotton, its most important cash crop, and produces much of the world's caviar. Other major agricultural cash crops are grapes, tobacco, citrus fruits and vegetables. The country has the resources to be self-sufficient, but still imports 70 per cent of its food. In recent years foreign products, especially from Turkey, Russia and Iran, have flooded the local market and local products cannot compete. Much of this trade is in foods from crops that are grown in Azerbaijan but cannot be processed locally because the food-processing sector is under-developed.

Under the Soviet Union, agriculture in Azerbaijan was collectivized in large state farms (*kolkhozi* and *sovkhozi*); agricultural priorities were determined by Moscow according to the needs of the USSR as a whole. Azerbaijan was the Soviet Union's main supplier of fruit, vegetables and wine. Accordingly, Azerbaijan had a fixed market for its agricultural output at fixed prices with no additional transportation costs. In turn, it received the products that it needed, such as meat, dairy produce and grain. These foodstuffs were imported into the country at artificially low prices subsidized by the government.

To reverse this trend, the government undertook a privatization programme in 1996 to dismantle the collective farm system and distribute land to individuals. Today, over 90 per cent of agricultural land is privately owned. The trend among farmers has been to move away from traditional crops such as wheat and cotton to fruit, vegetables and nuts, which require less fertilization and mechanization, can be cultivated in small plots and marketed directly. Farmers also produce dairy products, meat and poultry. State-owned agricultural sector businesses have been privatized and the prices of agricultural products deregulated. Though foreigners are barred from owning land, they can capitalize on opportunities through joint ventures with local landowners.

Arable farming is the leading sector. Cereals such as wheat, barley, maize and Azerbaijan's favourite food, rice, are grown. A great variety of vegetables and fruits, including the rare feikhoa fruit, are also produced.

Industrial crops include cotton, valuable types of tobacco, tea and sunflowers.

Sericulture (silk production) is a traditional specialization in some rural parts of north-west Azerbaijan.

Horticulture is developed along the sea coast where there are a variety of vegetable-growing regions. Lankaran specializes in early kinds of vegetables, while unique nut plantations and mulberry trees grow elsewhere. More than 200 types of industrial, table and sultana varieties of grapes are known in Azerbaijan. They are cultivated in the Kur-Araz lowland and the higher parts of Shirvan, Karabakh and Nakhchivan.

Livestock rearing is traditionally an important branch of agriculture in Azerbaijan. Livestock numbers are: beef cattle (cows and buffaloes) 1,138,047; sheep and goats 7,630,871; pigs 24,064; poultry 14,700,000. There is great potential for development in this sector.

Having been dependent on supplies of meat and meat products during the Soviet era, Azerbaijan reached self-sufficiency shortly after its privatization of livestock.

Fishing Azerbaijan is one of the few countries in the world to produce black caviar and exclusive kinds of fish (sturgeon) available only in the Caspian Sea. The Azerbaijani sector of the Caspian is the major fishing area for the famous Caspian herring. Mountain rivers provide tourist attractions to the adventurous.

The food industry has developed evenly throughout the country and manufactures nearly all known types of produce. Traditional flour-milling, butter and cheese production and canning stand alongside wine-making (some 10 types of wine, brandy and sherry are produced in Azerbaijan), fish processing (caviar from sturgeon) and tea and tobacco products. All have won international recognition.

36 What is the state of Azerbaijan's infrastructure?

The basic infrastructure in Azerbaijan is extensive and can be considered good for a low-income country. It includes a developed road network, an extensive rail network with links to the west, north and south, electricity generation capacity with substantial network penetration and functioning fixed line telecommunications. The existence of basic infrastructure is a major asset for the economy. Though it is in a poor state of repair, relatively small volumes of investment in upgrading and maintenance could yield very high returns.

TRANSPORTATION. The transport infrastructure in Azerbaijan includes aviation, railways, maritime transport and roads, with railways as the main mode of freight transport. The unresolved conflict with Armenia has resulted in the severing of a number of major transport links with Nakhchivan. International road and rail communications with the Black Sea and Russia are also dependent on the security situation in Georgia and Southern Russia. There are about 25,000 kilometres of roads. At the moment several projects signed with various international organizations to repair these roads are under way. The rail network consists of 2,089 kilometres of track. The most important routes are to Russia, Iran and Georgia. The tracks and rolling stock are poorly maintained and in need of repair or replacement.

There are three international airports in Azerbaijan, located in Baku, Ganja and Nakhchivan. The national airline is Azerbaijani Airlines, known as AZAL for short. There is an urgent need to develop a regional airline. Sea and water cargo transportation also has vital importance for the country. Azerbaijan has direct connections with other states bordering on the Caspian as well as international waters. Baku International Sea Port is the largest port on the Caspian Sea. It is undergoing major reconstruction supported by the EBRD to increase its efficiency and commercial viability. Several World Bank and EBRD financed projects to upgrade roads, railways and ports represent a start in addressing serious transport infrastructure needs. Upgrades of Azerbaijan's transportation system are being made in conjunction with the European Union's TRACECA (Transport Corridor Europe Caucasus Asia) programme.

POWER. The state-owned company Azarenerji controls Azerbaijan's electricity generation and transmission system. Total power generation capacity is 5,583.8 megawatts produced by eleven thermal and six hydroelectric power stations. Imports from Russia, Iran and Turkey make up the shortfall. The transmission and distribution network consists of more than 110,000 kilometres of transmission lines connecting 40 sub-networks to the central grid system. At the moment several projects signed with various international organizations in the energy sector are under way.

TELECOMMUNICATIONS. According to the latest statistics, there are 14 telephones to every 100 people in Azerbaijan and 31.4 to every 100 people in Baku. In order to attract investments many companies in the telecommunication sector have been declared open for privatization. Progress has been made in the installation and use of cellular mobile phones. Cellular mobile telecommunications were launched in 1994. The number of subscribers for the analogue service has since shown a regular increase. Demand for mobile communications has arisen due to the poor state of fixed lines, and the needs of oil-related economic activities. In 1996, the first GSM service was launched. With the arrival of a second operator in 1998 and a third in 2007 the authorities showed their commitment to greater competitiveness in the sector. In Azerbaijan as a whole there are 50 mobile phones for every 100 people. There are currently more than 4,300,000 mobile telephone subscribers. The Internet, one of the key fields of telecommunications, is rapidly developing in Azerbaijan. Azerbaijan leads the Caucasian states in Internet provision and the development of high technology.

37 With how many countries does Azerbaijan have diplomatic relations?

38 What international organizations has Azerbaijan joined?

39 What international and regional projects is Azerbaijan involved in?

International Relations

37 With how many countries does Azerbaijan have diplomatic relations?

When Azerbaijan restored its independence, many countries soon recognized the new republic. Turkey was the first to recognize Azerbaijan's independence. It is very important for Azerbaijan to play a respected role in the international relations system and to collaborate with the world's leading powers and the international organizations that direct global politics.

Azerbaijan's foreign policy is oriented towards strengthening its sovereignty and promoting economic development. Azerbaijan is also focusing on developing relations with the West - Turkey, the USA and Western Europe - while cultivating relations with Russia and Iran. The Azerbaijani government has identified several issues that currently guide foreign policy: settlement of the Mountainous Karabakh conflict and resolution of the consequences of the war, especially the refugee problem; the development of good relations with neighbouring countries and the development of the Eurasian Transport Corridor; the promotion of stability in the region; preventing weapons shipments into the area and establishing a nuclear-free zone in the South Caucasus; and integration into European and transatlantic security and co-operation structures including NATO and the European Union (EU).

To realize all these ambitions, Azerbaijan has formed diplomatic relations with 160 countries. It has consular relationships with all the member states of the Vienna Convention. To date 94 foreign embassies operate in Azerbaijan; 26 of them are in Baku itself, while the rest are accredited in Ankara, Moscow or Tehran. Azerbaijan, in turn, has 52 embassies, eight consulates and four permanent missions abroad.

38 What international organizations has Azerbaijan joined?

Co-operation within the framework of international organizations constitutes one of the most significant guidelines of Azerbaijan's foreign policy. After independence Azerbaijan joined the OIC (Organization of the Islamic Conference - in 1991), the United Nations (1992) and OSCE (1992). Azerbaijan is also a member of more than 20 UN economic organizations including ESCAP (the Economic and Social Commission for Asia and the Pacific), UNIDO (United Nations Industrial Development Organization), UNCTAD (the United Nations Commission on Trade and Development), the ECE (the Economic Commission for Europe), the IMO (International Maritime Organization), the World Bank (the World Bank Group including the International Development Association and International Finance Corporation) and the IMF (International Monetary Fund). It has observer status at the WTO (World Trade Organization) and is a member of the EBRD (European Bank for Reconstruction and Development), IDB (Islamic Development Bank) and ADB (Asian Development Bank). Azerbaijan has agreements with other organizations that assist the country in transitional reforms and developing its economy.

Azerbaijan also actively co-operates on the regional level as a member of the CIS (Commonwealth of Independent States), BSEC (Black Sea Economic Co-operation), ECO (Economic Co-operation Organization, which includes Turkey, Iran, Pakistan, Azerbaijan, the five Central Asian Republics and Afghanistan) and GUAM (Georgia, Ukraine, Azerbaijan and Moldova). Azerbaijan's integration into Europe is proceeding rapidly and in 2001 it became a member of the Council of Europe. The European Union and Azerbaijan signed a Partnership and Co-operation Agreement in 1996 which came into force in 1999. In 2004 Azerbaijan became part of the EU's European Neighbourhood Policy.

39 What international and regional projects is Azerbaijan involved in?

Azerbaijan takes part in many international projects, which are vital both for regional development and the international community. The projects are mainly economic and promote global development and Azerbaijan's integration into Europe.

One key project is TRACECA (Transport Corridor for Europe, Caucasus and Asia). In September 1998 representatives of 14 nations signed the Baku Declaration, thereby voting for the restoration of the Great Silk Road. The project is developing comprehensive transport and communications infrastructure (rail, road, maritime and telecommunications) and closely integrating all the countries of the region.

Azerbaijan is involved in other important international projects: the North-South Transport Corridor, the Economic-Social Commission for Asia-Pacific and SPECA, the Special Programme for the Economies of Central Asia.

Since Azerbaijan is rich in natural resources, particularly oil and gas, oil pipelines pass through the country. Oil is exported via the Western Route Export Pipeline (WREP) to Supsa in Georgia, the Northern Route Export Pipeline (NREP) to Novorossiysk in Russia and the newly built Baku - Tbilisi - Ceyhan Main Export Pipeline through Georgia and Turkey to the Mediterranean Sea.

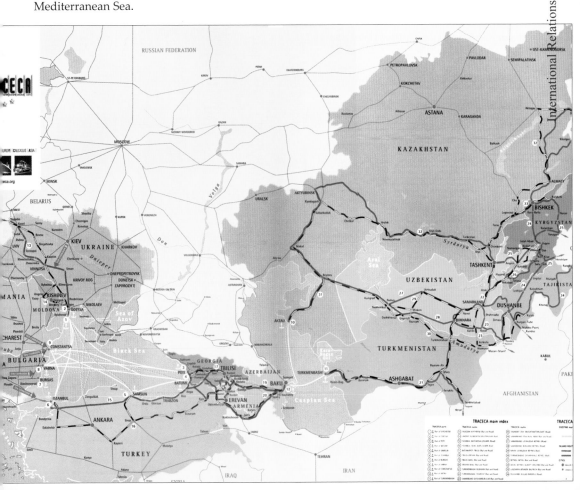

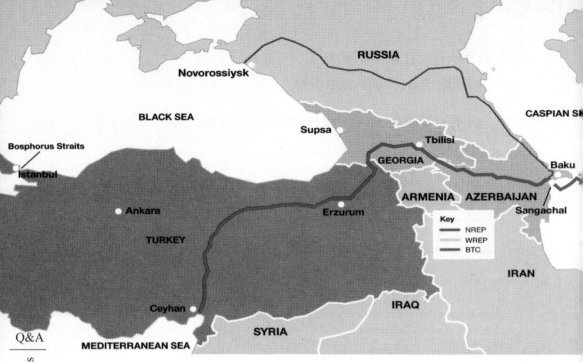

The Baku - Tbilisi - Ceyhan route, known as BTC, was approved in November 1999 by Inter-Governmental Host Government Agreements during the OSCE Summit in Istanbul. The project is a four billion-dollar investment for use by producers in Azerbaijan, Kazakhstan and other regional suppliers. The BTC pipeline unlocks a vast store of energy from the Caspian Sea by providing crude oil from Azerbaijan, through Georgia, to Turkey for onward delivery to world markets. Traversing 1,768 km, the BTC pipeline is able to transport up to one million barrels of crude oil per day (equivalent to 50 million tonnes per year) from the cluster of discoveries in the Caspian Sea, known collectively as the Azari, Chiraq and deep-water Gunashli fields. Linefill of the BTC pipeline began at the Sangachal oil terminal in Azerbaijan on 10 May 2005 and the first export of oil from the Ceyhan marine terminal in Turkey commenced on 4 June 2006. With demand for energy expected to increase 60 per cent by 2030, international interest in the BTC pipeline is high. It is a world class project, and one of the great engineering projects of the new millennium. The length of the BTC pipeline is the distance from New York to Miami in the USA, or from London to southern Spain in Europe.

The discovery of the giant Shah Daniz gas and condensate field in the Azerbaijani sector of the Caspian Sea led to a new project for Azerbaijan, the BTE (Baku - Tbilisi - Erzurum) gas pipeline. The pipeline transports natural gas from the Shah Daniz field through Georgia to Turkey where it will meet Turkey's demand for gas for many years. First deliveries of gas started in December 2006. Shah Daniz is the biggest discovery since Prudhoe Bay in Alaska back in the 1970s and, in the last five years it is second in size only to Iran's Kir Kabir discovery.

In November 2007, Azerbaijan, Georgia and Turkey inaugurated the construction of another international project - the Baku - Tbilisi - Kars railway. The actual agreement was signed in 2005. The railway will be 1,000 kilometres in length and will provide a link between China and Europe, making Azerbaijan an important transit country. The project is slated for completion by 2010.

Law & Order

40 What is Azerbaijan's legal system?

Azerbaijan's legal system is determined by statute, based on Civil or Roman law, and not precedence, so the decisions of the courts are not the source of law.

Under the Constitution of the Republic of Azerbaijan legislation consists of:

- the Constitution
- acts accepted by referendum
- laws
- decrees
- resolutions of the Cabinet of Ministers of the Azerbaijani Republic
- normative acts of central executive power bodies

The list is not simply a hierarchy, but one based on the relative legal authority or weight of the normative acts. A normative act lower down the list would be unlikely to prevail over one higher up.

The Constitution of Azerbaijan was adopted on 12 November 1995 by referendum and entered into force on 27 November 1995. It has the highest legal force in the territory of the republic and is implemented directly. It is the basic foundation of the legislative system in the republic.

The use and implementation of all normative acts are obligatory only after their publication. Neither acts accepted by referendum, nor others should contradict the Constitution. No normative act shown in the list above should contradict a higher normative act.

A referendum may be held on any matter concerning the interests of the people. The Constitution may be accepted or amended, and a change made in the state borders only by referendum.

Laws are accepted by the Milli Majlis and submitted to the president for signing within 14 days from the day (24 hours from the moment) of their acceptance. The president signs laws within 56 days from their presentation. If the president has objections to a law, he may return it to the Milli Majlis within the specified term without signing it, together with his comments. Should the president fail to sign constitutional laws, they will not come into force.

Deputies of the Milli Majlis, the president of the republic, the Supreme Court, the Public Prosecutor's Office and the Milli Majlis of the Nakhchivan Autonomous Republic have the right to submit draft laws for consideration by the Milli Majlis of the Azerbaijani Republic.

Decrees are issued by the president on the basis of, and in order to develop, laws to establish general rules. Government resolutions are adopted in the context of presidential decrees to regulate different economic, social, state governance and other issues.

As regards international law, the Constitution says that international agreements wherein the Azerbaijani Republic is one of the parties constitute an integral part of the legislative system of the republic. Whenever there is disagreement between normative-legal acts in the legislative system of the Azerbaijani Republic (except the Constitution of the Azerbaijani Republic and acts accepted by referendum) and international agreements wherein the Azerbaijani Republic is one of the parties, the provisions of international agreements shall dominate. So norms of international law that contradict the Constitution and acts accepted by referendum are not valid.

Ministries and state institutions have lawmaking authority in restricted spheres of social relations and issue their own normative acts.

41 How is Azerbaijan's judicial system organized?

Azerbaijan has a complex three-tier judiciary system, which includes courts of general jurisdiction, economic courts, military courts and a court for grave crimes. Any decision taken by the court of first instance can be appealed against in the Court of Appeal. A complaint about a decision of the Court of Appeal can be filed with the Supreme Court which is the highest judicial power in the country. Court judges are nominated by the president from candidates who have successfully passed a two-tier professional examination.

Commercial disputes are adjudicated by the Economic Court, which consists of general economic courts and economic courts for disputes arising out of international contracts. The Supreme Court of the Azerbaijani Republic has a dedicated panel on disputes.

Azerbaijan also has a Constitutional Court that is empowered to rule on the constitutionality of laws, the settlement of disputes among the branches of power and the banning of political parties and organizations. Currently, Azerbaijan is modifying its legal system to allow citizens to appeal directly to the Constitutional Court. At present this right is reserved for selected state bodies.

Since Azerbaijan is a member state of the Council of Europe, its citizens are entitled to complain to the European Court of Human Rights if they feel that their rights have been violated and all the national courts have failed to uphold their rights.

Members of the Constitutional Court

Q&A

Law & Order

42 How are the police organized?

The police in Azerbaijan are designed to protect citizens' life and health, their rights and freedoms, property and legal status. The police operate on the basis of respect for human rights and freedoms, lawfulness and human values.

The main responsibilities of the police are:

- the protection of public order and the provision of security
- identifying and tackling crime
- traffic safety

The whole range of policing, including reorganization and appointments, is governed by rules set by the appropriate executive authorities of the Azerbaijani Republic. The police are headed by the Ministry of Internal Affairs, which has offices in all regions of the republic. The minister of internal affairs and his deputies are appointed by the president of the republic. The local police offices are commanded by the chiefs of police. They operate by means of departments and local commissioners. Authorities and local government assist the police to accomplish their duties.

There are 23,000 police officers in the police forces of Azerbaijan. The traffic police regulate traffic. Policing is mainly done by police officers who are in constant contact with the public. They patrol the streets on foot or in cars, give advice and deal with disturbances. Each year, 2 July, the day of the organization of policing in Azerbaijan, is celebrated as Police Day.

Duty groups operate at every police unit and station. Operational and investigative groups are set up daily to respond rapidly and efficiently to appeals and information, to carry out urgent investigations and arrest criminals. Rapid response and investigative groups are sent to crime scenes, depending on the gravity of the crime.

Reports of crimes and accidents are received by duty officers and their assistants.

Anyone can call the police hot line by dialling 102 or approach duty officers for assistance round the clock.

Uniformed police officers usually carry a truncheon to protect themselves. Firearms are issued only to specially trained police officers and only on the authority of senior officers. A police officer can use firearms as a last resort, provided that other means have not been effective and that a violent criminal is dangerous and a threat to other lives.

Armed police officers are responsible for the decision to fire. Each instance in which force has been used or a gun fired is recorded by the relevant police department. A police officer is responsible before the courts for the illegal use of firearms and may be punished under Azerbaijani legislation.

A system of armed response vehicles - patrol cars with weapons in a locked box - provides a speedy initial response to a firearms incident in Baku.

In the past, in regions where armed gangs operated, police officers used to carry firearms for personal protection.

The Police Veteran medal is awarded to police officers for 30 or more years of exemplary service after retirement

Science & Education

43 At what age do children go to school in Azerbaijan?

Children in Azerbaijan usually go to school at the age of six. Before going to school many children attend kindergartens. Some parents send their children to kindergartens and pre-school classes attached to primary schools for one year in order to prepare them for formal schooling. After four years of primary education children enter the fifth form, where their basic education begins and carries on until the ninth form. One teacher usually teaches children in primary classes whereas different, specialist subject teachers usually teach the higher classes. Secondary education in Azerbaijan lasts 11 years and pupils usually complete it when they are 17. Every Azerbaijani citizen has the right to education. The state guarantees free compulsory secondary education and establishes minimum educational standards.

The system of education is under state control. Pupils who have completed secondary education (first to 11th forms) receive a certificate (*attestat*) that allows them to take the entrance exams to go on to higher education. Pupils who complete only the basic course (first to ninth forms) receive a certificate of incomplete secondary education (*shahadatnama*) and can continue their education only at secondary schools (vocational training, technical colleges etc.).

44 What are the types of secondary school in Azerbaijan?

General education in Azerbaijan is provided in secondary and specialized schools. Azerbaijan has:
- daytime secondary schools
- evening (irregular) secondary schools
- evening classes attached to daytime secondary schools
- irregular groups
- gymnasiums
- lyceums
- specialized schools

Education lasts 11 years in secondary schools. Secondary schools have three stages:
- primary education - first to fourth forms
- basic education - fifth to ninth forms
- secondary education - 10th to 11th forms

Lessons in secondary schools are taught in Azerbaijani, Russian and partly in Georgian, while English, French, German, Arabic and Persian are taught as foreign languages.

Under the Constitution of the Republic of Azerbaijan general secondary education is compulsory and free of charge. Pupils who have completed the basic level of education receive one type of certificate while pupils who complete the secondary level receive a different certificate.

In 2006-07, 1,552,000 pupils attended 4,516 secondary schools. Some 85,000 children attended 225 specialized schools and 33 gymnasiums. A further 20 educational institutions (14 boarding schools, five satellites and one home school) educate mentally and physically disabled children. There are also 1,761 institutions which deal with the developmental problems of 111,000 pre-school children. More talented children and teenagers attend specialized music and art schools (the Bul-Bul secondary music school, the Baku Choreography School etc.) alongside their secondary education. Education in these institutions is 11-12 years.

45 Is vocational training provided in Azerbaijan?

Vocational training, which is an important part of education in Azerbaijan, has been in place for a long time. The first vocational schools were opened in Shaki (1843), Nakhchivan (1879) and Baku (1887). Vocational training in Azerbaijan rapidly developed in the 1970s and 80s. Training in technical colleges lasts three years. Pupils with a basic education level (ninth form) receive secondary education alongside vocational training. Education in vocational schools lasts one to two years. Pupils here are taught a profession and secondary education. Pupils choose their own profession. Technical specializations include carpentry, painting, printing, electronics, hotel administration, farming and tourism.

At present 110 technical colleges operate in Azerbaijan, of which 48 are vocational colleges and 62 vocational schools.

The main building of Baku State University

46 When was the first university founded in Azerbaijan?

Azerbaijan's first secular institution of higher education is Baku State University (BSU). The university was founded on 15 November 1919 during the Azerbaijani Democratic Republic. When it was founded the university had 40 teachers and four faculties. Since then it has developed and today BSU has 16 faculties, attended by nearly 12,000 students who study for bachelor's degrees in 43 subjects and master's in 127. Since its foundation the university has educated up to 100,000 specialists, including more than 2,000 students from 51 foreign countries. The university has integrated Azerbaijani science into international science and played a big part in the development of Azerbaijani culture. World-renowned Azerbaijani scientists, writers, poets and statesmen have graduated from the university. BSU employs approximately 300 doctors and professors.

BSU used to have medical, history and philology faculties, but they were separated from the university and various institutions and universities emerged on their basis. The Azerbaijani Medical University was founded in 1930 on the basis of BSU's medical department. In 1920 the Azerbaijan Industrial Institute was established and consisted of the oil industry, electronics, construction and agriculture faculties. Over the following years the institute has been renamed and new faculties have opened. The institute is now famous at home and abroad as the Azerbaijani State Oil Academy. The Azerbaijani State Conservatory was founded in 1921 and the Azerbaijani State Pedagogical University was established in the same year. The Azerbaijani Physical Training and Sports Academy and Azerbaijani Agricultural Academy were founded in 1930 and 1929 respectively. There are also specialized centres: the Azerbaijani Technical University, the Azerbaijani State Languages University, the Baku Slavonic University, the Azerbaijani Cultural and Art Academy, the Azerbaijani Art Academy, the Azerbaijani State Economic University, the Academy of National Aviation and other private higher schools.

The statistics for 2007 show that 913 people have secondary or higher education out of every 1,000 people over the age of 15. The literacy level is 98.8 per cent; 99.5 per cent amongst men and 98.2 per cent amongst women. Azerbaijan provides full education to bachelor's and master's level.

93

47 Is science well-developed in Azerbaijan?

Azerbaijani manuscripts can be traced back to antiquity. A source from the Manna period, when southern Azerbaijan had its first form of statehood (9th - 6th century BC), reads "the scribe of Manna will record data about migrants from the Midian region and the region of Manna". The people of northern Azerbaijan adopted the Albanian alphabet in the 4th century (discovered by archaeologists in Mingachevir). Literate people in general and poets and scientists in particular were held in great esteem. It was highly prestigious to be well educated in various sciences and to express this knowledge in refined and delicate verse. With the Arab conquest of Azerbaijan and the subsequent adoption of Islam, the Arabic alphabet acquired popularity. Literate people gained access to ancient treatises, which had been translated and

Shamakhi Observatory

preserved by Arabian scientists, and to the treasures of Muslim culture. Khatib Tabrizi, an outstanding philologist of the 11th century, philosopher Abulhasan Bahmanyar, astronomer Fazil Firaeddin Shirvani, who drew a set of astronomical maps, and Abubakr Ajemi Nakhchivani, a prominent architect of the Middle Ages, all bequeathed a priceless scientific heritage to their nation.

Nizami Ganjavi and Khagani Shirvani were 12th century poets whose outstanding poetry sparkles with philosophy. Nasraddin Tusi was the most prominent Azerbaijani scholar of the 13th century. He inspired the development of science and culture in Azerbaijan which was the most important political and administrative entity of the state. In 1259 Nasraddin Tusi founded the observatory at Maragha, one of the most important scientific research centres of his time. His research, which outlived his era by centuries, was translated into Latin and published in Europe.

Early in the 14th century, a house of healing or Dar-ash-Shafa, was founded in the city of Tabriz. It was an entire scientific village with educational, treatment and scientific institutions, including an observatory. The Dar-ash-Shafa had a higher school, a kind of university. It hosted 6,000-7,000 students who

Nasraddin Tusi (1201-1274)

A prominent Azerbaijani academic and statesman, Nasraddin Tusi was an accomplished scholar in many disciplines. His work played a major role in the development of geometry and trigonometry not only in the East but also in Europe. It was Tusi who presented trigonometry as an individual science for the first time. He also wrote on astronomy, physics, medicine, philosophy, ethics and logic. Nasraddin Tusi improved upon earlier Arabic translations of Avicenna (*Canon of Medicine*), Euclid (*Elements*), Ptolemy (*Almagest*), Autolycus, Theodosius, Apollonius and others. Some 20 of his works concern mathematics and astronomy, the most famous of which is the four-volume *Astronomic Tables of Ilkhanis*, a compilation of the research carried out at the Maragha Observatory. His most popular book, *Ahlagi Nasiri*, deals with ethics.

Abbasqulu Agha Bakikhanov (1794-1847)

Bakikhanov wrote on a wide range of subjects but perhaps his most important work is *Gulustani-i-Iram (Paradise Flower Garden)*, the first historical review of the Eastern Caucasus from antiquity to 1813 when the Gulustan peace treaty was signed. He presents a range of evidence including on geographic features and sites around Guba and Karabakh. He also wrote on logic, Persian grammar, geography and religion. Bakikhanov was also well known as a poet and wrote under the penname Gudsi. He wrote many works on astronomy and the universe as well as on history, culture and religion.

came from all over Asia to study natural sciences, philosophy, history, medicine, astronomy and logic. Over this period, theses by Seyid Yahya Bakuvi (on philosophy, history, geography and astronomy), Abdurrashid Bakuvi (on history and geography), Fazlullah Rashidaddin (on medicine and history), the historians Mohammed Hindushah Nakhchivani and Iskandar Munshi and Mohammed Fizuli, a renowned Azerbaijani poet and philosopher, became popular. In the late 18th and early 19th centuries, Haji Zeynalabdin Shirvani gained renown as a scientist and geographer.

The main building of the National Academy of Sciences of Azerbaijan

In the 19th century, Azerbaijan made a contribution to modern science. The historian Abbasqulu Agha Bakikhanov, the philosopher Mirza Fatali Akhundov and the Darwinian Hasan bay Zardabi are just a few of the prominent scientists of that period. Mirza Jafar Topchubashov, Mirza Kazim bay and Mirza Shafi Vazeh made great achievements in Oriental studies. After the creation of Baku State University in 1919 and other research institutions, scientists were able to undertake research. They set up various societies and groups which became a basis for scientific and research institutions. The Azerbaijan Investigation and Survey Society performed a key role. The society was created in 1923 and underwent several structural reforms. In 1925 the society was put at the disposal of the Azerbaijani government. In 1929 the society was reorganized and named the Azerbaijani Scientific Research Institute and in 1932 it became the Azerbaijani department within the Caucasian branch of the USSR Academy of Sciences. In 1935 this department became the Azerbaijani branch of the USSR Academy of Sciences.

During the Second World War, Azerbaijani scientists, led by Yusuf Mammadaliyev, made several important discoveries, which became the cornerstone in the development of new fuels and explosives for the army. He was awarded the Stalin Prize in 1943 for these discoveries, the highest award in the former USSR.

By decree of the Soviet of USSR People's Commissars, issued in 1945, the Azerbaijani branch of the USSR Academy of Sciences became the Azerbaijani SSR Academy of Sciences. Later, in March of

Mirza Kazim bay (1802-70)

A founder of Oriental studies in Russia, Mirza Kazim bay wrote his first academic work, entitled *Experiments in Arabic Grammar*, at the age of 17. He spoke fluent Turkish, Russian, Persian, Arabic, English, German and French. Mirza Kazim bay was the founder and first dean of the faculty of Oriental Studies at the University of St Petersburg and the first researcher in Muslim law in Russia. He is also the first author of a grammar of the Azerbaijani language. His work *Derbendnama*, the peak of his academic research, was published in 1851 in St Petersburg.

One of the founders of the Academy of Sciences of Azerbaijan, Yusuf Mammadaliyev was the author of more than 200 scientific works, including six pieces of major research. He made a huge contribution to the country's chemical industry and laid the foundations of petrochemical research in Azerbaijan.

Yusuf Mammadaliyev proposed rubber production using natural oil and gas for the first time.

Yusuf Mammadaliyev (1905-61)

Mammadaliyev also applied the explosive substance toluol and high-octane aviation fuel to industrial use. He discovered solid fuel for missiles and successfully applied it in industry. As a result of this discovery, the cosmic missile industry prospered and in 1957 the first satellite was able to enter space. An official initiative was taken to nominate him for the Nobel Prize in 1957, but the initiative failed since USSR officials of Armenian origin rejected it.

that year, the Academy of Sciences of Azerbaijan held its General Assembly at which the outstanding medical scientist Mirasadulla Mirqasimov was named the academy's first president. The presidents of the academy over the following years were Y. Mammadaliyev (1947-50, 1958-61), M. Aliyev (1950-58), Z. Khalilov (1961-67), R. Ismayilov (1967-70), H. Abdullayev (1970-83), E. Salayev (1983-97), and F. Maqsudov (1997-2000). Mahmud Karimov has held the post since 2001. He was re-elected in the last elections for president of the Academy and correspondent members in 2007.

The Academy of Sciences is the main scientific institution in the republic. It plays a critical role in the study and development of Azerbaijan's natural resources and the development of the economy and culture. The Academy consists of six departments: Physics, Mathematics and Technical Sciences, Chemical Sciences, Earth Sciences, Biological Sciences, Social Sciences, and Language, Literature and Arts. Each department, in turn, has various research institutes assigned to it. There are 34 scientific-research centres, 30 institutes, three regional research centres, 10 construction-technology departments and two experimental plants.

The Academy of Sciences plays a leading role in the republic in undertaking fundamental research, creating new technologies and methodologies and in training highly qualified experts. Some of the scientific research carried out at the Academy has had an international impact including in solid state physics and semiconductors, mathematics and mechanics, petrochemicals, oil refining, crystal geology and the scientific basis for improving the productivity of arable and livestock farms.

Today in different countries Azerbaijani scientists are committed to scientific and educational work. The most well-known of them is Prof. Lotfi A. Zadeh (Lotfi Rahim oghlu Alaskarzada), founder of the

Prof. Lotfi A. Zadeh
(Lotfi Rahim oghlu Alaskarzada)
(1921)

fuzzy logic theory. Industrial and electronics companies, NASA and NATO work on the basis of his theory. Prof. Lotfi A. Zadeh is an honorary life professor of the University of California in Berkeley, where he heads the computer software institute.

Since independence, the Academy has sought to strengthen its international ties. Currently joint research projects are being carried out with scientists in the USA, Japan, France, Holland, Israel, Switzerland, Great Britain, Norway, Germany, Pakistan, Turkey, Iran and other countries. By decree of the Azerbaijan president issued in 2001, the Azerbaijani Academy of Sciences was given national status and became the Azerbaijan National Academy of Sciences.

Culture & Arts

Öö Üü Əə Çç Şş Ğğ

48 How many people speak Azerbaijani worldwide?

There are approximately 50 million Azerbaijanis worldwide. Azerbaijan was divided into two parts under the Gulustan (1813) and Turkmenchay (1828) treaties which gave the northern part to Russia and the southern part to Iran. At present 8.3 million Azerbaijanis live in northern Azerbaijan (the Republic of Azerbaijan) while 30 million live in southern Azerbaijan, which is part of Iran. Azerbaijanis live in 67 countries in all, including Turkey (three million), Russia (three million), Iraq (one million), the USA (one million.), Egypt (900,000), Pakistan (650,000), Afghanistan (450,000), Georgia (300,000) and Germany (300,000). Taking into consideration all these figures, more than 50 million people can be said to speak Azerbaijani.

49 What is the origin of the Azerbaijani language?

The Azerbaijani language belongs to the Turkic group of languages. Azerbaijani, together with the closely associated Turkish, Turkmen and Gagauz languages, form the south-western group of Turkic languages.

From the traditional morphological and typological point of view, the Azerbaijani language belongs to the group of agglutinative languages (in which a suffix is added to a word's root to make different grammatical forms).

The Turks, who make up the ethnic foundation of the Azerbaijani people, appeared in the territory of modern-day Azerbaijan early in the first millennium. Alongside many other tribes they were the ancient inhabitants of this land. The emergence of a nation of Turkish origin speaking the Azerbaijani language was a long process that took several centuries. As the number of Turkish tribes and their economic, political and cultural influence increased, the language was enriched. Ethnic groups united into a nation with a unique culture and language and have managed to preserve their ethnic and anthropological characteristics into the 21st century.

The Azerbaijani language has evolved over many centuries. The epic *Book of Dada Qorqud* shows that Azerbaijani has been the means of communication amongst our people for more than 1,300 years, whilst other sources indicate that the history of written literary Azerbaijani begins in the 13th century.

The 800-year evolution of literary Azerbaijani can be divided into two main periods. The old period covers the 13th to 18th centuries, while the new period began in the 18th century and continues today.

Thanks to the efforts of the then leader of Soviet Azerbaijan, Heydar Aliyev, the Azerbaijani language was afforded the status of state language. The following article was included in the 1978 Constitution of the Azerbaijani Soviet Socialist Republic: "The Azerbaijani language is the state language of the Azerbaijan Soviet Socialist Republic." The constitutions of other Soviet republics did not refer to state language.

The Constitution of independent Azerbaijan, accepted in a nationwide referendum in 1995, confirmed Azerbaijani as the state language of the country. Article 21 of the Constitution reads: "The state language of the Azerbaijani Republic is the Azerbaijani language. Azerbaijan ensures the development of the Azerbaijani language."

As one of the Turkic languages, modern Azerbaijani has specific grammatical and phonetic properties.

Azerbaijani consists of 15 vowel and 25 consonant phonemes. These 40 phonemes are represented by the 32 letters of the Azerbaijani alphabet.

Name	Print	Script	Name	Print	Script
a	A a	*Aa*	qe	Q q	*Qq*
be	B b	*Bb*	el	L l	*Ll*
ce	C c	*Cc*	em	M m	*Mm*
çe	Ç ç	*Çç*	en	N n	*Nn*
de	D d	*Dd*	o	O o	*Oo*
e	E e	*Ee*	ö	Ö ö	*Öö*
ə	Ə ə	*Əə*	pe	P p	*Pp*
fe	F f	*Ff*	er	R r	*Rr*
ge	G g	*Gg*	se	S s	*Ss*
ğe	Ğ ğ	*Ğğ*	şe	Ş ş	*Şş*
he	H h	*Hh*	te	T t	*Tt*
xe	X x	*Xx*	u	U u	*Uu*
ı	I ı	*Iı*	ü	Ü ü	*Üü*
i	İ i	*İi*	ve	V v	*Vv*
je	J j	*Jj*	ye	Y y	*Yy*
ke, ka	K k	*Kk*	ze	Z z	*Zz*

Azerbaijani Alphabet

The current Azerbaijani alphabet of Latin letters was created in the mid-19th century. Since the 8th century the Arabic alphabet had been used in Azerbaijan as in other nations of the Near and Middle East. In 1923 the Soviet government adapted the Azerbaijani Latin alphabet and in 1929 banned the Arabic script. In 1939 the Soviet government applied the Cyrillic alphabet in Azerbaijan. In 1991 when independence was restored, the Latin alphabet was once again deemed the country's official alphabet. Since 2001 this has been the only alphabet to be used in Azerbaijan.

The vowel "ı" and consonant "ğ" are not used at the beginning of a word in Azerbaijani.

According to the rules of Azerbaijani syntax, the subject comes at the beginning of a sentence and the predicate at the end, while an attribution precedes the word it modifies.

Azerbaijan now uses an Azerbaijani alphabet, established on the basis of Latin letters.

The Azerbaijani language has four dialect groups: 1) the *eastern* group (Baku, Guba, Shamakhi, Lankaran and Mughan dialects; 2) the *western* group (Ganja, Gazakh, Karabakh and Ayrym dialects); 3) the *northern* group (Shaki and Zagatala-Gakh dialects); 4) the *southern* group (Nakhchivan and Ordubad dialects).

50 What are the main minority languages in Azerbaijan?

Representatives of several ethnic groups live in Azerbaijan. Some are considered to be distinct ethnic groups and have their own languages. There are five widely-spoken minority languages in Azerbaijan: *Talysh, Lezgi, Avar, Tat* and *Kurdish*.

The *Talysh* language is spoken by the Talysh and belongs to the north-western group of Iranian languages. The Talysh people mainly live in the southern part of Azerbaijan: the Talysh Mountains, Lerik, Astara, Lankaran and Masalli districts. The *Lezgi* language is spoken by the Lezgis and belongs to the Lezgi group of Dagestani languages. The Lezgis mainly live in the north and north-eastern part of Azerbaijan in districts such as Gusar and Guba and in parts of Gakh and Oghuz. *Tat* is the language of the Tats and belongs to the Iranian language group. The Tat people live mainly on the Caspian coast, in Davachi, Khizi and Absheron. The Avar people live in northern Zagatala and Balakan districts and speak *Avar*, a language of the Caucasian language group. *Kurdish* is spoken by the Kurdish population that mainly live in the western regions of the country, the districts of Lachin, Kalbajar, Gubadli and Zangilan. The language belongs to the western Iranian group.

51 Who is Dada Qorqud?

Kitabi-Dada Qorqud (The Book of Dada Qorqud) is the most significant Turkic literary epic of the Middle Ages. For hundreds of years the stories that make up this collection were handed down as part of the oral tradition of the Turkic peoples. Two manuscripts are known to exist - one in Dresden and one in the Vatican. The Dresden manuscript, which was discovered by H. F. von Dietz in 1815, is the more complete with 12 stories, and its language is very close to modern Azerbaijani. The Vatican manuscript consists of only six stories and is considered to be closer to the Old Turkic language. It was discovered in 1950 by Ettore Rossi. The manuscripts are believed to date to the 15th or 16th centuries, although scholars are still debating the actual dates and which is older. The epic describes the life and heroic deeds of Oghuz Turks during the Middle Ages. (In ethnic and linguistic terms, the Oghuz are related to three contemporary Turkic peoples - the Azerbaijanis, Turks and Turkmen.)

Dada Qorqud, after whom the book is named, narrates the stories. Medieval scholar Rashid ad-Din refers to Dada Qorqud as a real person. In the epic, he is high priest and bard of the Oghuz tribe. He composes tales and often sings them to the accompaniment of music from his *qopuz* (lute). It is also his job to bestow names upon young men after they have proven their bravery and to give advice and help when they are in trouble. Turkish traveller Evliya Chelebi (1611-79) and German scholar Adam Oleari (1603-71) said that Dada Qorqud, Qazan Khan and his wife Burla Khatun were buried in Derbent, an ancient Azerbaijani city now in Dagestan.

A scene in the film *Dada Qorqud* (1975), performed by Azerbaijani actor Hasan Mammadov

Events in *Dada Qorqud* concern three time periods. The first is antiquity, usually shown by motifs closely related to those in Homer's

Illustrations for *Dada Qorqud* by USSR People's Artist Mikayil Abdullayev

Odyssey. Scholars often compare events and characters in these two epics. For example, the protagonists in both have very similar adventures, while the wives offer their lives as a sacrifice to save their husbands. The tales of Tapagoz (a creature with one eye) and Cyclops are also thought to come from a common source. Scholars still debate whether or not Homer borrowed these stories while they were circulating orally in western parts of Central Asia. The second period is the 7th-12th centuries, in which the life of the Oghuz tribes is mainly described. The epic itself refers to the time when Dada Qorqud appeared and mentions that historically it was very close to the period when Mohammed lived (570-632 AD). The third period of time, referred to in the manuscripts themselves, is the 15th century when these stories were written down.

In Azerbaijan, serious study of *Dada Qorqud* started in the late 1950s. During the years of the Stalinist repression, research had been prohibited, probably because Turkish scholars were already working on it. Soviet policy at the time was generally anti-Turkish, as the Soviet authorities did not want relationships to develop between Azerbaijan and Turkish academics. Investigating history was viewed as potentially dangerous, as the Turkic peoples share much in terms of language, culture and literature today and in earlier periods, the similarities were even closer.

Kitabi-Dada Qorqud was translated into German in 1958 by Ihsan Hayn. In 1973 Professors Faruk Sumer, Ahmed Uysal and Warren Walker translated it into English in Texas and in 1974 Geoffrey Lewis translated the book in London.

A number of events were held to mark the 1,300th anniversary of the epic *Dada Qorqud* and a special encyclopaedia was published by decree of Azerbaijani President Heydar Aliyev. The anniversary was marked by UNESCO at international level too. In April 2000 the heads of Turkic states and Koichiro Matsuura, director-general of UNESCO, participated in a ceremony in Baku.

Monument to *Dada Qorqud* in Brussels
by Namiq Zeynalov

101

52 Who are Azerbaijan's best known poets and writers?

**Nizami and philosophers, 1485,
Azerbaijan Institute of Manuscripts, Baku**

Literature has held a special place in Azerbaijani culture over the centuries and folklore is at its heart. Ethnic and cultural values are enshrined in folklore. Lullabies are the first literature that an Azerbaijani hears and spark a love of words and of the harmony of language. Azerbaijani folklore is rich because everyone is a potential creator of folklore. Elegies are said at funerals and commemorative events. The Zoroastrian scripture *Avesta*, completed in the 6th century BC, and the legends of Midia, passed down through the works of Greek historian Herodotus, are derived from this rich folklore. Ancient Turkic myths and legends provide another source of Azerbaijani folklore. They are the basis of the heroic tales of *The Book of Dada Qorqud*.

In the early 5th century the 52-letter Albanian alphabet emerged in Azerbaijan. Catholicos Viro, head of the Albanian Church, translated Persian myths into Albanian. Albanian literature reached its peak in the 7th century. The most prominent poet of that era was Davdak, whose elegy on the death of Azerbaijani ruler Javanshir is a unique work that survives to this day.

Writing in the 7th century, Moisey Kalankatuklu included tales and stories in his *History of Albania*. This is one of the rare extant works in Caucasian Albanian and shows that Azerbaijan had a highly developed culture in the 4th to 7th centuries. Another historian of the period, Mkhitar Gosh, records history and culture in his *Chronicle of Albania*.

From the mid-7th century, after the adoption of Islam, most literature in Azerbaijan was written in Arabic. Azerbaijani poets of the 7th and 8th centuries such as Musa Shehavet, Ismail bin Yaser and Abdul Abbas wrote in Arabic. From the 10th century Persian began to dominate in the region as the language of poetry.

After Azerbaijan left the Caliphate in the 9th century, Persian gradually replaced Arabic as the language of literature. This was partly a result of the environment at court and the preferences of Azerbaijan's rulers. Moreover, Azerbaijani writers wanted to maintain links with countries in the Near East where Arabic and Persian were state languages.

From the 11th century onwards written literature was mainly created at court and became known later as "palace literature" or "*divan* literature". Most of the authors of this period wrote in Persian. One of the best known Azerbaijani authors of the 11th century was Qatran Tabrizi (1012-88). He wrote a collection of poems, *Divan*, and a dictionary, *At-Tafasir*, both in Persian. Some poets and scholars of the 12th century, such as Abu Nasr Mansur Tabrizi, Khatib Tabrizi, Iskafi Zanjani and Khattat Nizami Tabrizi wrote in Arabic.

The 12th century was an important period for literature in Azerbaijan. Poets from this period include Abul-ula Ganjavi, who was awarded the title *Melikush-Shuara* (chief poet), Feleki Shirvani, Izaddin Shirvani, Mujiraddin Beylaqani and Givami Ganjavi, who all wrote in Persian. From the 13th century poetry in Azerbaijani began to dominate. The earliest surviving work in Azerbaijani is a poem by Hasanoghlu.

Creative genius Fizuli grew from the roots put down by Nizami and others. (See below for more about Nizami.) Before Fizuli, Azerbaijani literature was distinguished by the work of Hasanoghlu (13th century), Qazi Burhanaddin (1344-98), Nasimi (1369-1417) and Khatai (1487-1524), and earned renown in the Middle and Near East. Like Nizami, Fizuli (who developed the former's compassionate traditions) surpassed national and regional borders, giving fine expression to joy and sorrow, and declares the freedom and honour of the individual: "I am not weak, look, I won't bow to anyone." He also wrote about grief, which was to become a major theme of Romantic poets such as Byron and Heine. Epic and other types of storytelling poetry also developed in Fizuli's era. Later poets include Qurbani (16th century), Ashiq Abbas (17th century) and Khasta Qasim (1684-1760) while Sari Ashiq developed the four-lined *bayati* in the 17th century. In the 19th century Dada Ali, Ashiq Pari and Ashiq Alasgar wrote works that retain their interest today. The heroic epics *Koroghlu* and *Shah Ismayil* and the love epics *Ashiq Qarib*, *Asli and Kerem* and *Abbas and Gulgaz* date back to the Middle Ages and were influenced by *The Book of Dada Qorqud*. They have become masterpieces of Azerbaijani folklore.

Molla Panah Vaqif is an outstanding poet and statesman of the early modern era. He created a realistic and lyrical body of work that broke the fascination with Fizuli. Other writers of this period include the poets Molla Vali Vidadi (1707-1808), Mirza Shafi Vazeh (1794-1852) and Qasim bay Zakir (1784-1857).

Mirza Fatali Akhundov (1812-78) brought Azerbaijani literature within the context of Western literature and in so doing brought Azerbaijani culture closer to Europe. Azerbaijani literature has developed along European lines in the modern era, but with age-old traditions at its foundation. Patriotic poets and writers such as Jalil

Fizuli's Divan, 1682, Azerbaijan Institute of Manuscripts, Baku

Nizami reading his play *Treasure of Secrets*, to a prince.
Nizami, 1538, Bukhara

Mammadquluzada, Mirza Alakbar Sabir and Najaf bay Vezirov promoted national freedom and the cultural development of the people in their works. Playwright Huseyn Javid (1882-1941) developed the traditions of Mirza Fatali. Jafar Jabbarli (1899-1934) and Ilyas Afandiyev (1914-97) are other well-known dramatists.

The poetry of Abdulla Shaiq (1881-1959), Ahmad Javad (1892-1937), Aliagha Vahid (1895-1965), Samad Vurgun (1906-56), Mahammadhuseyn Shahriyar (1906-89), Suleyman Rustam (1906-89), Mikayil Mushviq (1908-38) and Rasul Rza (1910-81) remains popular. The same can be said of the novels of Nariman Narimanov (1870-1925), Mammad Said Ordubadi (1872-1950), Yusif Vezir Chemenzeminli (1887-1943), Suleyman Rahimov (1900-83), Mir Jalal Pashayev (1908-78), Mirza Ibrahimov (1911-93), Gilman Ilkin (1941), Imran Qasimov (1917-81), Ismayil Shikhli (1919-95), Aziza Jafarzada (1921-2003), Huseyn Abbaszada (1921-2008) and others.

The literature of independent Azerbaijan has been integrating into world literature for more than a decade. The writers of the 1960s played a big role in this process. But it is the rich Azerbaijani language that has carried our literature on its shoulders throughout the centuries.

Some of the best known figures of contemporary Azerbaijani literature are the poets Mirvarid Dilbazi (1912-2001), Balash Azaroghlu (1921), Nabi Khazri (1924-2007), Huseyn Arif (1924-92), Sohrab Tahir (1926), Qabil (1926-2007), Nariman Hasanzada (1931), Khalil Rza Uluturk (1933-94), Mammad Araz (1933-2004), Ilyas Tapdiq (1934) and Vahid Aziz (1945). Contemporary writers include Isa Huseynov (1928), Chingiz Huseynov (1929), Maqsud Ibrahimbayov (1935), Yusif Samedoghlu (1935-98), Akram Aylisli (1937), Rustam Ibrahimbayov (1938), Anar (1938), Vagif Samedoghlu (1939), Elchin (1943) and Chingiz Abdullayev (1959).

Khaqani Shirvani (1126-99)

Khaqani was prominent in Azerbaijan's literary renaissance in the 12th century. Born in Shamakhi, Khaqani wrote the first poetry in Azerbaijani and made the genre *qasida* popular in the Near East. Like other writers of the period, he wrote about the reality of life around him and the struggle between good and evil. His work is marked by a deep compassion. He left a collection, a Divan, of lyric poems of 17,000 couplets and a poem *Tohfet-ul-Iraqeyn* (A Gift from the Two Iraqs) as well as letters written in prose.

Nizami Ganjavi (1141-1209)

Azerbaijani poet Nizami Ganjavi is known worldwide, as his beautiful, compassionate work has stood the test of time. Nizami Ganjavi's *Khamsa* or Quinary includes the five books *The Treasury of Secrets* (1174-75), *Khosrov and Shirin* (1181), *Leyli and Majnun* (1188), *Seven Beauties* (1197) and *Iskandernama* (*The Book of Alexander,* 1200). His collected poetry or divan consisted of 20,000 couplets, but, unfortunately, only a small part of the *divan* survives to this day. Nizami Ganjavi was a great poet, scholar and philosopher. It is obvious from his works that he had a deep knowledge of astronomy, medicine, philosophy and education. It was Nizami who first fought for the idea of a "utopian community", before Italian philosopher Tomazo Campanella (1568-1639). Writing about the Sun, Moon and stars, Nizami argued that the Moon did not have its own light and called it a "lightless spot". In the development of geometry he also praised the works of Euclid (3rd century BC) and Ptolemy (2nd century BC).

Imadeddin Nasimi (1369-1417)

Classical Azerbaijani poet Nasimi was born in Shamakhi. He wrote the first socio-philosophical poem in Azerbaijani. In his philosophical poetry Nasimi praises humanity, its capacity

for thought, beauty and joy. Nasimi wrote that the essence or pearl of the world is mankind. He first compared man with God. He said that nature, the earth and sky derive their beauty from mankind. In 1417 Yashbey, ruler of Aleppo, ordered that he be skinned alive. Nasimi is said to have recited his poem *Aghrimaz* (Without Pain) during the flaying. Other well-known poems by Nasimi are *Sigmazam* and *Dilbera, men senden ayri* (*My sweet, I am away from you*).

Mohammed Fizuli (1496-1556)

The most prominent Azerbaijani classical poet was born in Karbala, Iraq. Fizuli was from the Bayat tribe that had moved to Iraq from Azerbaijan. Fizuli wrote poems in three languages - Arabic, Persian and Azerbaijani. He is Azerbaijani literature's most prominent prose writer. Fizuli wrote mainly on love and humanity and his *Leyli and Majnun* is a literary gem. Fizuli also wrote allegorical works. His poem *Bangu-Bade (Opium and Wine)* is about the politics of his day and describes various types of ruler. He also wrote the *Shikayetnama, Rindu-Zahid* (in Persian) and *Enus-ul Qalb*. Fizuli is one of the creators of the literary Azerbaijani language and wrote in the style of Nasimi. He formed a literary school, which greatly influenced Azerbaijani and Near Eastern poetry.

Molla Panah Vaqif (1717-97)

A talented diplomat and statesman, Molla Panah Vaqif wrote some of the classics of Azerbaijani literature. He was born in the village of Salahli in Gazakh District. In 1757 he moved to Karabakh and started a school there. Later in 1769 Ibrahimkhalil Khan (1759-1806), the then ruler of Karabakh, invited him to his palace where Vaqif worked, first as a butler and later as chief vizier. His most famous poems are *Stop flapping your wings awhile, Cranes, It is a holiday, My honey, Your lips are the colour of rubies* and *Look*.

Mirza Shafi Vazeh
(1794-1852)

Classical poet Mirza Shafi Vazeh was born in Ganja. Vazeh writes in his poetry of the joys of life, and the wisdom and goodness of mankind. In 1844 he established a literary society, the Divan-i-Hikmat, in Tbilisi, where Azerbaijani and foreign intellectuals gathered. One member of the society was German poet and traveller Friederich von Bodenstedt. Vazeh rarely wrote down his verse, but Bodenstedt recorded his poetry and upon his return to Germany translated it into German. In 1851 *The Songs of Mirza Shafi* was published to such acclaim that it was translated into nearly all European languages. Bodenstedt denied Vazeh's authorship, claiming that it was his own work. Only in the 20th century did Azerbaijani scholars discover the deceit and put the record straight.

Khurshudbanu Natavan
(1832-97)

Natavan, a well-known figure in Azerbaijan literature in the 19th century, was born in Shusha into the family of Mehdiqulu Khan, heir to the rulers of Karabakh. She was educated at home and from an early age was interested in poetry, music and art and spoke Near Eastern languages. In 1872 she founded the *Majlisi Uns* (Friends' Assembly), a literary assembly of well-known poets writing in the classical style. In 1858 she met Alexandre Dumas Pere in Baku and gave him a few handicrafts. Dumas, in turn, gave her a fine chess set. In 1850 she started writing in the traditional Eastern genre. Most of her poetry forms a series in praise of nature and or devoted to her son who died young. Her most famous poems are *Violet, Carnation, Without You* and *Gone*.

Mirza Alakbar Sabir
(1862-1911)

Satirical poet Mirza Alakbar Sabir was born in Shamakhi. Humanitarianism and the ideals of freedom are a key part of his work. In defending the principles of realism Sabir said that his duty was to write that "bad is bad, wrong is wrong and right is right". In its craftsmanship and literary form, Sabir's poetry influenced literature in Azerbaijan and the Near and Middle East. He also wrote parodies, for instance, *I have nothing to do with how the people are pillaged*, and, *God, you won't need that*.

Huseyn Javid
(1882-1941)

Huseyn Javid was a prominent Azerbaijani poet and playwright, born in Nakhchivan. He is one of the founders of progressive Azerbaijani romanticism in the 20th century. Huseyn Javid is the author of lyrical poems, lyrical epic and epic poems and verse dramas, a first in Azerbaijani literature. He is best known as a playwright. Huseyn Javid's philosophical and historical tragedies influenced national theatre and represented a new stage in terms of style and content. They became known as "Javid's theatre". Historical dramas such as *Prophet* (1921), *Topal Teymur* (1925), *Seyavush* (1933) and *Kheyyam* and the tragedy *Satan* (1918) all brought him fame. As a democrat, Huseyn Javid did not adapt to "Soviet demands" and was arrested in 1937. He was exiled to Siberia, where he died in 1941. At the initiative of Heydar Aliyev his remains were buried in his native town, Nakhchivan, in 1982 and, later, in 1996 a big monument was erected there.

Samad Vurgun
(1906-56)

Born in Gazakh, Samad Vurgun was awarded the Soviet title of People's Poet for his contribution to the development of poetry in Azerbaijan. His early poems are known for their intimate lyrics. Pessimism, unrequited love and admiration for nature are the main topics in his early work. Some of Samad Vurgun's best known poems are *Ahead, A Long Way Off* and *Azerbaijan*. He is also the author of several verse dramas, including *Vaqif* about Azerbaijani poet Molla Panah Vaqif. Samad Vurgun's best known later works include *Mugan, Aygun, Old Friends* and *A Negro's Dreams*. His work is marked by patriotism, internationalism and compassion.

Mahammadhuseyn Shahriyar
(1906-88)

Shahriyar is a well-known figure in 20th century Azerbaijani and Iranian poetry. He started writing lyric poems in the 1920s and his first book of poems was published in 1931. The poem *Salute to Heydarbaba (Heydarbabaya salam)* is well known in Azerbaijani literature. His work, written in both Azerbaijani and Persian, skilfully combines the two poetic traditions. The motifs of his poetry are justice, freedom, moral purity and optimism. Shahriyar praises the beauty of Azerbaijani nature, customs and traditions and honours endless love for the motherland.

Muhammad Asad bay
(1905-42)

Muhammad Asad bay (Leo Nussenbaum, Qurban Said) was an Azerbaijani emigre author of the 20th century. Born in Baku, Asad bay emigrated to Turkey in 1920 after the fall of the Azerbaijani Democratic Republic. He moved from there to Germany and then Italy, where he died near Naples. Asad bay is the author of the bestselling novel *Ali and Nino* (1937), which, like all his work, he wrote in German. His other works include *Oil and Blood in the Orient* (1929), *Twelve Mysteries of the Caucasus* (1930), *Stalin* (1930), *Caucasus. Mountains, Nations and History* (1931), *Muhammad* (1932), *DSI. Plot Against the World* (1932), *White Russia* (1932), *Russia at the Crossroads* (1933), *Liquid Gold* (1933), *Manuela* (1934), *Milosh and Oil* (1934), *Lenin* (1935), *Rza Shah - Teacher, Padishah and Reformer* (1935), *Nikolay II. Grandeur and Development of the Last Tsar* (1935), *Great Allah. The Decline and Rise of the Islamic World. From Abdul Hamid to Ibn Saud* (1935), *Mussolini* (1937) and *Altunsach* (1938).

Ali and Nino **is the story of a young Azerbaijani who falls in love with a Georgian princess. It is the story of the search for truth and reconciliation between different religions and ways of life - Islamic and Christian, East and West, young and old. Most of the events in the story happen in 1918 in Baku in the Ichari Shahar (Old Walled City) on the eve of the Bolshevik Revolution. Muhammad Asad bay wrote his novel under the pseudonym Qurban Said. It was first published in German in 1937 in Austria.**

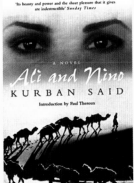

The novel has been translated into 29 languages - Arabic, Azerbaijani, Bengali, Cantonese, Catalan, Czech, Dutch, English, Finnish, French, Georgian, German, Greek, Hebrew, Hungarian, Indonesian, Italian, Japanese, Norwegian, Persian, Polish, Portuguese (Brazilian and continental), Russian, Serbian, Spanish, Swedish, Turkish and Urdu.

Bakhtiyar Vahabzada
(1925)

Born in Nukha (Shaki), Bakhtiyar Vahabzada has been awarded the title People's Poet. He has played an important part in the formation of modern Azerbaijani verse. Love, patriotism and human values feature prominently in his poetry. His poems *Mugham* and *Gulustan* talk about the dreams of national liberation of the Azerbaijani people; *Shabi-Hijran* is dedicated to Fizuli and *Martyrs* to those who perished in January 1990. He has also written dozens of poems and plays.

Anar Rzayev
(1938)

Anar Rasul oghlu Rzayev is one of Azerbaijan's most famous contemporary writers. He has written more than 50 books, many of which have been translated and published in many countries. His best known works are *Longing for the Holiday, The Rain Stopped, White Port, A Person's Person, The Sixth Floor of the Five-Storey Building, Opportunity, I've Come to You, Without You, Summer Days in the City, Hotel Room* and *Me, You, Him and the Telephone*. Anar's plays are often performed. He has written the scripts for of 11 feature films, including *Dada Qorqud*, and some documentaries. Since 1991 he has been chairman of the Writers' Union of Azerbaijan.

Chingiz Abdullayev
(1959)

Another well-known figure in Azerbaijani contemporary literature, Chingiz Abdullayev is often rated amongst the top three most popular authors in the CIS. He has written some 600 books which have been published in 23 countries in 16 languages. More than 20 million copies of his work have been printed. One of his best known novels is *Azerbaijan's National Export*. His novels *Blue Angels, The Law of Scoundrels, Better to be a Saint, The Shadow of Herod* and *Three Colours of Blood* have been included in the golden fund of world detective literature.

53 What are Azerbaijan's traditional instruments?

Primitive cultural artefacts found in archaeological excavations in Azerbaijan show that music has an ancient tradition here. Pictures on a ceramic vessel from the 6th millennium BC found in the Azerbaijani town of Gilqamish are thought to show the *buq* and *chang* wind instruments. Ancient musical instruments, some preserved intact and others damaged, dating from the 4th-3rd millennia BC, have been found near the modern Azerbaijani towns of Ujar, Aghstafa, Mingachevir, Barda, Gabala and Masalli. In all 88 musical instruments have been found here, including 32 string, 23 wind and 16 percussion instruments.

The oldest known musical instrument in Azerbaijan is the *qavaldash*, made out of two large stones, at the prehistoric settlement of Gobustan, near Baku. Dating back to the Stone Age, the *qavaldash* is flat piece of limestone balanced on two pillars of rock and is an early percussion instrument. The ancient people of Gobustan are thought to have played the instrument to accompany ritual dances.

The most popular traditional instruments still played today are the *tar, kamancha, saz, ud* and *qanun* (all string instruments), the *balaban, tutek, zurna* and *ney* (wind instruments) and the *naghara, qoshanaghara, qaval, daf* and *dumbak* (percussion instruments).

The naghara (drum) is a folk percussion instrument, mentioned in the 7th century in the epic of *Dada Qorqud*. It has a cylindrical, double-faced frame covered with goatskin. There are large, medium and small *naghara*. The medium-sized drum is 330-360 mm in diameter. The large drum is played with large sticks, while the medium-sized and small ones are played with sticks or the hands. The drum is used both as a solo instrument and in accompaniment.

The *qoshanaghara* (double drum) is another ancient percussion instrument. It consists of two different sized drums, covered with goatskin and connected to one other. The *qoshanaghara* is played with sticks. Its size can vary, but as a rule, the two bodies of the *qoshanaghara* are equal in height, 300-330 mm. One of them is 240-280 mm in diameter and the other 110-140 mm.

Qoshanaghara

Naghara

The *qaval* (tambourine) belongs to the group of single percussion instruments. It is an ancient percussion instrument depicted in the work of medieval Azerbaijani painters and poets. The *qaval* was included as a lead instrument in the Traditional Instruments Orchestra founded by Azerbaijani composer Uzeyir Hajibayov, who also wrote the first musical scores for the instrument. Nowadays, the *qaval* is an important part of ensembles and orchestras composed of traditional instruments. The *qaval* has wide performance capabilities because it can produce trills, tremolos, mordents and other musical features. The *qaval* is a key part of a mugham trio - a group consisting of a singer, tar player and *kamancha* player that performs traditional Azerbaijani music such as *mugham* modes and rhythmic *mughams*.

The *qaval's* cylindrical frame is 60-75 mm tall, and its diameter is 340-450 mm. The *qaval* is made of walnut wood, with 60-70 small copper rings fitted to the inner side of its frame along the perimeter. Specially tanned sturgeon skin is stretched over the round frame. The thinness and transparency of the fish skin makes the sound of the instrument especially pleasant. To play the instrument, the musician holds it in his hands and plays with his fingers; sometimes the performer slaps the *qaval* as well.

The *zurna* (a sort of flute) is an ancient wind instrument, common in Azerbaijan. Many types of *zurna* were widespread in the Middle East and Caucasus. Four types of *zurna* made of deer horn were found during archaeological excavations of an ancient settlement in Mingachevir. Researchers say these instruments are 3,000 years old.

Ney

Qaval

The *zurna* is usually made of apricot, walnut or mulberry wood. The diameter at the top of the instrument is 20 mm, while at the lower part it is 60 mm. The *zurna* is 302-317 mm long and has seven apertures on the front. The player produces sound from the instrument by breathing out through the mouthpiece. The air passes through the mouthpiece, pivot and plug and enters into the body of the instrument. The player plays the *zurna* by opening and closing the apertures with his fingers. There are different types of *zurna* such as the *qarazurna* and *jurazurna*. The *zurna* usually accompanies both wedding parties and wrestling tournaments in some regions of Azerbaijan.

The *balaban* is a wind instrument, made of hazel, mulberry, walnut or apricot wood. It has eight holes (seven on the front, one on the back) on its 280-300 mm long cylindrical frame. A flat mouthpiece made of cane is fastened to the topside of the frame. The *balaban* has a soft, mournful sound. It is used as a solo and ensemble instrument.

Balaban

The *ney* is an ancient wind instrument, common in both Iran and Central Asia. It is usually made of cane, but sometimes of bronze. The 60-70 mm *ney* has six or nine holes on its pipe-shaped frame. Some musicians consider the *ney* an ancestor of the modern flute.

Kamancha

The *kamancha* (a kind of fiddle or violin) is played with a bow. It is made of walnut, apricot or mulberry wood and consists of an oval wooden cup or main body, a round neck, a top called an *ashiqlar* and iron rest called a shish. The instrument is 700-800 mm long and has four strings, although it used to have one to three strings. The *kamancha* has a soft, mournful sound. It is played either as a solo or ensemble instrument and is part of a *mugham* trio.

Tar

The modern *tar* is considered one of the most developed of the Azerbaijani string instruments. The tar emerged in the Near East and is mentioned in the work of medieval poets including Qatran Tabrizi (12th century) and Fizuli (16th century). Until the mid-19th century the *tar* had five strings and limited capabilities. In the 19th and 20th century Sadiqjan (1846-1902), a prominent Azerbaijani *tar* player, developed the *tar*.

The *tar* was and still is the main instrument

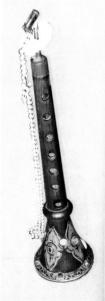

Zurna

in a *mugham* trio (*tar*, *kamancha* and *qaval*) and continues to play a significant role in the development of the art of *mugham*.

The structure and form of the *tar* is different from that of other string instruments. The *tar* has three main parts: the body, neck and head. The body is made of mulberry wood and the neck and head are made of walnut. Its total length is 850 mm. The body is 165 mm tall and 185 mm wide.

Ramiz Quliyev, well known Azerbaijani tar player

There are 22 frets fastened to the neck of the instrument. The body is covered with film made from the membrane of a cow's heart. The *tar* has 11 strings of varying thickness. The instrument is played with the help of a plectrum made of ebonite or bone. The *tar* is held horizontally against the chest. The performer pushes the *tar* against his chest with the help of his right wrist and holds the neck in his left hand. He holds the plectrum in his right hand and presses the frets with the fingers of his left hand.

The *saz* is another string instrument played with a *mizrab* or plectrum. In medieval times any string instrument of the Turkic people was called a *saz*. Its origin is connected with the *qopuz* (the name of the saz until the 15th century), *setar* and *dutar*. The *saz* has a pear-shaped frame, a long neck and top. There are small holes on the upper part of the frame and the side. There are three kinds of *saz*: the small *saz* (600-700 mm long), the medium-sized *saz* (900-1,000 mm long) and the large *saz* (1,200-1,500 mm). The strings are made of metal and the eight to 10 stringed *saz* is the most common. The main melody is played with a high-pitched string (soprano). The *saz* is played in ensembles and folk groups.

Saz

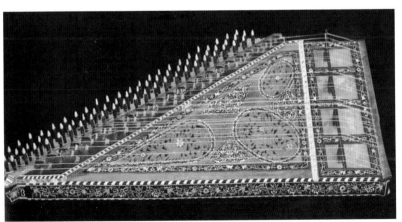

Qanun, decorated with mother-of-pearl

Ud

111

54 What is *Mugham*?

A master of *mugham*, Alim Qasimov (1957) is one of the world's truly gifted singers. He has been praised for his vocal dexterity and emotional delivery. The recipient of the international IMC/ UNESCO Music Prize in 1999, Alim Qasimov was described as "one of the 20th century's greatest singers" by *Folk Roots*, who praised him for his "pure vocal excitement".

Mugham is a unique form of Azerbaijani classical music that has been passed down orally to the present day. The art of *mugham* is deeply rooted in Azerbaijani cultural history and is considered by Azerbaijanis to be an invaluable part of their heritage. In 2003 the United Nations' cultural organization, UNESCO, declared Azerbaijani *mugham* a Masterpiece of the Oral and Intangible Heritage of Humanity

The concept of *mugham* has many meanings in Azerbaijani musical culture. First of all, the term refers to the tonal or *lad* system in Azerbaijani music, a meaning it has had for seven centuries. Nowadays Azerbaijanis associate mugham with types of melody with rhythmically free improvisation (*bəhərsiz hava*) as well with a broader musical genre. *Mugham* is the general name for the largest genre in Azerbaijani traditional music and comes in a variety of forms. The largest form in term of size and concept is the *dastgah* or mode. A *dastgah* is a vocal and instrumental composition similar to a suite. The *mughams* (rhythmically free melodies) alternate with *tasnifs* (rhythmic melodies similar to songs) and *rangs* (instrumental dance melodies). Another type of *dastgah* is the *zerbi mugham* or rhythmic *mugham*. *Zerbi mughams* are one-part compositions whose instrumental accompaniment keeps to a regular meter and whose vocal line is based on rhythmically free improvisation. The most popular *zerbi mughams* include *Simayi-Shams*, *Heyrati*, *Karabakh Shikastasi*, *Shirvan Shikastasi*, *Kasma Shikasta* and *Kurd Afshar Zerbi-Mansuriyya*. The separate parts that make up modes or *dastgahs - mughams*, *tasnifs*, *rangs* and *zerbi mughams* can also be performed independently. The popular longer *mugham dastgahs* include *Rast*, *Shur*, *Segah*, *Bayati-Shiraz*, *Humayun* and *Mahur*.

Dastgahs are usually performed by a small ensemble or trio that consists of a singer (called a *khananda*) and two instrumentalists (*sazanda*) who play the *tar* and *kamancha*, traditional string instruments. During rhythmic pieces the singer accompanies himself or herself on the *qaval*, a percussion instrument similar to the tambourine. The *mugham* trio has been widespread in Azerbaijan since the late 19th century.

Azerbaijani *mugham* was first recorded in the early 20th century. It was first written down in 1928 by Muslim Magomayev (1885-1937). Composers Niyazi (1912-84), Qara Qarayev (1918-82) and Fikrat Amirov (1922-84) also notated *mughams*.

The art of *mugham* is inextricably linked to classical poetry. Poems written in the *aruz* meter of oriental poetry are sung in *mughams*. The *ghazal* of classical poetry - that is, a poem made up of rhyming couplets with a refrain - is the main poetic form used in *mugham* performance. Singers or *khananda* in the past preferred *ghazals* by medieval poets such as Khagani Shirvani (12th century), Nizami Ganjavi (12th century), Imadaddin Nasimi (14th century), Muhammad Fizuli (16th century) and Shah Ismayil Khatai (16th century). Contemporary singers often use the *ghazals* of Molla Panah Vaqif (18th century), Khurshudbanu Natavan (19th century), Seyid Azim Shirvani (19th century) and Aliagha Vahid (20th century).

In the early 20th century *mugham* began to be performed on stage rather than in the domestic or chamber surroundings in which it had previously been performed. Public *mugham* concerts gave the impetus to improve the capacity of traditional instruments and to the creation of instrumental

Khananda (singer) Haji Husu

Khan Shushinski, Bahram Mansurov and Talat Bakikhanov play *mugham*

Khananda (singer) Jabbar Qaryaghdi oghlu

forms of *mugham*. The *tar* and *kamancha* alone can now perform whole modes or *dastgahs*. *Mughams* can also be performed by clarinet, oboe, *qarmon*, piano and even electric guitar, although the sound is not considered authentic.

The performance of *mugham* requires an exceptional musical memory, as the performer has to know the traditional *mugham* repertoire, and also a talent for improvisation and composition. A *mugham* mode is not performed from a written score but follows a framework within which the performer adapts and improvises. According to the unwritten rules, a performer must have a perfect knowledge of this art before he or she can be raised to the rank of master, *ustad*. A master has the moral authority to make changes to the rules of mugham. It takes a musician a long time to become a master. Since the 1920s musical education in Azerbaijan has been in three stages - primary, secondary professional and higher musical education. Azerbaijani

Azerbaijani musicians after recording at the Sport Record Company in Warsaw, 1912, sitting (from left to right): Jabbar Qaryaghdi oghlu, Davud Safiyarov, Mashadi Muhammad Farzaliyev, Kechachi oghlu Muhammad,Below: Qurban Primov, Sasha Oqenazashvili; **Standing: company owners**

A recording made at Monarch Record studio in Tbilisi. The inscription in Russian reads *Karabakh Shikastasi, performed by Jabbar Qaryaghdi oghlu*, and in English *Persian song, male performing*

mugham performers have, therefore, had a musical education for 14-15 years.

Although *mugham* does have melodies that were once composed by individuals, *mugham* art is generally anonymous. Performers with a talent for composition create *tasnifs* and *rangs* which are then taken up by other musicians and gradually become "folk music".

Generations of brilliant musicians have created the culture of *mugham* performance. The best known *mugham* singers of the 19th and 20th centuries include Mirza Sattar, Abulhasan Khan Azar Iqbal, Jabbar Qaryaghdi oghlu, Alasgar Abdullayev, Mirtaghi Mirbabayev, Kechachi oghlu Muhammad, Islam Abdullayev, Meshadi Mammad Farzaliyev, Huseynqulu Sarabski, Said Shushinski, Khan Shushinski and Zulfi Adigozalov. The tar players include Mirza Sadiq Asad oghlu, Mirza Faraj Rzayev, Mashadi Jamil Amirov, Shirin Akhundov, Mirza Mansur Mansurov and Qurban Pirimov, whose fame spread beyond Azerbaijan to the rest of the Caucasus, Iran, Turkey and Central Asia.

Azerbaijani musicians began to tour Europe at the beginning of the 20th century. Between 1900 and 1920 several record companies in Europe made and released recordings of Azerbaijani *mughams, tasnifs* and *rangs*. The best known Azerbaijani *mugham* performers today - UNESCO prize-winning singer Alim Qasimov, *tar* players Malik Mansurov and Ramiz Quliyev, *kamancha* players Habil Aliyev, Shafiqa Eyvazova and Elshan Mansurov - perform concerts all over the world and make recordings with major companies.

Mugham gives creative inspiration to Azerbaijani composers, painters, sculptors and poets.

115

55 What art festivals does Azerbaijan have?

International
Baku
JAZZ
Festival
2005

Local art festivals are very popular in Azerbaijan. Music, film and theatre festivals are held every year and attract interest from abroad.

Music and film festivals are the most popular. Azerbaijani cinema is more than 100 years old. A festival held in 1998 to mark its centenary was attended by French cinema stars Regis Varnier and Pierre Richard. The Azerbaijani Cinema Centenary Fund was established as a result. The East-West Film Festival has been held annually since 1999 and maintains close links with other international film festivals and organizations, such as the American Cinema Foundation's Freedom Film Festival. During the festival in 2000 the Azerbaijani president declared 2 August to be Azerbaijan Cinema Day.

The Bul-Bul singing competition has been held regularly since 1997. Vocalists from Russia, Georgia, Ukraine and other CIS countries, Iran, South Korea and the USA compete.

Another music festival is the International Baku Jazz Festival. Jazz came to Baku in the mid-20th century, although saxophone music was banned between 1945 and 1953 (problematic for a thriving jazz scene). In the 1940s, Azerbaijani conductor and bandleader Niyazi formed a 15-strong jazz orchestra in Baku with the composer and pianist Tofiq Quliyev, a popular figure throughout the 1950s and 60s. Despite the saxophone ban, by the 1950s the mesmerizing jazz *mugham* of Vaqif Mustafazada and Rafiq Babayev were in full swing.

The open-air Green Theatre hosted the first jazz festival in Baku in June 1967. The All-Union Jazz Festival Baku 1987 was a great success with all the popular jazz groups of the Soviet Union in attendance. In 2002 the Caspian Jazz & Blues festival was first held in Baku and brought together musicians from America, Europe and Azerbaijan. Since 2005 the festival has been held as the International Baku Jazz Festival.

Theatre festivals include the One-Act Play Festival, the Festival of Experimental Performances and the Him-Jim International Mime Festival. Theatre troupes from the CIS countries take part in this festival.

Vaqif Mustafazada (1940-79)
A well-known Azerbaijani jazz musician and composer, Vaqif Mustafazada skilfully used Azerbaijani music to create a new musical genre, a synthesis of jazz and *mugham*. He was awarded the title Honoured Artist of the Azerbaijani SSR.

Famous jazzman Herbie Hancock performing at the International Baku Jazz Festival in 2006

116

56 What is *meykhana*?

Meykhana is Azerbaijan's own ancient version of rap. *Meykhana* is a Persian word meaning "a place where people get together to drink and talk or recite poems". *Meykhana's* roots in Azerbaijan can be traced back at least a millennium to the Sufi tradition. Today it is widespread on the Absheron Peninsula in particular. *Meykhana* is a form of poetry, recited spontaneously without any preparation or premeditation. At least two people are needed to perform *meykhana*. *Meykhana* is similar to Western rap but traditionally is performed with total spontaneity.

Performers can choose any topic. One performer creates a four or five line stanza and the second performer picks it up without missing a beat. Gifted performers can develop any subject - cars, money, women, work, contemporary events. But more important than the topic itself is the ability to maintain the performance with its rhyme and rhythm. Performances can go on for hours. The language of *meykhana* is the language of the street and Russian words are often mixed in with Azerbaijani.

The ability to recite *meykhana* is often thought of as a gift since it is so difficult to respond spontaneously and sustain the pattern for any length of time.

Meykhana has various forms and structure: a) rhyming *meykhana*; b) *meykhana* with a refrain; c) couplet *meykhana*; d) non-rhyming *meykhana*.

Meykhana has had three distinct periods of development in the 20th century - pre-Soviet (before 1920), Soviet (1920-1991) and post-Soviet (1991 to the present). *Meykhana* developed freely during the first period but was tightly constrained during the second. Today it is free again.

Aliagha Mammadqulu oghlu Isgandarov (Aliagha Vahid) (1895-1965)
A prominent writer of *ghazals* (lyric poems) in contemporary Azerbaijani literature and a famous *meykhana* master, Aliagha Isgandarov was awarded the title Honoured Artist of the Azerbaijani SSR (1943). His satirical poems exposed flaws in society, fanaticism, oppression and injustice. His work continues the traditions of Fizuli and his *ghazals* form an important part of the repertoire of performers. Aliagha Isgandarov also translated *ghazals* by classical poets Nizami, Khagani, Fizuli and Navai.

The quality of *meykhana* used to be much higher. Pre-Soviet *meykhana* was the best, as it had not been separated from its own roots and traditions and performers were incredibly skilled. Today *meykhanas* are typically four or five line stanzas and even one of the lines is likely to be total nonsense.

Few *meykhanas* have actually been recorded, so many have been lost. Verses often survive only in popular memory.

Nowadays there is a tendency towards writing down *meykhana* and performing it from memory. This will probably enrich and sharpen the content and may make *meykhana* more like Western rap - polished critiques on society performed by a skilful individual. Azerbaijan's best known *meykhana* performer was Aliagha Vahid. Aghasalim Childag (1930-2008) and Nizami Ramzi (1947-97) followed in his footsteps. At present Balasadiq Aslanov, Karim, Aghamirza, Mehman Ahmadli, Namiq Mena and Namiq Qarachukhurlu are well known *meykhana* poets.

57 What are Azerbaijan's national dances?

Dance is an important part of Azerbaijan's rich national heritage. Azerbaijani dances are known worldwide and performed in the repertoires of many troupes.

Azerbaijan's well-known dances include *Uzundara, Vaghzali, Tarakema* (Nomadic Herder), *Papaq, Innabi, Jeyrani, Mirzayi, Jutju, Shaki Zorkhanasi, Nakhchivan* and *Gazakh Yallisi*. The *Zorkhana* - a men's dance - symbolizes courage, bravery and youthful enthusiasm. The *Gazakh yallisi* shows unity and togetherness. The dance is performed by a group of people and whoever doesn't dance properly is "fined" by the chieftain who makes him sing a song or dance another dance. *Vaghzali* is played when a bride is seen off from her parental home to the bridegroom's house and her departure is reflected in this dance. *Jangi* (martial music) inspires a sense of unity, friendship and invincibility. *Uzundara* (literally "a long valley") is a long dance, which was traditionally performed when the bride and bridegroom were on the road. The dancer performing the *Banovsha* (Violet) shows how the violet grows from the ground, blooms and fades. *Jeyran bala* is an old and delicate dance. This dance shows the gazelle's gracefulness and elegance. It is performed by men and women. *Mirzayi* is traditionally played at wedding parties and performed by men and women with handkerchiefs in their hands. *Innabi* is the name of a fruit. It is a dance performed by one or two girls who show feminine airs and graces

and coquetry. *Tarakema* is a dance of nomadic people, full of a sense of freedom and expansiveness. The dancers, both men and women, extend their arms and go forward with their heads held high. Other dances include the coquettish *Nazlana-nazlana*, *Nalbekilerle raqs* (a dance with plates) and *Neftchilar sultani* (Sultan of Oilmen).

Azerbaijani dances convey a sense of friendship, invincibility and courage.

58 When did theatre, opera and ballet emerge in Azerbaijan?

Theatre. Azerbaijan leads the Near East in the arts and culture. Performances of national games such as *Qaravelli, Kosa-kosa, Qaragoz* and *Kilimarasi* go back a long way. In medieval times religious theatre *Shabih* emerged in Azerbaijan. Performances of *Shabih* told the tragedy of the family of Imam Huseyn, grandchild of the Prophet Mohammad.

Mirza Fatali Akhundov's drama *Sarguzashti veziri-khani Lankaran (The Adventures of the Vizier of the Lankaran Khan)* was first performed in Azerbaijani in the Baku Society's meeting hall during the Novruz holiday on 22 March 1873. The performance had been organized by Hasan bay Zardabi and Najaf bay Vezirov and laid the foundation of professional theatre in Azerbaijan and the whole Muslim world.

Various groups - the Azerbaijani Artists' Union, Nijat, Hamiyyat, Shafa and the brothers Zulfuqar bay and Uzeyir bay Hajibayov - put on theatre performances in Baku until 1919. The performances were mainly held in the buildings of Taghiyev, Mayilov and Musa Naghiyev.

On 24 October 1919 the Azerbaijani State Theatre was established in Baku. In 1959 the theatre was granted academic status and survives to this day under the name of the National Academic Drama Theatre. This group is also heir to the troupe founded in 1873.

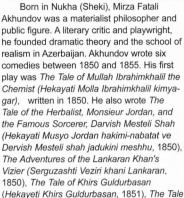

Born in Nukha (Sheki), Mirza Fatali Akhundov was a materialist philosopher and public figure. A literary critic and playwright, he founded dramatic theory and the school of realism in Azerbaijan. Akhundov wrote six comedies between 1850 and 1855. His first play was *The Tale of Mullah Ibrahimkhalil the Chemist (Hekayati Molla Ibrahimkhalil kimya-gar)*, written in 1850. He also wrote *The Tale of the Herbalist, Monsieur Jordan, and the Famous Sorcerer, Darvish Mesteli Shah (Hekayati Musyo Jordan hakimi-nabatat ve Dervish Mesteli shah jadukini meshhu*, 1850), *The Adventures of the Lankaran Khan's Vizier (Serguzashti Veziri khani Lankaran*, 1850), *The Tale of Khirs Guldurbasan (Hekayeti Khirs Guldurbasan*, 1851), *The Tale of the Miser (Serguzashti-Merdi khesis or Haji Qara*, 1852) and *The Tale of the Bribe-taking Advocates (Murafia vekillerinin hekayati*, 1855). Akhundov was also the first to write realist novels in Azerbaijani literature with *Hekayati Yusif shah* or *Aldanmish kavakib (Deceived Star)*. He is known for his *Oriental Poem on the death of Alexander Pushkin* (1837) and *Kemalluddovle mektublari*, a philosophical piece.

In 1857 Mirza Fatali Akhundov devised a new alphabet based on Arabic script. He went to Istanbul in 1867 in the hope of having the project adopted in the Islamic world. He gave the alphabet to the then Turkish prime minister, Fuad Pasha. The project was discussed in the *Cemiyyeti Elmiyyeyi Osmaniyye* (the Ottoman Scientific Society) but failed to be adopted.

Mirza Fatali Akhundov (1812-78)

**Najaf bay Vezirov
(1854-1926)**
One of the first tragedians in Azerbaijani literature, Najaf bay Vezirov staged Akhundov's comedies *Haji Qara* and *The Adventures of the Lankaran Khan's Vizier (Serguzeshti veziri khani Lankaran)* in 1873 in Baku.

The founders of Azerbaijani theatre include Abdurrahim bay Haqverdiyev, Eyneli bay Sultanov, Huseyn Arablinski, Abbasmirza Sharifzada, Aleksandr Tuganov, Sultan Dadashov, Adil Isgandarov, Ismayil Hidayetzada, Zafar Nematov, Mehdi Mammadov and Tofiq Kazimov. Some of the best known actors were Mirzagha Aliyev, Jahangir Zeynalov, Marziya Davudova, Fatma Qadirli, Hokuma Qurbanova, Rza Afqanli, Aghadadash Qurbanov, Ismayil Osmanli, Nasiba Zeynalova, Huseynqulu Sarabski, Haqiqat Rzayeva, Shovkat Mammadova and Bul-Bul.

Azerbaijan now has 27 state theatres, which perform plays, opera, musical comedies, puppet shows and mime, two municipal and four private theatres. The Azerbaijani State Cultural and Art University teaches different theatre skills. Baku also has the Russian Drama Theatre Company, which performs in Russian, and the Young Spectators' and Musical Comedy theatres. The National Academic Drama Theatre's repertoire today includes *Oedipus* by Sophocles, *King Lear* and *Hamlet* by Shakespeare, the *Socrates' Commemoration Night* by Chingiz Aytmatov, *Aydin* by Jafar Jabbarli, *Farhad and Shirin* by Samad Vurgun and *The Prince and His Daughter* by Ilyas Afandiyev.

Azerbaijani playwrights Najaf bay Vezirov, Abdurrahim bay Haqverdiyev, Jalil Mammadquluzada, Huseyn Javid, Sabit Rahman, Anvar Mammadkhanli and Ilyas Afandiyev have all followed in the wake of M.F. Akhundov.

Opera in Azerbaijan is basically a 20th century phenomenon which has incorporated elements of Azerbaijani traditional music. The first opera performances in Baku were staged at the old Taghiyev Theatre.

The Azerbaijan State Theatre of Opera and Ballet was built in 1910. The building was designed in the Renaissance style. Today it is one of the most beautiful and majestic symbols of cultural life in Azerbaijan.

**Nasiba Zeynalova
(1916-2004)**
A popular Azerbaijani theatre and film actress, Nasiba Zeynalova began her career in 1937 and worked in the Shikhali Qurbanov Azerbaijani State Musical Comedy Theatre for many years. Her father, Jahangir Zeynalov (1865-1918), was a professional actor.

**Rashid Behbudov
(1915-89)**
A famous Azerbaijani singer and actor, Rashid Behbudov performed both opera and popular music and created many roles on stage and in film. He sang in various languages - Azerbaijani, Russian, Persian, Turkish, Hindi, Urdu and others - and gave concerts in many countries. He was awarded the honours People's Artist of the USSR, Hero of Socialist Labour and Knight of the Order of Lenin. Rashid Behbudov received the Stalin Prize for his performance of the role of Asgar in the musical comedy *Arshin Mal Alan*. He founded and led the Azerbaijani State Song Theatre in 1966, which is now named after him.

**Uzeyir Hajibayov
(1885 - 1948)**

An outstanding Azerbaijani composer, public figure and teacher, Hajibayov wrote the first Azerbaijani operas, including six *mugham* operas. He wrote *Leyli and Majnun* in 1908 and the best of his operas, *Koroghlu* in 1937. Hajibayov also wrote musical comedies, cantatas, compositions for chorus and chamber, instrumental compositions, romances and songs.

Uzeyir Hajibayov was involved in setting up the Music Conservatory, the Academy of Sciences, the Folk Instruments Ensemble and many other fundamental institutions that provide a formal music infrastructure in Azerbaijan. He wrote down the basic principles of Azerbaijani modal music, *mugham*, in his book *The Principles of Azerbaijani Folk Music* (1945).

Uzeyir Hajibayov received the highest artistic awards. He was the first Azerbaijani musician to be honoured with the title People's Artist of the USSR.

Bul-Bul (1897-1961)

Bul-Bul, whose name means *nightingale*, achieved fame as a tenor, teacher and founder of the professional singing school in Azerbaijan. He was honoured with the title People's Artist of the USSR and won a USSR State Prize. Bul-Bul synthesized the best traditions of Azerbaijani and European songs, creating a new vocal school in Azerbaijan which influenced cultural life across the Middle East. Bul-Bul sang the lead roles in most Azerbaijani operas.

Niyazi (1912 - 84)

The first Azerbaijani conductor to gain international recognition, Niyazi founded the school of professional conducting in Azerbaijan. He was honoured with the title People's Artist of the USSR and won an Azerbaijan State Prize and Nehru International Prize. As a composer, Niyazi wrote the opera *Khosrov and Shirin* (1940) and the ballet *Chitra* (1971), as well as other works of symphonic and chamber music.

**Fikrat Amirov
(1922 - 84)**

A prominent composer, Fikrat Amirov wrote numerous compositions, including the opera *Sevil*, the ballets *1001 Nights* and *Nizami*, and symphonic mughams. He also wrote music for stage and film, chamber compositions, romances and songs. Fikrat Amirov was awarded the title People's Artist of the USSR and won an Azerbaijan State Prize.

The development of national opera is inextricably linked with the founder of Azerbaijani professional music, the famous composer Uzeyir Hajibayov. Azerbaijan prides itself on having created the first opera in the Middle East - *Leyli and Majnun* (1908). Uzeyir Hajibayov wrote the opera on the basis of Fizuli's poem. Hajibayov went on to write several operas and musical comedies, including, in 1913, *Arshin Mal Alan (The Cloth Peddler)* which was successfully performed in many countries and made into a film more than once.

Inspired by Hajibayov, composers Zulfuqar Hajibayov, Muslim Magomayev, Niyazi, Qara Qarayev, Fikrat Amirov, Shafiqa Akhundova, Vasif Adigozalov, Suleyman Alasgarov and others wrote operas and musical comedies.

Many opera singers have displayed their talent on the stage of the Opera and Ballet Theatre, including Bul-Bul, Shovkat Mammadova, Huseinqulu Sarabski, Sona Hajiyeva, Haqiqat Rzayeva, Rashid Behbudov, Muslim Magomayev, Lutfiyar Imanov and the sisters Fidan and Khuraman Qasimova.

The conductors to have wielded the baton include Niyazi, Ashraf Hasanov, Afrasiyab Badalbayli, Rauf Abdullayev and Yalchin Adigozalov.

***The Maiden Tower* ballet by Afrasiyab Badalbayli**

**Muslim Magomayev
(1885 - 1937)**
A contemporary of
Uzeyir Hajibayov,
Muslim Magomayev
was heavily involved in
documenting Azerbaijani
folksongs throughout
the countryside. He is
best remembered for his
outstanding operas
Shah Ismayil (1919) and
Nargiz (1935).

**Qamar Almaszada
(1915-2006)**
Well-known as a bal-
lerina, teacher and bal-
let master, Qamar
Almaszada was the first
ballet dancer in the
Near East. She was
honoured with the title
People's Artist of the
USSR and won an
Azerbaijan State Prize.

**Qara Qarayev
(1918 - 82)**
A well-known compos-
er and teacher, Qara
Qarayev wrote two bal-
lets, three symphonies, a
violin concerto, sym-
phonic poems, numerous
chamber and vocal com-
positions and music for
stage and screen. He
was awarded the title
People's Artist of the
USSR and won an
Azerbaijan State Prize.

The Qasimova sisters - Fidan and
Khuraman - are both brilliant opera
sopranos, a rare combination

Culture & Arts

Ballet. The first Azerbaijani ballet is *The Maiden Tower*, staged by composer Afrasiyab
Badalbayli (1907-76) in 1940, based on motifs in the eponymous poem by playwright Jafar Jabbarli.
The ballet was composed on the basis of national dance music, *mugham* and classical ballet.
Azerbaijani ballet began to develop from this time onwards. The ballet *Gulshan* by Soltan
Hajibayov was performed in 1950. Qara Qarayev's *Seven Beauties* (1952) and *Along the Thundering
Ways* (1958), Fikrat Amirov's *Nizami* (1947) and *1001 Nights* (1979), Niyazi's *Chitra* (1971),
Arif Melikov's *Legend of Love* (1961) and Faraj Qarayev's *Shadows of Gobustan* (1969)
have made Azerbaijani ballet music famous all over the world.

The great dancers to have performed at the Opera and Ballet Theatre include Qamar
Almaszada, Leyla Vakilova, Alasgar Abdullayev, Rafiqa Akhundova, Maqsud
Mammadov, Vladimir Pletnev, Chimnaz Babayeva, Medina Aliyeva, Tatyana Sukhorukova
and Zaur Fetullayev.

1001 Nights Ballet by Fikrat Amirov

122

The Amazing History of the Construction of the State Opera and Ballet Theatre of Azerbaijan

In 1910, famous Bolshoy Theatre soprano Antonina Nezhdanova visited Baku and performed at various clubs and venues. The local audience were fascinated by her glamour and incomparable voice. One of the older Mailov brothers, who were millionaires, fell head over heels in love with the singer and showered her with gold and other jewellery. Nezhdanova spent a month in Baku, giving concerts in the Exchange Office, the Winter Club and in the wooden hall that housed the circus. When the tour was over, a ceremonial ball was organized at the casino to mark Nezhdanova's departure. During the supper the singer was asked: "When will you give us the pleasure of seeing you in Baku again?" She shrugged her shoulders and replied: "Most probably never. I am not accustomed to performing at the casino or the circus. I'm just surprised that your beautiful, wealthy city, which has such generous and chivalrous gentlemen, should have no opera theatre where singers can demonstrate their skill." Mailov asked: "Khanum, where are you going now?" The singer replied that she had to tour Japan and in a year would return to Russia. Mailov said: "Come back to our city in a year's time. We will have built a building worthy of your skill and you will inaugurate it." It was all agreed. Mailov discussed the project with the architect Bayev and asked him to erect a building similar to the Tbilisi Opera Theatre, but much more beautiful and impressive.

Oil baron Haji Zeynalabdin Taghiyev heard the story. When Mailov told him that Bayev was planning to build the theatre within a year, Taghiyev said: "I cannot imagine how

The Azerbaijan Akhundov State Academic Opera and Ballet Theatre, known also as the Mailov Brothers' Theatre, Baku

it is possible to construct such a building in a year. I was a mason and contractor and have built not a few buildings. I can say I have a great deal of experience in this sphere. And I'm sure that it is almost impossible." Mailov smiled in response and said: "Haji, let's have a bet. If the building is not ready within a year, I will stop construction and offer the Opera building to you as a gift. But if I manage to get the theatre built on time, you will reimburse me for the expenses. And the building will belong to me." Taghiyev agreed.

The theatre was built in the classical style, with foyers, an auditorium and stage. The Mailov Theatre takes a special place in the history of theatre construction during the pre-revolutionary period as it was built at record speed, all the more remarkable considering that building technology was not very advanced. The rapid pace of construction was kept up from beginning to end. The 1,800-seat theatre was completed in less than 10 months. Throughout the construction period (from 29 April 1910 to 27 February 1911) the builders worked in three shifts with 200 workers on every shift and the building site was floodlit. With careful organization Bayev was able to complete his building in a short time. On 18 February 1911 Baku mayor Peter Martunov and engineer E. Ribchinskiy examined the newly built theatre and confirmed its safety.

On 28 February 1911 the Baku Opera and Ballet Theatre was opened. Mailov notified Nezhdanova of the ceremony by telegram and she came to Baku to participate in the celebration. On the opening day the opera *Boris Godunov* was performed with Moszhukhin in the title role. The opening of the theatre was a major event for Baku.

In October 1916 Baku had its first permanent drama group, when Pavel Amirago's opera troupe took up residence at the Opera Theatre. Until then all the performances in Baku had been by touring groups.

On 17 May 1920 the first decree was issued nationalizing theatres, cinemas and museums. On 1 June 1920 all the theatres in Baku passed into government ownership and the Opera Theatre became known as the Azerbaijani State Opera and Ballet Theatre under a special resolution.

In 1925 the Azerbaijani Opera Troupe separated from the Drama Troupe and united with the Russian Opera Troupe. In 1927 the theatre was named after writer Mirza Fatali Akhundov and in 1959 it was granted the status of an academic theatre.

Restoration work in 1987 gave the theatre its modern-day appearance.

59 When did cinema emerge in Azerbaijan?

In late 1897, just two years after the Lumiere brothers showed the first motion pictures, one of their patented cinematographs (film camera and projector) was brought to Azerbaijan. On 8 January 1898 the first film was shown in Baku. On 31 March the Baku Scientific Photographic Circle organized a public stroll for charity in the Mikhaylov Garden (now named the Vahid Garden) and

had it filmed. This chronicle and sequences such as *Arrival of a Train at the Railway Station, Departure of a Steamboat* and *Market Street at Dawn* were shown on 21 June. On 2 August a second programme of films was shown, which included *The Ceremony of Departure of the Amir of Bukhara in the Velikiy Knyaz Aleksey Steamboat and The Ruler of the Caucasus.* These sequences and some more films such as *Oil Gusher in Bibiheybat* and *Oil Gusher in Balakhani* were made by Aleksander Mikhailovich Mishon, a film maker and photographer who lived in Baku for 25 years. The *Oil Gusher* films were successfully shown at the world cinema show in Paris in 1900. In 2001 at the initiative of the Azerbaijani Cinema Foundation the films were brought to Azerbaijan from Paris and are now kept in the cinema archives. Following the discovery of these films, Azerbaijan's then president, Heydar Aliyev, issued a decree on 18 December 2000 declaring 2 August National Cinema Day in Azerbaijan.

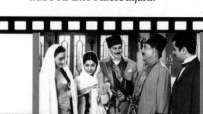

Belgian entrepreneurs the Pirone brothers established a stock company, Filma, in Baku in 1915. Supported by local entrepreneurs, Filma made several films in 1915-16 including *In the Country of Oil and Billions,* based on a novel by Ibrahimbay Musabayov, and Uzeyir Hajibayov's love story *Arshin Mal Alan.* The films made their name both in Azerbaijan and abroad.

A new stage in the history of Azerbaijani cinema began after occupation by the Soviets in 1920. On 28 April 1923 the first state cinema workshop was opened in Baku on the basis of the Cinema and Photo Office. Films made between 1920 and 1930 covered the events of the day such as women's emancipation and the changes in the country, including *Bismillah, Haji Qara, A Game of Love, Latif, Ismat* and *Peasants.* The first cartoon film, *The Fate of Abbas,* was made at this time, as was the first film with a soundtrack, *On the Shore of the Blue Sea.* In 1937 the film *Chapayev* was dubbed into Azerbaijani.

Abbas Mirza Sharifzada (1893-1938)
Azerbaijan's first cinema producer

Samad Mardanov (1909-39)
Azerbaijan's first professionally educated cinema producer

Huseyn Seyidzada (1910-79)
A well-known Azerbaijani producer

The decade 1940 to 1950 saw further development in Azerbaijani cinema. A group of young cinema graduates from the All-Union Cinema Institute in Moscow returned to work in Azerbaijan. They included also Qamar Salamzada (1908-97) - the first woman film-maker in the Near East. The films of this period are *Sabuhi, Arshin Mal Alan, Mashadi Ibad, Bakhtiyar* and *His Big Soul*. In 1946 a group of actors in *Arshin Mal Alan* were awarded USSR Supreme State awards.

Innovations in style and content were made in the 1960s. Feature films were made for the wide screen including *Telephone Girl, Our Teacher Jebish, In a Southern City, Investigation, The Choppy Kur, Stars Don't Go Out, I would Like Seven Sons* and *Dada Qorqud*.

The economic changes of the late 1980s brought problems for Azerbaijani cinema, but a few films were made by state order or with sponsorship: *Nizami, Uzeyir Hajibayov: the Chords of a Long Life, Another Life, Night without Shore, Yaramaz (Good-for-Nothing), The Day of Murder, Tehmine* and *Scream*.

Rustam Ibrahimbeyov (1939)
A well-known Azerbaijan author, producer and script-writer. In 1997 he won an Oscar for his script for *Burnt by the Sun*, the first Oscar in Azerbaijani cinema history. He is a member of the film academies of Europe and America.

Some of the most important films of the independence years are *White Horseman, Sari Gelin (Blonde Bride), The Frenchman, The Other Time* and *Bat*.

Some of the best known directors and producers in Azerbaijani cinema are Rza Tehmasib (1894-1980), Agharza Quliyev (1898-1976), Jafar Jabbarli (1899-1934), Mikayil Mikayilov (1903-86), Hasan Seyidbeyli (1910-76), Tofig Taghizada (1919-98), Ajdar Ibrahimov (1919-93), Latif Safarov (1920-63), Rasim Ojaqov (1933-2006), Eldar Quliyev (1941) and Oqtay Mirqasimov (1943). Over the years a talented body of screen actors has emerged. They include: Agahuseyn Javadov (1894-1981), Alasgar Alakbarov (1910-63), Adil Isgandarov (1910-78), Mammadrza Sheikhzamanov (1915-84), Hasan Mammadov (1938-2003), Hasan Turabov (1938-2003), Seyavush Aslan (1935), Mukhtar Maniyev (1935), Haji Ismayilov (1941), Aliabbas Qadirov (1946-2006) and Arif Quliyev (1950).

Vaqif Mustafayev (1953)
A well-known Azerbaijan producer and script-writer who has received both local and international prizes. He is a member of the European Cinema and Television Academy.

Rasim Balayev (1948)
A well-known Azerbaijani film actor

Azerbaijani film-makers M. Dadashov, H. Seyidbeyli, R. Ibrahimov, V. Mustafayev, R. Ojaqov, A. Salayev and Y. Rzayev have received international awards. Playwright Rustam Ibrahimbayov won an Oscar for his screenplay for *Burnt by the Sun* while Vaqif Mustafayev was elected a member of the European Cinema and Television Academy for his work *Good-for-Nothing*.

The first issue of *Akinchi*   *Ziya*   *Fiyuzat*   *Azerbaijan*

60 When was the first newspaper published in Azerbaijan?

A national press emerged in the mid-19th century and proved an important feature in Azerbaijan's public life.

The publication of *Tbilisi Akhbari (Tbilisi News)* in 1832 and the *Trans-Caucasus News* supplement in Azerbaijani to *Zakavkazskiy Vestnik* in 1845 were the first steps towards the formation of the national press. They were official newsletters but not real newspapers.

The first national newspaper in Azerbaijan was *Akinchi (Ploughman)* which first appeared on 22 June 1875. The naturalist Hasan bay Zardabi, one of the founders of the national enlightenment movement (1842-1907), was publisher, editor and proof-reader of *Akinchi*. Mirza Fatali Akhundov, S.A. Shirvani, N. Vezirov, Asgar Gorani and others promoted the ideals of enlightenment and democracy in the newspaper, thereby influencing the formation of public, political and artistic views in society.

Akinchi was published fortnightly from 1875 to 1877 in Baku, with 56 issues appearing during this period. The newspaper, a tribune for democratic ideas, published material about the development of science, enlightenment, culture, realism in literature and art as well as the need for a new style of education. The newspaper's greatest achievements were its closeness to the language of the people, simplicity and fluency. *Akinchi* promoted science and culture and was the first to fight for the emancipation and education of women. It sharply criticized superstitions and backwardness and published scientific material on agriculture and natural sciences. It was distributed in Georgia, Dagestan, Uzbekistan and other countries. Censorship, police pressure, disturbances in Dagestan and the outbreak of the Turkish-Russian war resulted in the closure of *Akinchi*. The tsarist government thought it dangerous for editor Hasan bay Zardabi even to live in Baku.

The date 22 July, the day of *Akinchi*'s first publication, is marked every year as National Press Day in Azerbaijan.

Hasan bay Zardabi
(1842-1907)

A well-known Azerbaijani publisher and naturalist and one of the founders of professional theatre, Hasan bay Zardabi began publishing the newspaper *Akinchi* on 22 June 1875. Hasan bay Zardabi was compiler, editor and proof-reader of *Akinchi*. He worked with other newspapers in tsarist Russia and edited the newspaper *Kaspi* for some time. Hasan bay Zardabi also played a key role in the establishment of the first charitable organization. He opened a school for girls and began education in Azerbaijani. He was known as the Teacher and Moral Father of Trans-Caucasian Muslims.

**Jeyhun Hajibayli
(1891-1962)**

An outstanding Azerbaijani public figure, journalist and translator, Jeyhun Hajibayli graduated from the University of St Petersburg and the Sorbonne. His articles appeared in many European publications, including *La Revue du monde musulman* and *Le Figaro*, as well local newspapers, *Kaspi, Progress, Irshad, Taraggi* and St Petersburg paper *Ruskaya molva*. In 1917 he was editor of *Ittihad* newspaper and the *Newsletter of the Muslim National Committee*. Jeyhun bay used the pen-names *Daghistanli, Jeyhun Daghistanli* and *Azeri*. In 1920 he emigrated to France and took an active part in the founding of *Qafqaz* magazine in Paris and *Azerbaijan* magazine in Munich and Paris. His writing on Azerbaijani press history, Karabakh dialect and folklore was well-known. He was a brilliant linguist and knew Arabic, Persian, ancient Turkish, German and French.

**Ahmad bay Aghayev
(1869-1939)**

A prominent Azerbaijani journalist, scientist and writer, Ahmad bay Aghayev graduated from the Sorbonne in Paris. He was well-known in Europe as an Islamic scholar and his articles were published in the Parisian *Nouvelle Revue* in the 1890s. He was the editor of Azerbaijani newspapers *Kaspi, Hayat, Irshad* and *Taraggi*. He founded the *Turk Yurdu* magazine, *Akhin* newspaper in Turkey and the Anadolu News Agency on the order of Ataturk. He was the editor of Turkish newspapers *Hakimiyyeti-milliye, Cumhuriyyet* and *Millet*. Ahmad bay Aghaoghlu was a member of the Azerbaijani and Turkish parliaments, a professor at Istanbul and Ankara universities and led Turkey's policy to promote the press. He was fluent in Arabic, Persian, Russian, Greek, English, German and French.

The traditions of *Akinchi* were continued by *Ziyayi Qafqaziye, Keshkul, Sharqi Rus, Dabistam, Heyat, Fiyuzat, Kaspi* and *Azerbaijan*. They all reached the standards of the international press.

In 1988-91 the first independent media appeared after 70 years of Soviet rule. Censorship was officially cancelled in August 1998, boosting the country's independent media. Nowadays there are some 650 media organs in Azerbaijan - newspapers, magazines, information agencies, TV and radio companies.

The media are free in Azerbaijan and regulated under the law on the mass media. Anyone can found a print publication without official permission but the founders must apply to the Ministry of Justice for official registration. The ministry is obliged to respond within seven days. The media may be financed from any source. The media publish both in Azerbaijani and other languages.

61 Why is *Molla Nasreddin* magazine so popular in Azerbaijan?

Azerbaijanis say *"The pen is mightier than the sword"* to convey the importance of the written word. It is an apt description for Molla Nasraddin, an eight-page weekly magazine that was one of the most influential publications in the history of Azerbaijan. It had a profound effect on intellectual life and activism in the early 20th century. Even today its impact is still felt in the region, especially in the Caucasus, Turkey and Iran.

The journal takes its name, *Molla Nasraddin*, from a wise man of folklore who is believed to have been a real person. Jokes and satirical stories about the mullah have been widespread in the region since the 13th century.

Molla Nasraddin managed to stay in print for 25 years (1906-31) throughout the turbulence following the revolution of 1905 and then the First World War, the Russian Bolshevik Revolution of 1917, the establishment of the Azerbaijani Democratic Republic in 1918-1920 and the Soviet takeover of Azerbaijan.

The editor of *Molla Nasraddin*, Jalil Mammmadquluzada, and his staff of cartoonists, writers and poets did battle with every major social and political issue of their time. The magazine played on certain themes over and over.

Molla Nasraddin was the first Azerbaijani satirical magazine. It was first published on 7 April 1906 and brought a new style, content, language and way of thinking to Azerbaijani society. It was ironical and satirical and laughed at reality. The journal's writers, Sabir, M.S. Ordubadi, A. Nazmi, M.N. Zeynalov and A. Haqverdiyev published their articles under pen-names. The magazine primarily fought against fanaticism and backwardness. *Molla Nasraddin* was the first magazine to print pictures, mainly because of the illiteracy of society. Between 1906 and 1918 *Molla Nasraddin* was published in Tbilisi, in 1921 in Tabriz and in 1921-31 in Baku.

The magazine especially attacked the backwardness of that time and the snobbery and egotism of "the so-called intelligentsia" who were so involved in Russian language and culture that they considered it shameful to speak Turkic.

Jalil Mammadguluzada (Mirza Jalil) (1866-1932)

Mirza Jalil deeply influenced society and literature in Azerbaijan. His literary work affected not only Azerbaijan, but also the life of the people of the Near and Middle East. Mirza Jalil founded satirical journalism in the Near East with his *Molla Nasraddin* journal, which was first published on 7 April 1906. The democratic and liberal ideas he promoted created a good image for the journal in the community and international arena. *Molla Nasraddin* had a wide range of readers in Russia, Iran, Egypt, India and Turkey.

Jalil Mammadquluzada played an exceptional role in promoting Azerbaijani realism by creating many works in various genres (plays, novels, poems, essays, literary criticism and memoirs) in his 40 years of writing. His stories such as *The Post Box* and *Freedom in Iran* and a comedy called *The Dead* are masterpieces of realism. His other work includes *My Mother's Book, The Meeting of Mad Men* and *The Stories of the Village of Danabash*.

Azim Azimzada (1880-1943)

A well-known caricaturist, Azim Azimzada founded critical realism, realist painting and caricature in Azerbaijan. Although not a professionally educated artist, Azimzada made his name with his work for the *Molla Nasraddin* journal. His cartoons and sharply critical pictures have become national classics.

Molla Nasraddin observed that the main reason why people were so ignorant and naive was that they did not read and study, as they considered it a waste of time. The magazine also severely criticized parents who prevented their children, especially girls, from attending school. *"Why should a girl attend school?"* Molla asks. *"The only thing a girl should learn is how to cook and how to put her mother-in-law and father-in-law in their places when necessary."* Education at *madrasas* (religious schools) was strongly criticized, as children had to learn phrases by heart in the Arabic language, without having a clue as to their meaning.

The rights of women were among the editorial staff's greatest concerns. They constantly wrote about the conditions that kept women ignorant, especially since women took on the main care and nurture of children. Rarely did women get the chance to go out and be exposed to new ideas. Most were illiterate; few had opportunities to receive formal education. They lived in a dark world, shrouded from head to toe in black chadors. While men were involved in gambling and love affairs with attractive, Western-dressed Russian women, Azerbaijani wives stayed at home, slaving at housework and caring for the children. Finally *Molla Nasraddin* inspired the establishment of other satirical journals in the Near and Middle East, in Iran, Turkey and Turkmenistan.

62 What is Azerbaijani architecture like?

**Ajami Nakhchivani
(12th century)**

He is the best known medieval architect in Azerbaijan and a founder of the Nakhchivan architectural school. Ajami Nakhchivani signed himself Abubakr oghlu Ajami or a Nakhchivan architect in inscriptions on his buildings and had the nickname Sheikh ul-Muhendisin, architect-in-chief. His first work, built in Nakhchivan, is the harmonious tomb of Yusif ibn Kuseir (1162). He also built the tomb of Momunekhatun (1186), the double-domed Bashtagh (1187) which partly survives, the Juma Mosque and Dar-ul-mulk Palace. His work had a great influence on architecture in the Near East.

The earliest surviving examples of architecture in Azerbaijan date back to the Neolithic and Bronze Ages. They can be found in Nakhchivan, Khojali, Gadabay, Tovuz and Dashkasan. Fortifications, castles, shrines and fire temples were built in the ancient Azerbaijani states of Midiya and Manna.

Urban construction developed during the Caucasian Albanian period (4th century BC-7th century AD). Fortress walls and earthenware water-pipes in the town of Gabala, the defensive system or "long walls" of Damirgapi (Derbent), Chiraqqala Castle (6th century), the Round Church in the village of Lakit (5th-6th centuries), the basilica in the village of Gum (approximately 6th century AD) and the temple complexes in Mingachevir (7th century) all show that urban

The Khan's Palace, Sheki, 1762

construction was well advanced. When Christianity was prevalent in the 6th and 7th centuries in Caucasian Albania, round and basilica-style temples and fortifications were built. After Azerbaijan became part of the Arab Caliphate, religious buildings became widespread. Both pre-Islamic and Islamic buildings from the Albanian period in Azerbaijan played an important role in architectural development.

Ancient buildings can be seen in the villages of Pashan and Mukhakh in Zagatala District (4th and 5th centuries). Govurqala castle survives in the village of Boyuk Galdak in Sheki District (6th century). Boyuk Amirli in Gabala District has Albanian monuments from the 4th to 8th centuries. A medieval Albanian church can be seen in the town of Oghuz and a first century Albanian church in the village of Garakand in Khojavand District, Mountainous Karabakh. Albanian

Yusif ibn Kuseir's tomb, Nakhchivan, 1162

From left to right: Ismailliya Palace, the adminstrative office National Academy of Sciences, Baku, 1908-13; Heydar Aliyev Park, Baku. In the background is the Heydar Aliyev Palace, 1972; Architectural detail, Baku; Government House, Baku, 1951

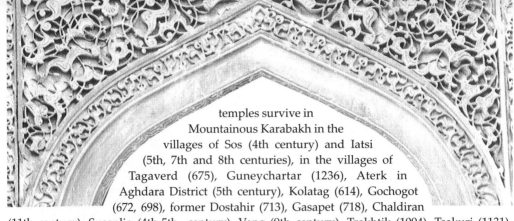

temples survive in
Mountainous Karabakh in the
villages of Sos (4th century) and Iatsi
(5th, 7th and 8th centuries), in the villages of
Tagaverd (675), Guneychartar (1236), Aterk in
Aghdara District (5th century), Kolatag (614), Gochogot
(672, 698), former Dostahir (713), Gasapet (718), Chaldiran
(11th century), Susanlig (4th-5th century), Vang (9th century), Trakhtik (1094), Tsakuri (1131),
Mammadadzor (1147) and Tug (1197). Albanian churches are also preserved in the villages of
Shushikand (905), Chanagchi (1065 and 1100), Khachmaz (1100), Khantsk (1122) and Khndzristan
(1202) in Asgaran District.

During the rule of the Arab Caliphate, Barda became the architectural centre of Azerbaijan. The
best examples of medieval architecture in Baku are Siniqqala minaret (1078), the Maiden Tower
(12th century), the Shirvanshahs' Bayil Castle (built in the 13th century and now under water just
outside Baku port) and the Shirvanshahs' Palace (15th century). The Khan's Palace in Sheki (18th
century) and the Palace of Panah Khan Javanshir in Shusha (18th century) are fine examples of later
architecture. The Blue Mosque in Tabriz (1465) and the Sheikh Safiyaddin complex in Ardabil
(16th-17th centuries) are fine pieces of architecture in Iranian Azerbaijan.

Azerbaijani architects and *naqqashlar* or painters also worked in other countries in the 15th-16th
centuries. Azerbaijani architects left their "signatures" on architectural monuments in Bursa, Cairo,

Baku Mayor's Office, 1900-04

132

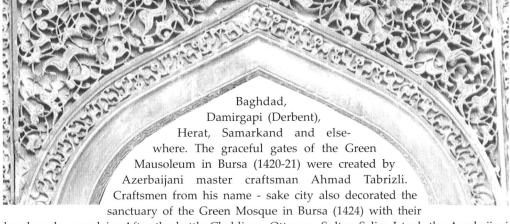

Baghdad,
Damirgapi (Derbent),
Herat, Samarkand and else-
where. The graceful gates of the Green
Mausoleum in Bursa (1420-21) were created by
Azerbaijani master craftsman Ahmad Tabrizli.
Craftsmen from his name - sake city also decorated the
sanctuary of the Green Mosque in Bursa (1424) with their
hand-made porcelain. After the battle Chaldiran, Ottoman Sultan Selim I took the Azerbaijani
architect Ali Tabrizli (who was also known as Ali the Prisoner and Adjam Ali) back to Istanbul
where he built the general arch of the Topkapi Palace and the Sultan Selim Mosque (1522). Mirek
Mirze Qiyas, a 16th-century Azerbaijani architect, lived for a time in the palace of Humayun, the
shah of the Great Moghuls in Delhi, and built his tomb.

In the 19th century towns expanded in Azerbaijan following the principles of Russian town-
planning. Azerbaijan's architecture developed in two main directions - it followed local traditions,
which could often be seen in house-building, and European architectural traditions. Local architects and popular craftsmen created their own houses using traditional architectural forms.
Graduates of the European schools of architecture (St Petersburg Civil Engineering Institute and
the Tsar's Academy of Arts) also contributed to the construction of housing in Baku. At the end of
the 19th and early 20th centuries buildings of architectural interest were erected in Baku,
Shamakhi, Ordubad and Lankaran: the Rustam Mustafayev State Art Museum, the Academy of
Sciences' Muhammad Fizuli Manuscript Institute, Baku City Hall, the Opera and Ballet Theatre
and Saadat Palace and the building housing the Institute of Scientific Research and
Ophthalmology.

Nizami Literature Museum, Baku, 1915

Ziver bay Ahmadbayov (1873-1925)

The first professionally educated Azerbaijani architect

Modern architecture mainly encompasses classical national and European styles. Examples are the building of the Cabinet of Ministers, the small city complex of the National Academy of Sciences, the Akhundov National Library, the new building of the President's Palace, Government House, the Absheron Hotel, the tomb of Nizami Ganjavi in Ganja, Molla Panah Vaqif's tomb in Shusha, Huseyn Javid's tomb in Nakhchivan, the Heydar Aliyev Palace in Baku, the Chemists' Palace in Sumqayit, the Azerbaijani State Philharmonic building, the reconstructed Shikhali Qurbanov State Musical Comedy Theatre and the buildings of the National Olympic Committee of Azerbaijan, the National Bank and Heydar Aliyev Foundation.

The traditions of fine architecture were continued by Kerbalayi Safikhan Qarabaghi (1788-1910), Qasim bay Hajibababayov (1811-74), Sadikh Dadashov (1906-46) Shafiqa Zeynalova (1922-79), Enver Qasimzada (1912-69), Alasgar Huseynov (1928-76), Hasan Majidov (1914-78), Talat Khanlarov (1928-2003), Nazim Hajibayov (1928), Rasim Aliyev (1937) and Hajimurad Shugayev (1940).

Mikayil Huseynov (1905-92)

One of the founders of modern Azerbaijani architecture, Mikayil Huseynov created his first theoretical works together with academic Sadiq Dadashov (1905-46), a well-known Azerbaijani architect and scientist. He was the author of up to 200 projects in Azerbaijan and abroad, including houses, public buildings and monuments.

Q&A

Culture & Arts

From left to right: SOCAR Building (1891-96) with the Heydar Aliyev Foundation (2004) on the right, Baku; Puppet Theatre, Baku, 1912; Church of the Saviour - German church in Baku,1897; Hajinski building, Baku, 1912; National Academic Drama Theatre (1961), in the front the Fizuly statue, Baku

Azerbaijani State Philharmonic Hall
The Azerbaijani State Philharmonia, now named after Azerbaijani composer Muslim Magomayev, was built in 1912 in the Renaissance style and took its inspiration from the Casino buildings in Monte Carlo. The building is unique as the stage is not opposite the entrance. The Azerbaijani State Philharmonic Hall has two international-standard concert halls seating 515. The winter hall is built in an oval shape. It is crowned with a cupola and has two towers on either side. The building was refurbished in 2003

Architectural ornamentation, Baku

63 Who are Azerbaijan's best known artists?

Sultan Muhammad (1470-1555)

A famous miniaturist and founder of the Tabriz miniature school in the 16th century, Sultan Muhammad headed the workshop at Shah Ismayil's Palace in Tabriz. He illustrated the work of some Azerbaijani poets and painted miniature scenes of life, portraits and carpet designs. His work is kept at the Saltykov-Shchedrin Library in St Petersburg and in museums in Istanbul, London, Paris, Washington and Krakow.

The Ascension of the Prophet by Sultan Muhammad, 1563

Painting developed as an independent art form in Azerbaijan in the early Middle Ages. Artists of the Tabriz miniature school laid the foundation of medieval painting in Azerbaijan in the early 13th and 14th centuries. Tabriz was a major arts centre of the Near and Middle East. German Orientalist F. Schultz described the Tabriz miniature school as the *Mutter Schule* or mother school, because it played a big part in the development of art in neighbouring Near Eastern countries. To date, the oldest samples of miniature art are *Verqa and Gulsha* from the 13th century, which can be seen in the Topkapi Palace museum in Istanbul, *Menafi al-heyvan* by Ibn Betutushi from 1297-98 which is in the Morgan Library in New York, and *Jami et-tevarikh* from 1306 which is in Edinburgh University library in Scotland.

Refugees by Bahruz Kangarli, 1918

Spring Melody by Sattar Bahlulzada, 1972

Bahruz Kangarli (1892-1922)
The founder of realism in Azerbaijani art, Bahruz Kangarli painted both realist portraits and landscapes. He was Azerbaijan's first professional artist. His work is characterized by simplicity, realism, artistic and aesthetic values and harmony. He also worked on theatre sets and costumes.

Classical Azerbaijani art flourished in the 13th and 14th centuries and reached its peak in the 16th century. Valuable works of art were created by Mir Said Ali, Aghamirek Isfahani, Farrukh bay, Mir Zeynalabdin Tabrizi and Sadiqi bay Avshar, successors to Sultan Muhammad, founder of the Tabriz miniature school. The most famous pieces of this period are the miniatures of *Khosrov and Shirin* (1405-1410, Freer Gallery in Washington) and *Khamsa* (1481, Topkapi Museum in Istanbul), the manuscripts of *Khamsa* by Muzaffar Ali, miniatures painted by Farrukh bay for *Khamsa* by Amir Khosrov Dehlevi, miniatures by Sadiqi bay Avshar entitled *Garshasp Fights Monsters, Portrait of the Amir, Portrait of Teymur Khan Turkman* and *Dervish Sitting under a Tree*. All these works of art are both complete and original. Kamaladdin Behzad is another well-known artist of the period.

In the late 16th and early 17th centuries traditional Near Eastern art genres faded in Azerbaijan. During this period the art of miniatures was in crisis and painters began to use more realist methods.

Sattar Bahlulzada (1909-74)
One of the founders of the landscape genre in modern Azerbaijani art.

The new realist style in painting was welcomed by the noble feudal societies. The new methods of fine art, based on visual realism, had great democratic potential for publicity, but Azerbaijani fine art would need 200 years to absorb the new European traditions. The framework of strict rules concerning miniature painting was destroyed in the 19th century and a turning point reached in appropriating the "new language" of art. This period saw the strengthening of cultural relations with Europe and Russia, the formation of a new bourgeois society, the development of national self-identity and the formation and development of the democratic movement.

Togrul Narimanbeyov (1930)
One of modern Azerbaijan's best known artists.

137

Tahir Salahov (1928)
A world-renowned Azerbaijani artist and painter, he has made a great contribution to the development of modern portrait painting. Prof. Salahov is a member of several prestigious international institutes and honorary president of UNESCO's International Association of Plastic Arts.

Repairmen **by Tahir Salahov, 1960**

Fuad Abdurrahmanov (1915-71)
One of the founders of modern Azerbaijani sculpture, he was also an alternate member of the Artists' Academy of the USSR.

Mirza Qadim Iravani and Mir Mohsun Navvab were well-known figures from the democratic tendency in Azerbaijani fine art in the 19th century. They used personal expression in their portraits and searched for style. They depicted likenesses and tried to express psychological points while preserving Eastern conservatism.

European sensitivity and lyricism can be seen in the drawings of the poet Khurshudbanu Natavan. The caricatures of Azim Azimzada from 1918-20 reflect socio-political problems, while the series of pictures of *Refugees* by Bahruz Kangarli mirror the atrocities of Armenian aggression. *The Portrait of Sheikh-ul Islam* and *The Mosque of Bibi Heybat* by Ali bay Huseynzada (1864-1940) are examples of patriotic realism.

Azerbaijani artists from the modern period worthy of note include Latif Karimov (1906-91), Huseyn Aliyev (1911-91), Qasim Qasimzada (1913-92), Maral Rahmanzada (1916-2008), Najafqulu (1923-90), Vajiha Samadova (1924-65), Mikayil Abdullayev (1921-2002), Oqtay Sadiqzada (1921), Boyukagha Mirzazada (1921-2007), Elbay Rzaquliyev (1926) and Kamil Najafzada (1929).

The first examples of sculpture in Azerbaijan are on the rocks of Gobustan. In the 4th and 7th centuries AD carvings in stone and metal were widespread in Caucasian Albania. Examples are a female statue excavated in Khinisly village, Shamakhi, a picture of two parrots found in Mingachevir and the Bayil stones near Baku. Many valuable examples of sculpture were created in Azerbaijan in medieval times. The works

Zivar Mammadova (1902-80)
Azerbaijan's first female sculptor

Statue of Zarifa Aliyeva by Omar Eldarov, 1989

of this period are known for their fine ornament and style. The Spout of Shirvan made in 1206 by Ali ibn Mohammed ibn Abdul is at present in the State Hermitage in St Petersburg. The most popular pieces of sculpture are those created in the late 19th and early 20th centuries on gravestones in Absheron, Guba, Ganja and Shamakhi.

Omar Eldarov (1927)
A prominent Azerbaijani sculptor, he is an associate member of the Azerbaijani National Academy of Sciences and of the Russian Academy of Arts.

The best work by modern Azerbaijani sculptors includes Fuad Abdurrahmanov's statues of Nizami Ganjavi in Ganja, Baku and Luxemburg, Tokay Mammadov and Omar Eldarov's statue of Fizuli, Tokay Mammadov and Ibrahim Zeynalov's statue of Nasimi, Tokay Mammadov's statues of Mashadi Azizbayov and Uzeyir Hajibayov, Fuad Abdurrahmanov's statue of Samad Vurgun in Baku and J. Qaryaghdi's Samad Vurgun in Gazakh, Omar Eldarov's statues of Heydar Aliyev in Nakhchivan and Cheboksari, Azad Aliyev's statue of Beethoven in San Salvador, Anar Eyniyev's statue of Ataturk in Izmir, Turkey, and Omar Eldarov's statue of Ihsan Dogramaji in front of Bilkent University. Other well-known sculptors include Huseyn Ahmadov (1915-55), Aghasalim Quliyev (1918-56), Miralasgar Mirqasimov (1924-2003), Munavvar Rzayeva (1929-2004) and Nijat Mammadov (1929-66)

Some of the best works of art are exhibited in the Rustam Mustafayev Azerbaijan State Art Museum in Baku. The museum was established in 1936 on the basis of the Azerbaijan State Museum's Art Department, which was founded in 1920. It is the country's largest art gallery and in 1943 it was named after Rustam Mustafayev, a prominent Azerbaijani painter. The museum has about 12,000 items in its collection. It exhibits paintings, graphics, sculpture and works of decorative and applied art by Azerbaijani, European and Near Eastern artists and samples of folk art from various periods.

Q&A

Culture & Arts

Statue of Nasimi
by Vaqif Nazirov, 2003

139

64 What kinds of applied art are popular in Azerbaijan?

Decorative applied art is mainly related to daily life. The field is divided into two in terms of raw materials (metal, ceramics, textiles and wood) and technique (carving, casting, minting and weaving). Works of applied art reflect the outlook of society, daily life, custom, traditions and aesthetic vision. The various fields of decorative applied art in Azerbaijan include ceramics, copper-work, jewellery, weaving, carpet-weaving, stone-carving and wood-carving.

Ceramics have been known in Azerbaijan since the Bronze Age. Archaeological excavations have found potters' kilns in Mingachevir, Gabala and Ganja. The oldest was found in Mingachevir and dates to the late Bronze Age and early Iron Age. Various items of pottery made on a potter's wheel survive from the Bronze Age. Archaeological research has revealed that ceramics were made on potter's wheels and baked in kilns. More than 20 types of ceramics (churns, jugs, pitchers, lamps, bowls and cups) were made in Azerbaijan. Guba, Khachmaz, Oghuz and Gabala specialised in pottery. In medieval times fine pieces of pottery decorated with human, animal and natural images were popular. One example is a ceramic bowl made in the early 14th century in Sultaniyye, Southern Azerbaijan, devoted to the poem *Khosrov and Shirin* by Nizami Ganjavi. It is now in a collection in London. Ceramics developed in the 19th and 20th centuries and were sold or bartered. Items for daily use enjoyed a large market before

the development of industry, but with the arrival of mass production interest in hand-made ceramics fell. Some domestic items in Azerbaijan are still made by master potters. This ancient art is still practised in Guba, Khachmaz and Oghuz districts of Azerbaijan, where potters create valuable pieces for both the foreign and local markets.

Jewellery-making is a widespread decorative art. Decorative items found in archaeological excavations in Mingachevir, Yaloylutepe, Khojali, Gabala and Ismayilli show that jewellery has a long history and played a big role in daily life. The main items are rings, earrings, necklaces, bracelets and different kinds of beads. The bronze belts found in Mingachevir and Khojali (3,000 BC) as well as a gold bowl (9th-8th centuries BC), dug out in Hasanlu near Lake Urmiya, and a belt (8th century BC) found in the region of Ziviya are classic pieces of jewellery. During the period of Caucasian Albania (4th century BC to 8th century AD) jewellery was a leading field of the economy.

European travellers and diplomats have left a wealth of information about the development of jewellery-making in Azerbaijan. For example, a new stage in jewellery-making began in the Middle Ages. Decorative items such as bracelets, rings, belts and knick-knacks were very com-

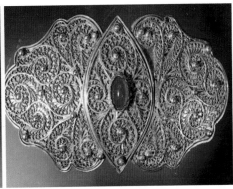

mon in that period. The golden belt of Safavid ruler Shah Ismayil I, kept in Topkapi Museum in Istanbul, is an example of work from that period.

Jewellery continued to develop in the 19th and 20th centuries and Azerbaijani master crafts-men made different ornamental items in metal. Research shows that jewellery was particularly developed in Nakhchivan, Shamakhi, Lahij, Ganja, Baku and Shusha. Most of the jewellery con-sisted of women's ornamental items, such as rings with or without precious stones, earrings and necklaces. This ancient art continues to develop today. One of Baku's streets is called *Zargarpalan* or Jewellers' Quarter, because it used to have many jewellery workshops. Fine ornamental pieces for women made by Azerbaijani master craftsmen can be seen in Azerbaijan's museums.

Copper-smithing is an ancient handicraft in Azerbaijan. From late 2000 BC copper wares were

used widely. The medieval cities of Baku, Ganja, Shamakha and Guba all had coppersmiths' quarters in the bazaars and city centres. The centre of metalwork in this period was Tabriz. Marco Polo, the Venetian traveller who visited Azerbaijan in the second half of the 13th century, dealt in cop-per wares. A figurative vase (1319), one of the well-known works of that time, is now in the Victoria & Albert Museum in London. In 1399 in Tabriz master craftsman Abdul Aziz made a two-tonne copper bowl on the order of Amir Teymur (Tamerlane). One of the biggest bowls in the Near East, it is now kept in the State Hermitage in St Petersburg. A silver astronomic instru-ment from the 15th century *(istirlab)* is kept in the USA. The script on it shows that it was made by Shukrullah Mukhlis in 1486 in Shirvan.

Lahij, a village in Ismayilli District, has been the centre of cop-per-smithing in Azerbaijan since the 18th-19th centuries. Copper jugs, vases and cauldrons made by Lahij

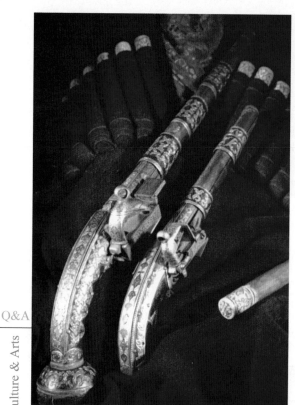

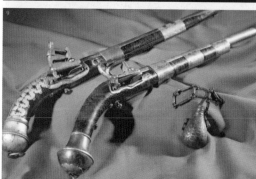

master craftsmen were renowned in the Caucasus, Turkey and Iran. One of the oldest samovars in the former USSR was made in 1717-18 by master craftsman Najafqulu from Lahij. About 200 workshops are thought to have been operating there in the mid-19th century. In the early 19th century the master craftsmen of Lahij applied their experience in the arms plant in Izhevsk, Russia. Today copper-smithing is still practised in Lahij, passed down through the generations.

Armour has been made by skilled craftsmen in the Caucasus for centuries. Adorned with many artistic and technically superb decorations, Caucasian weaponry constitutes a truly unique phenomenon in the culture of the Near East. Silver was the material most widely used in the Caucasus to decorate weaponry.

Caucasian pistols and guns, despite the simple technology of their manufacture, were of excellent constructional design and high-firing power. In the 17th and 18th centuries, Caucasian pistols and rifles earned fame and popularity throughout the Near East. Caucasian firearms were sumptuously and lavishly decorated: the barrels were adorned with gold damascene; the gunstocks, straight and narrow, were made of plane and nut wood, inlaid with bone, silver or different types of wood. The bands used to secure the barrel and stock were often made of solid, engraved silver. The inscribed names of the gunsmith and/or owner of the weapon, enclosed in decorative cartouches, served as an elegant addition to the artistic ornamentation of the piece.

In the 19th and early 20th centuries Caucasian armourers produced a special kind of cavalry sword, the *shashka*, or "long knife", which resembled a sabre but with the blade only slightly curved and without a cross-guard.

In the late Middle Ages hauberks, breast-plates, armlets, leggings and greaves, shields and sabres and all kinds of halberds and helmets were produced. Used by Caucasian warriors, these weapons and armour were both made in the Caucasus and imported.

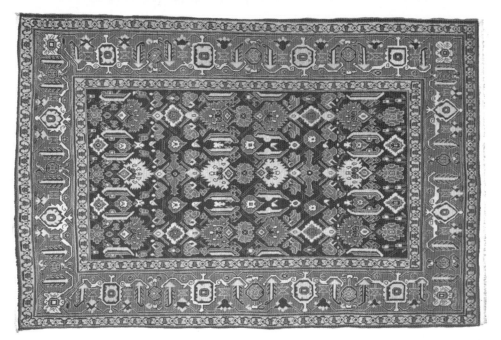

Carpet-weaving is another ancient art in Azerbaijan, according to archaeological excavations and literary sources. In some sources Azerbaijani carpets are referred to as Persian carpets. Xenophon (5th century BC) noted that the Iranians, who expanded their influence in the regions of Azerbaijan, had appropriated the arts of local stone and metal craftsmen and were using their carpets, garments and decorative items. North-eastern Azerbaijan was a centre of high-quality carpet production in the 6th-7th centuries. Chinese traveller Xuanzang, who visited Iran in the 7th century, wrote in his memoirs: "Azerbaijan is one of the largest centres of carpet-making." Historian Moisey Kalankatuklu noted in *Agvan Tarikhi* (History of Agvan) that silk textiles and multi-coloured carpets were manufactured in northern Azerbaijan.

A 10th century manuscript by an otherwise unknown author, Khudud-Al-Alem, says that the

Azerbaijani town of Mugan was famous for its *chuvals* or sacks and *palases*, a type of narrow carpet without pile; the towns of Nakhchivan, Khoy and Salmas were known for their *zili* and *khali* pileless carpets and sashes and Ardabil and Shirvan for coloured silk and woollen textiles. Tenth century historiographer Abu Jafar Muhammad at-Tabari wrote that carpets of high quality were manufactured in north-eastern Azerbaijan. Historian and traveller Al Mukaddassi, describing the Azerbaijani town of Barda and its market in the 10th century, noted that "the silk and clothes have no equal in the world".

In the 13th century Venetian traveller Marco Polo wrote "there are many skilful craftsmen, producing textiles, carpets and sabres for the whole world in Azerbaijan". In the 13th-14th centuries Azerbaijani jewellery and carpets attracted European, especially Venetian merchants. Traders, travellers and ambassadors from different countries exported carpets from Azerbaijan as commodities and presents. Azerbaijani carpets can be found on the canvases of famous European artists. They can be seen in Hans Holbein's *Ambassadors*,

while Dutch artist Jan Van Eyck painted his *Madonna of Canon Van der Paele* with a Guba carpet in the background.

In the 16th-17th centuries during Safavid rule the Azerbaijani art of carpet-making developed rapidly. At this time the cities of Tabriz, Ardabil, Shamakhi, Baku, Ganja and Barda were considered to be centres of carpet-weaving. The magnificent Sheikh Safi carpet was woven in 1539 by Azerbaijani carpet-makers and given to the mosque of Sheikh Safiyaddin in Ardabil. In 1893 it was sold to the Victoria & Albert Museum. It is the biggest carpet of the 16th century: 10.51m long and 5.34m wide with a total area of 56.21 sq.m.

Carpets woven centuries ago in Shirvan, Karabakh, Absheron, Guba, Gazakh, Ganja, and Talish-Mughan now decorate the great museums of the former Soviet Union, Western Europe and the USA. Ninety per cent of the carpets, especially the flat-woven ones known as Caucasus carpets, are original Azerbaijani carpets.

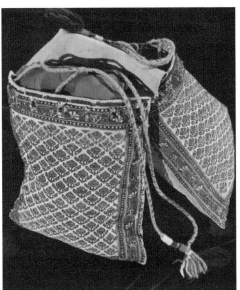

Carpets evolved from everyday domestic items to works of art. Azerbaijani carpets had different designs and were made using different techniques, depending on local features, traditions and raw materials (wool, silk, cotton etc).

Azerbaijani carpets are divided into four groups according to their design and production technique - Guba-Shirvan, Ganja-Gazakh, Karabakh and Tabriz. Study of Azerbaijani carpet-weaving and carpet-weaving in general includes the principles of decoration, colour and composition. The composition, size, decoration and even colours of Azerbaijani carpets vary according to the carpets' purpose. For instance, small carpets are woven for *namaz* or prayers, larger carpets for the wall and a set of carpets to decorate living rooms - a big carpet *(khali)* on the upper side of the room, with a top carpet and border carpet.

The compositions of Azerbaijani carpets con-

sist of two interrelated components: the middle of the carpet and the *yelan* or border. The centre and *yelan* give the carpet its character, while the decoration completes the composition.

The oldest surviving Azerbaijani carpets date back to the 13th-14th centuries. Shirvan carpets from the 13th-14th centuries are in the Turkish and Islamic museums in Istanbul, while the Museum of Berlin's Eastern Department has Gazakh and Shirvan carpets from the 15th century.

Carpet-weaving continued to develop in the 19th and 20th centuries. The most valuable masterpieces of different carpet schools are Baku (the Metropolitan Museum in New York), *Ancient Ganja* (a private collection in Brussels), *Four Seasons* (the Rustam Mustafayev State Art Museum in Baku) and *The Meeting of Leyli and Majnun in the Desert* (the Nizami Literary Museum in Baku).

Carpet-weaving in Azerbaijan is still developing. Today women and girls over the age of seven in towns and villages usually make carpets in winter. They follow the harmony of colour from memory. In 1928 the Azerbaijani Carpet Union was established to manage all the carpet work-

shops in the country. The workers of the union make fine, vivid carpets. These carpets have been exhibited in international fairs in Baghdad, Leipzig, Montreal, Plovdiv, Algiers, Cairo, Izmir, Damascus, Tripoli and Tehran. There are specialised schools in all Azerbaijan's carpet-weaving regions which teach the art and technique of carpet-weaving.

In 1967 the State Carpet Museum, the first carpet museum in the world, opened in Baku. The museum has all kinds of Azerbaijani carpets and carpet-wares and is constantly improving its collection.

Decorative needlework has always been popular in Azerbaijan. All household items - curtains, tablecloths, bedding, garments, accessories and horse cloths and saddles - are decorated with needlework. Some written sources comment on Azerbaijani needlework. Marco Polo in the 13th century noted the beauty of silks in Shamakhi and Barda. In 1561 Anthony Jenkinson, an English diplomat, writing about the luxury of the summer residence of Shirvan's ruler Abdullakhan, said that "the Khan was sitting in a tent embroidered with silver and fine needlework. But his garment was decorated with pearl and precious stones." French traveller Chardin, who lived in Azerbaijan for a short time in the 17th century, compared the big workshops where only needlework was done with those in France.

Cotton, silk and wool produced in Shamakhi, Ganja, Sheki and Shusha were used in embroidery. Silk, golden and silver thread combine with brilliant golden beads and pearls in some of the best examples of embroidery. Azerbaijani decorative needlework uses colourful techniques: *takalduz* (dense embroidery with pearls and beads) and *gulabatin* (sewing with golden threads and applique).

Traditionally, *takalduz*, pearled embroidery and *gulabatin* were widespread in Sheki, Shusha, Ganja, Gazakh and Baku. Both women and men were involved in decorative needlework, but in

Sheki mainly men did embroidery. Their work received golden and silver medals in Moscow (1872), Paris (1900) and St Petersburg (1913).

Gulabatin is an ancient kind of needlework in Azerbaijan. The fabrics produced in Baku were substantial while in Shamakhi they were decorated with fine pictures. Golden and silver threads were used on deep red and green smooth velvet cloth. *Gulabatin* embroidery was most advanced in Shamakhi. Dutch traveller Y. Streis, who visited Shamakhi in the 17th century, was astonished when he saw "garments and other items with silver and golden threads".

Embroidery with pearl and beads was also very colourful. This technique was an integral part of some designs in the 19th century in Shusha, Ganja and Gazakh. Geometrical shapes, such as stripes, rhombuses and squares, and astral symbols from the rocks of Gobustan (10,000 BC) were the main motifs in decorative works. Flowers, birds and stylised human motifs were rarely used in embroidery.

146

questions

65

72

Customs & Traditions

65 What are Azerbaijan's public holidays?

New Year (1-2 January)

Since Azerbaijan uses the Gregorian calendar, New Year begins on 1 January. Every year New Year's Day is celebrated in Azerbaijan as in much of the rest of the world. On that day Christmas trees are decorated, people congratulate each other and Grandfather Frost (or Father Christmas) and the Snow Queen give presents to children. People gather together round the table to celebrate the New Year. Wishes made on New Year's Eve are believed to come true.

International Women's Day (8 March)

On 8 March 1908 a peaceful women's meeting in New York was broken up by the police. This day has been marked since 1911 throughout the world at the initiative of Clara Zetkin, a leader of the women's movement in Germany. International Women's Day was first marked in Azerbaijan in 1917.

Novruz Holiday (20-21 March)

This is the oldest holiday in Azerbaijan and reflects the ancient traditions of the Azerbaijani people. It is believed from historical records that *Novruz* has been celebrated in Azerbaijan since the 3rd millennium BC, the time of ancient Babylon. It was first celebrated at state level in 1921, when a decision of the Azerbaijani Revolutionary Committee declared 20-21 March a holiday. But the repression of the 1930s forbade the state celebration of the holiday. Although *Novruz* was officially prohibited during most of the Soviet period, people celebrated it in secret and kept the festival alive. In spring 1967 the Central Committee allowed the celebration of the holiday for the first time. It was an initiative by the secretary of the Azerbaijani Communist Party for ideological affairs, writer and dramatist Shikhali Qurbanov.

A decree of the Supreme Soviet of the Azerbaijani SSR, issued on 13 March 1990, permitted *Novruz* celebrations at the state level.

Victory Day over Fascism (9 May)

The holiday marks the end of the Second World War. At Stalin's initiative it was decided to celebrate 9 May as the day that fascist Germany signed the act of capitulation. Since then the holiday has been celebrated in Azerbaijan. Azerbaijan played a big part in the victory: it provided 70 per cent of the oil and oil products and 85-90 per cent of aeroplane fuel produced in the USSR for Soviet fighter planes. Some 681,000 Azerbaijanis joined the army, of whom 250,000 died on the battlefields.

148

Republic Day (28 May)

The emergence of this holiday dates back to the beginning of the 20th century. On 28 May 1918 the Azerbaijani Democratic Republic was proclaimed, the first democratic republic in the Near East. But in April 1920, after the occupation of Azerbaijan by Soviet troops, the republic collapsed and celebration of this day was banned. On 19 May 1990 the Supreme Soviet of the Azerbaijani Soviet Socialist Republic made a decision to celebrate 28 May as Republic Day.

Salvation Day (15 June)

On 15 June 1993 Heydar Aliyev was elected chairman of the Supreme Soviet of the Republic of Azerbaijan. Heydar Aliyev had come to Baku from Nakhchivan in June 1993, where he was chairman of the Supreme Majlis of the Nakhchivan Autonomous Republic, to rescue Azerbaijan from disunity and civil strife. The very existence of the state was under threat. On 27 June 1997 the Milli Majlis or parliament of the Azerbaijani Republic declared 15 June National Salvation Day.

Azerbaijan Army Day (26 June)

After the declaration of Azerbaijani independence in 1918, the Azerbaijani Democratic Republic began to build its army. On 26 June the republic's government adopted a decision to establish the first national army bloc, the Caucasian Islamic Army. But on 28 April 1920 Soviet occupation meant the army was dissolved. After the restoration of independence at the end of the 20th century, the Azerbaijani president issued a decree on 22 May 1998 declaring 26 June Armed Forces Day.

Independence Day (18 October)

With the collapse of the USSR in 1991 the Azerbaijani people had the chance to win the struggle for national liberty, begun in 1988. On 18 October 1991 the Supreme Soviet of the Azerbaijan Republic adopted a constitutional act "On the restoration of state independence" and on 29 December a referendum confirmed the act's legal force. Since 5 October 1994 the date 18 October has been marked as Azerbaijan's Independence Day.

Constitution Day (12 November)

Since the adoption of the first Constitution of the independent Azerbaijan Republic on 12 November 1995, this day has been celebrated annually as Constitution Day.

Revival Day (17 November)

This significant holiday is the result of the Azerbaijani nation's struggle for liberty and independence. In 1988 as debate opened up in the Soviet empire, dissatisfaction in the regions increased. It was on 17 November that the Azerbaijani people began to express their dissatisfaction in protest demonstrations. Revival Day has been celebrated since 11 November 1992 by decree of the Azerbaijan Republic.

Day of Solidarity of Azerbaijanis Worldwide (31 December)

At the end of the 1980s when the Soviet regime began to decline, the Azerbaijani people increased their efforts to establish relations with their compatriots. Azerbaijanis cut through the barbed wire laid by Soviet border troops, which separated them from their compatriots in Iran and Turkey. This historic event took place on 31 December 1989 after the restoration of Azerbaijani independence. On 16 December 1991 at the initiative of Heydar Aliyev, chairman of the Supreme Majlis of the Nakhchivan Autonomous Republic, 31 December was declared the Day of Solidarity of Azerbaijanis Worldwide. This holiday has been celebrated since 1991. The holiday plays an important role in establishing relations among Azerbaijanis living in different countries, creating unity and solidarity among them.

Azerbaijanis also celebrate Holy Ramadan and the Muslim Festival of Sacrifice which change according to the Muslim calendar. These holidays are marked by two non-working days each.

Customs & Traditions

149

66 How do Azerbaijani people celebrate national and religious holidays?

Novruz

Novruz is the oldest holiday of Azerbaijan. A symbol of spring and the revival of nature, the holiday is marked on the equinox (21-22 March) in the northern hemisphere. Before the holiday people usually clean their yards and homes and plant trees. On the eve of the holiday different delicacies *(qogal, kulcha, feseli, pakhlava, shakarbura)* are prepared. Delicious meals are cooked in every home for *Novruz* evening. The menu may vary, but one obligatory dish is *plov (pilaff)*. Eggs are dyed various colours and a *Novruz* tray *(Novruz khonchasi)* is prepared. The tray is decorated with candles and holds dried fruit and nuts. Bonfires are also lit as part of the celebrations. An important *Novruz* tradition is to grow *samani*, green shoots grown from wheat seeds. The *samani* symbolize Azerbaijanis' wish for an abundant harvest and form part of the decorations for the holiday evening party. *Samani halvasi*, a delicacy made from wheat, is also a delicious sweet. *Novruz* is a family holiday, celebrated at home.

It is also a tradition to give a *Novruz* present. A *Novruz* tray or different gifts are sent to neighbours and friends. And the dishes must not be returned empty or, according to tradition, the households will lose their wealth. Therefore, whoever receives a *Novruz* present returns the dishes with different *Novruz* gifts. Special effort is made to send a *Novruz* tray to non-Azerbaijanis so that they can enjoy the sweetness and happiness of the holiday.

Four weeks before the holiday the Azerbaijani people acknowledge their belief in the sun and fire by making bonfires every *charshanba* (Wednesday) and by dancing and singing. The tra-

ditions of making and jumping over bonfires, burning torches and decorating tables
with candles dates back to the Zoroastrian
period when fire was an important symbol of
the divine. Azerbaijanis retain these
Zoroastrian traditions today. When you
jump over a bonfire before or at Novruz,
pain, bitterness and misfortune will be burnt
up in the fire and not continue into the new
year.

It is an unwritten rule that quarrels must
be settled and people reconciled at their own
initiative without a mediator. It is a sin not to
forgive the penitent. Azerbaijanis call the second day of *Novruz* Grandfathers' and
Fathers' Day (*Ata-baba gunu*) and go to the
cemetery to remember their relatives. During
or on the eve of the holiday people visit those
who are in mourning and unable to celebrate
Novruz and usually take them *samani* and
khoncha.

On the *Novruz* holidays children put their
caps or small bags outside the doors of hous-

151

es and apartments, knock on the doors and then hide. The home owner puts various *Novruz* gifts into the caps.

Musical events are held to mark *Novruz*. *Ashugs* or minstrels welcome spring with songs and the *yalli* folk dance. Young men compete in horse-riding and wrestling. People dance folk dances such as *Hakhishta, Banovsha* and *Kosa-kosa*.

Azerbaijan is a multi-ethnic country with people of different religions. However, the tradition is so old that people of all ethnic groups look forward to *Novruz* and celebrate it as theirs.

Azerbaijan's largest *Novruz samani* are grown on the Maiden Tower in Baku. The beauty queen who has been elected *Bahar xanim* (Miss Spring) sets light to the flame on top of the tower to mark the arrival of spring.

Novruz is an official celebration and public holiday. The head of state usually congratulates the people on *Novruz* and participates in the popular celebrations.

The media report on the holiday for several days, describe its history and broadcast concerts and special holiday programmes.

Ramadan

In *Ramadan* Muslims fulfil one of the five pillars or main provisions of their religion, which is fasting. Fasting has been considered necessary since 623 AD and is believed to be one of the sacred duties imposed by God on any Muslim. According to the Qur'an, the faithful must fast from early dawn till dusk. Fasting shows peoples' love for God and their endurance of suffering and that all people are equal before God. All Muslims, apart from children, the sick, pregnant women, the mentally disabled and those who are travelling, must fast. The fasting ends with the *Ramadan* Festival. People pray early on the holiday at their homes or in public at mosques, a special festive ritual of Islam is performed and food is given to the poor. The Qur'an is believed to have been brought by Archangel Jabrail or Gabriel to the Prophet Muhammad in the month of *Ramadan*.

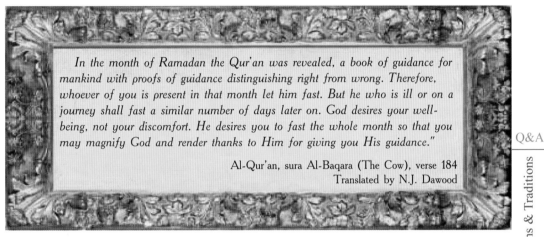

In the month of Ramadan the Qur'an was revealed, a book of guidance for mankind with proofs of guidance distinguishing right from wrong. Therefore, whoever of you is present in that month let him fast. But he who is ill or on a journey shall fast a similar number of days later on. God desires your well-being, not your discomfort. He desires you to fast the whole month so that you may magnify God and render thanks to Him for giving you His guidance."

Al-Qur'an, sura Al-Baqara (The Cow), verse 184
Translated by N.J. Dawood

The Muslim Festival of Sacrifice, *Eid ul-Adha (Qurban Bayrami)*

According to the Muslim calendar, the Festival has been marked since 623 AD on 10 *Zilhija*, the Lunar Muslim month. Traditionally Muslims going on pilgrimage to Mecca perform rituals, pray and make a sacrifice. However, those unable to go on the pilgrimage also make a sacrifice, fulfilling this sacred duty. On the day of the festival, which is a public holiday in most Muslim countries including Azerbaijan, people perform the special festive ritual prayers of Islam and sacrifice healthy sheep. The holiday begins with public prayer at home or in mosques. This religious holiday derives  from the story that God took pity on the prophet Abraham, when he was about to sacrifice his son to God, and sent a sheep to him from paradise to sacrifice instead.

153

67 What is *Novruz chershenbe*?

Azerbaijanis name the last month of the winter (22 February to 22 March) the Grey Month, because the weather at this time is often changeable, murky and dull. The Wednesdays of this month have been named after the natural elements - earth, wind, fire and water.

Novruz Wednesdays *(charshanbalar)* are connected with ancient beliefs, Turkic mythology and Zoroastrianism. According to superstition, cherishing the sacred elements every Wednesday helped people in their work during the year. Every Wednesday each natural element is thought to have come into existence and people perform ceremonies and hold parties in its honour. Azerbaijanis maintain the tradition of celebrating the last four Wednesdays on the eve of *Novruz* as the last Wednesdays of the year *(ilakhir charshanbalar)*.

Su Charshanbasi (Water Wednesday) - Water is traditionally believed to become fresher at new year. On Water Wednesday everybody goes to a source of water, washes their face and hands in fresh water,

Customs & Traditions

splashes one another with water and jumps over it, making a wish to leave all illnesses in the past. Water Wednesday is a symbol of health and different rituals are peformed with water: songs are sung, pools and canals are cleaned. Water drunk early in the morning on that day is considered to have healing properties.

Od Charshanbasi (Fire Wednesday) - Fire is connected with ancient Turkic mythology and Zoroastrianism. It is believed that the more people like the Sun and fire, the warmer their climate will become and happiness will come to the people. In Zoroastrian belief heat is connected with the tree stump. In olden times in Azerbaijan, known as the Land of Fire, the Azeri people used to hold the *Shahrivar, Sadda, Azarkan* and *Azar* festivals to honour fire.

Hava Charshanbasi (Air Wednesday) - On this day the wind (air) is believed to wake up and go around the world, waking water and fire. Warm wind on this charshanba is a sign of the coming spring. The wind blowing from different directions means air is cleaned. There are four anthropomorphic types of wind in ancient Turkic mythology that symbolize God's mercy and anger: White Wind, Black Wind, *Khazri* (blue) and *Gilavar* (red). The wind is described as goddesses and gods in Holy Scriptures such as the Koran, *Avesta* (Zoroastrian scriptures) and Bible. And today there are many rituals and songs about wind in our folklore.

Torpaq Charshanbasi (Earth Wednesday) or *Akhir Charshanba* (the last Wednesday) - According to traditional Azerbaijani belief, with the revival of the last element of nature the other elements gain in strength and change their form, protecting people from hardship. The earth, which is thought to be sacred, has since olden times been the origin and final resting place of mankind. On this day different rituals are performed and people go to the fields to hold feasts and parties and clear out their vegetable plots. On the evening of the last Wednesday and during *Novruz* a candle is lit for each family member and allowed to burn down without being blown out.

68 What are Azerbaijan's national costumes?

National costume reflects more than any other part of material culture the specific features of a nation. The ethnic, aesthetic and artistic creativity of a people finds expression in their garments, embroidery, weaving and knitting.

Traditional clothes among Azerbaijanis changed little up to the beginning of the 20th century. The dress of Azerbaijani women used to vary according to social status and ethnic identity. Female costumes consisted of under and outer garments and the latter were subdivided into shoulder and waist garments. Poor women wore a short waist-length tunic of calico, cotton or satin while the rich wore silk. The most famous national female garments were the *ust koynek* (outer shirt), *arkhaliq* (a blouse often gathered at the waist), *chapkan* (a long jacket or blouse) and *labbada* (a short jacket or blouse). On top of an *arkhaliq* or *chapkan* women wore a *kamar* or belt, usually made of leather with coins sewn on and a buckle made of a rough grade of silver.

Female headgear is traditionally very colourful and attractive. Best known is the *kalaghayi*, a decorative silk shawl. *Kalaghayi* varied in accordance with the age and social status of the wearer. A lavishly embroidered *tesek* (cap for women) was also widely worn. The *lachak* is another headdress, worn while doing housework or dying hair with henna. In the past Azerbaijani women did

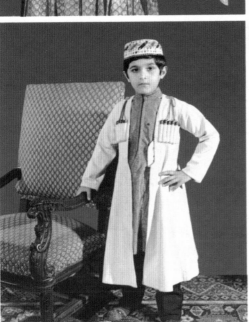

not appear in public without their *chadra* (a large veil) and sometimes they covered their face with a light scarf or veil called a *ruband*. When they saw strangers, village women simply covered their mouths and lower part of their face with a corner of their head shawl which is called a *yashmaq*. Women's costume also included jewellery for the head, neck, bosom, waist and wrist.

Traditional men's costume is similar to that of the rest of the Caucasus, with minor differences in cut and decoration. Urban and rurual dress varied, as did the clothes of the rich and

poor. Peasants wore wide pantaloons with a belt made from home-spun cloth and a simple tunic made from a variety of materials, including cotton and satin, and a woollen (occasionally silk) *kaftan* or coat called an *arkhaliq*. The better-off wore a *chukha* (tight-fitting jacket) and a *kurk* (sheepskin coat) in winter, and *shalvar* (trousers). City-dwellers at the turn of the 20th century began to wear European-style trousers, but otherwise dress remained traditional.

The men's outfit was completed with a fluffy sheep's wool hat *(papaq)*, woollen or silk socks and home-made, rawhide slippers. Headgear is an essential element of traditional Azerbaijani male clothing and has its own significance. It used to be a disgrace for men to go out bareheaded. Hats still vary and include the *bukhara papaq* and *charkazi papaq*. The *arakhchin* (a silk cap with rich embroidery) is also popular. Old men wear a *tasak* (a small stitched skullcap) under their *papaq*.

Traditional children's clothing is similar to adults', but tends to be less decorative.

Traditional shoes for men and women are similar. The best known are the *chariq* (bast or plant fibre sandals) and *bashmaq*. Woollen or silk knitted socks called *jorab* are very widespread.

Traditional national costume is not widely worn nowadays, but elements from it can be seen in everyday garments. Full national costume tends only to be worn on ceremonial occasions.

69 Who is the religious leader of Caucasian Muslims?

Sheikh-ul-Islam Haji Allahshukur Pashazada is the 12th *sheikh* and a prominent religious figure. He was elected *Sheikh-ul-Islam* in 1980. Since 1985 he has been a member of the Royal Academy of Jordan, researching the culture of Islam. He has contributed to the translation of the Qur'an into the Azerbaijani language and is the author of some academic works.

The majority of people living in the Caucasus are Muslims. The development of Islam in this area played a big part in the history of the Caucasian people. But the development of Islam in the Caucasus begins with Azerbaijan. Islam spread all over Azerbaijan from the 7th century and laid the foundation of the national and moral values of the Azerbaijani people. That is why Azerbaijan later played a big role in the development of Islamic culture in the Caucasus.

In the early 19th century the South Caucasus was annexed to tsarist Russia. The tsarist regime pursued a discriminatory policy among the Caucasian people, as it did all over the empire, and ignored the national feelings of the local Muslims. The regime's colonial policy extended to religion too. The main purpose was to win over the local Muslim clergy and make them obey the government. To that end a Muslim religious centre was founded. In 1823 the post of *Sheikh-ul-Islam* was established in Tbilisi, which was the centre of the Caucasian governorate.

In 1832 the idea of founding a Religious Office of the Affairs of the Transcaucasus Muslim People was proposed. The structure of the Russian Orthodox Church was the basis of the organization of the office. In 1872 Alexander II approved "the regulations for the Sunni and Shia Muhammadan Religious Department of the South Caucasus" and two Muslim administrative bodies were established in the South Caucasus; the Sunni Religious Office (*muftiyat*) was led by the *mufti*, and the Shia Religious Office by the *Sheikh-ul-Islam*. *Sheikh-ul-Islam* is an Arabic term for "the chief of Islam" or "the leader of Islam". Since the 10th century in Islam respected *feqihs* (religious lawyers) and Sufi thinkers have been give the title of *Sheikh-ul Islam*. The office was first situated in Tbilisi and later moved to Baku.

The first *Sheikh-ul Islam* of Caucasian Muslims was *Akhund Mohammed Ali Huseynzada*, who was appointed in 1823 and led the office until 1852.

Pope John Paul II meets Sheykh-ul-Islam Haji Allahshukur Pashazada

Taza Pir mosque, the official residence of the *Sheikh-ul-Islam*

Since 1980 Haji Allahshukur Pashazada has been the *Sheikh-ul-Islam*. All of the religious leaders elected *Sheikh-ul-Islam* have been educated Azerbaijanis, well-known in their day.

In 1920, after the collapse of the Azerbaijani Democratic Republic and the foundation of the Soviet regime, the institution of *Sheikh-ul-Islam* was disbanded. In 1944 during the first Congress of Caucasian Muslims in Baku the office was re-established and *Akhund* Agha Alizada was elected *Sheikh-ul-Islam*. He was the first elected *Sheikh-ul-Islam* in the history of the office (all the former *Sheikh-ul-Islams* had been appointed by the government).

After the demise of the USSR, all religious organizations in Azerbaijan found themselves in a critical situation, but the Office of the South Caucasus Muslims, under the newly elected *Sheikh-ul-Islam* Pashazada, continued to promote its influence in the Caucasus. Today the Office of Caucasian Muslims leads the Islamic communities in Azerbaijan and supervises the observation of Islamic practice. The office publishes yearly its official Muslim calendars and supervises the different religious ceremonies and holidays all over the country, ensuring they meet religious standards.

161

70 Why is 20 January a National Day of Mourning?

On 20 January 1990 Soviet troops were sent onto the streets of Baku to suppress peaceful demonstrations. They killed 141 civilians and wounded hundreds more. What happened that day was an act of terror by a totalitarian regime. The crime committed against the Azerbaijani people is, in fact, a crime against humanity.

The people were infuriated by the territorial claims and acts of Armenian aggression against Azerbaijan (tacitly backed by Soviet authorities in Moscow) as well as by the anti-nationalist behav-

Martyrs' Avenue in Baku

iour of the local authorities. Azerbaijanis were being expelled from Karabakh and the surrounding territories, land where they had lived for centuries. Since 1988 the national movement for liberty had been growing. This was a protest against the policy of the USSR and, consequently, in favour of the independence of Azerbaijan. Thousands of people protesting against Soviet policy held demonstrations all day long in the central square (now Azadliq or Freedom Square) and the streets of Baku.

On 18 January 1990 the Presidium of the Supreme Soviet of the USSR issued a decree "On the enforcement of a state of emergency in the city of Baku from 20 January", which had not been co-coordinated with the parliament of Azerbaijan. The decree aimed to choke the people's voice, to stop the demonstrations and the freedom movement. Later on the night of 20 January a big contingent of USSR Armed Forces was sent onto the streets of Baku. The Soviet Army displayed particular cruelty against the people. They used chemical weapons, shot at ambulances and the wounded and mutilated dead bodies. According to official sources, 131 people died, 774 were wounded, 400 imprisoned and four went missing in this atrocity. The day after the tragedy,

despite the pressure of the Soviet Army, people on the streets displayed their hatred both for those who had enforced the clampdown and for the Communist Parties of the USSR and Azerbaijan. On the night of the tragedy, the leader of the republic, fearing the people's anger, escaped to Moscow.

Azerbaijanis living in Moscow arranged a meeting about the tragedy. At that time Heydar Aliyev was living in Moscow and he went to Azerbaijan's permanent representation in the city to present his condolences to the people of Azerbaijan. In a speech he emphasized that the initiators of the tragedy were the then officials of the USSR and Azerbaijan who had done nothing to calm the people down. Heydar Aliyev, who considered the tragedy a crime against the Azerbaijani people, emphasized that the initiators bore responsibility for it and should be properly punished.

The Azerbaijani people buried the martyrs who perished on 20 January for the independence of the country in the hilltop park overlooking the city, the highest spot in Baku. Since then this place has been called Martyrs' Avenue and people mark 20 January as a National Day of Mourning. The Martyrs' Avenue is a sacred place for every Azerbaijani. Every year millions of Azerbaijanis visit the avenue and lay carnations on the graves. The ceremony begins in the early morning when the president of the republic and representatives of foreign countries lay wreaths at the eternal flame. Traditionally the head of state, accompanied by guards of honour, approaches the monument erected to commemorate the martyrs, lays a wreath, bows and keeps a minute's silence. Then officials of the diplomatic corps, dignitaries and martyrs' relatives offer their condolences to the president.

The general public visit Martyrs' Avenue until midnight. All national TV channels broadcast directly from the avenue. On that day the underground and public transport to Martyrs' Avenue operate free of charge in order to allow the crowds to move freely. According to official protocol, every guest or delegation paying a visit to Azerbaijan begins their journey by visiting the Avenue.

The Azerbaijani people named an underground station after 20 January, near the place where the tragedy occurred (before this the tube station was named after the 11th Army that committed the atrocity). The interior of the station is decorated with compositions by well-known Azerbaijani artists, who painted various scenes from the tragedy, and red carnations, the symbol of 20 January. Every 20 January the tube station and nearby streets, pavements and walls, which were riddled with bullet holes where civilians were shot en masse, are covered with red carnations.

Though the Azerbaijani people suffered military, moral and political aggression, on 20 January, 1990 they displayed their ability to maintain the traditions of historical heroism and resist the cruellest attacks for the sake of the freedom and independence of the motherland, even becoming martyrs. And today the Azerbaijanis are proud of those who are ready to perish for the sake of the people's national identity. On 20 January Martyrs' Avenue looks like a sea of carnations, a symbol formerly associated with the nuptial joy, but now with martyrdom.

71 What are the tales of Azerbaijani folklore?

If you really want to know what influences the way people think and act, delve into their folk epics, proverbs, anecdotes and traditions. It isn't always easy to penetrate the layers of belief that have been passed down for centuries, or, in the case of Azerbaijan, perhaps millennia.

The Azerbaijani people have a rich folklore heritage. Azerbaijani literature covers up to 100 genres and can be epic, lyrical or dramatic. Proverbs and sayings, folktales, legends, myths, anecdotes, toasts, curses, oaths, puzzles, tongue-twisters, *bayati* or couplets, elegies, lullabies and love songs are all oral literature and play a big role in passing information down the generations.

A few specific genres of Azerbaijani literature are connected with everyday life. They mainly include *holavarlar*, counting songs, and ploughman's songs which are connected with cattle breeding and farming. Historically the *ashuqs*, a kind of bard or people's musician, created and immortalized the lyrical and epic genres of Azerbaijani folklore, known as *qoshma, gerayli, mukhemmes, tajnis, divani*, epics and legends. The art of the *ashuqs* probably emerged in the 16th century and was at its highest point in the 19th century thanks to professional *ashuqs* such as Agh Ashuq, Ashuq Ali and Dada Alasgar.

The ancient patterns of artistic thinking and poetry of the Azerbaijani people have been preserved in the literary texts of the people's ancestors, the *Oghuz*. The texts are *Oghuz khagan, Kitabi-Dada Qorqud* and *Oghuznama*, and *Divani-lugat et-turk* by Mahmud Kashqari, a prominent Turkic scientist who lived in the 11th century. The epic *Koroghlu (Son of a Blind Man)* of the Azerbaijani people and its varied versions later became very popular amongst neighbouring peoples including the Kurds, Georgians, Afghans, Tajiks and Armenians and other Turkic peoples. The epic was written down in 1834 in Tabriz, Southern Azerbaijan, and in 1842 was published in London (A. Chodzko). The adventures and improvisations of Koroghlu, the bandit minstrel of Northern Persia, contain examples of the popular poetry of Persia and songs from the shores of the Caspian Sea. This is the full version of the Koroghlu epic.

Although some Azerbaijani folklore is retained from the Middle Ages, it was mainly collected and published in the 19th century. At that time *The Caucasus* newspaper, published in Tbilisi, devoted special sections to Azerbaijani folklore. Later, by the mid-20th century S. Mumtaz, H. Zeynalli, V. Khuluflu, A. Akhundov, A. Tahirbayov, M.H. Tahmasib and H. Alizada were all working to collect Azerbaijani folklore.

From 1994 the Folklore Cultural Centre, and from 2003 the Institute of Folklore, an independent structure of the Academy of Sciences, has been collecting and systematising Azerbaijani folklore. The institute collects folklore in all the regions of the country and publishes an anthology of Azerbaijani folklore. The Institute of Folklore also publishes academic publications including *Research on Oral Azerbaijani Literature* and the *Dada Qorqud* magazine.

Children's folklore

As in every society, there are many examples of oral folklore for children - obviously many created by adults for children and many that children themselves invent spontaneously in response to a situation. We have included some of the favourite examples which have been passed down through many generations and continue to intrigue and inspire children (and adults) today.

Jirtdan is one of the most popular fairy tales in Azerbaijan. *Jirtdan*, meaning "tiny" in Azerbaijani, is about a child, much smaller than other children his age, who finds strength in being intelligent. There is a hairy, scary monster in the story, the div, who loves to eat children, and he is the embodiment of the gigantic forces of evil. By creating a hero out of *Jirtdan*, the story challenges children, though physically small and weak, not to be afraid to outwit forces much larger than they are.

"Beauty is nine-tenths how you dress"
To be attractive what is most important is how one dresses and presents oneself. One does not have to be a natural beauty to be attractive, but one does need to know how to dress well.

Jirtdan closely resembles the German fairy tale of *Hansel and Gretel*, in which a brother and sister, who lose their way in the forest, finally outsmart and escape an evil witch who plans to eat them. As these stories are passed down the generations by word of mouth, variations to the tale occur.

Proverbs - "Father's words"

In the Azerbaijani language, "proverb" translates literally as "father's words" - *atalar sozu*. For many generations, father's words have been valued as an expression of the collective thought and experience of the community. These short sayings encapsulate the wisdom of the past, making it available to present and future generations. There are thousands of Azerbaijani proverbs and no-one knows how old they might be - centuries, possibly even millennia. Azerbaijanis are extremely fond of spicing up their conversation with these pithy sayings to convince others of the "rightness" of their opinions and actions.

"I wish God had not created the left hand to need the right hand"
Sometimes family and society strangle an individual's initiatives, making him or her long for the chance to be independent of them.

Proverbs are traditional answers to recurring ethical problems - meanness, deceit, treason, cunning, unreliability, jealousy, etc. They provide an argument for a course of action which conforms to the expectations of society. Like proverbs and expressions found all over the world, Azerbaijani proverbs cover a broad range of topics. In fact, if you look hard enough, you can probably find a saying to prove any point of view, even ideas that contradict one another.

"Wish your neighbour two cows so that you may have one for yourself"
Have a spirit of generosity towards others and in the end God will bless you, too.

165

72 What are the most common superstitions in Azerbaijan?

Superstitions are the oldest genre of beliefs in Azerbaijani folklore. The main superstitions are connected with daily life, flora and fauna, natural phenomena, myths and spirituality.

They include such ideas as, "Do not touch someone who is drinking water", "A white flower is a symbol of parting", "Do not cut bread with one hand", "A yellow flower brings bad things" and "A house where a horseshoe hangs will enjoy abundance". An empty plate and coming across a black cat or grey-haired or hunch-backed woman are believed to be unlucky. Some superstitions are connected with Zoroastrianism and fire-worship in Azerbaijan and some with ancient Turkic myths. Some are reflected in the *Kitabi-Dada Qorqud*, the ancient Azerbaijani epic. "People who have fallen out should be reconciled with one another on the holiday eve", "It is lucky to wear new clothes on the holiday eve" and "It is wrong to kill a swallow" are beliefs connected with the *Novruz* spring new year holiday and are observed.

An ancient tradition is to burn the herb rue and waft the smoke around family members and livestock and through the home. Rue smoke is believed to ward off the evil eyes and negative energy.

Another form of superstition is *jadu* - sorcery typical to Azerbaijanis and other Near Eastern nations. It does not differ greatly from western forms of the black arts.

Tourist Information, Sites & Landmarks

73 What's the history of the rock drawings in Gobustan?

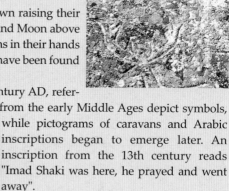

The cultural history of the people of Azerbaijan dates back millennia. Primitive humans had settlements in Gobustan, (60 km southwest of Baku) where their rock drawings show their spiritual culture. The Gobustan engravings, now a UNESCO World Heritage site, are unique. The first drawings were created over 12,000 years ago in the Stone Age and drawings were added until medieval times. The tribes inhabiting those areas were nomads, and isolated from the main areas of development.

The eruption of volcanoes and gas and oil gushers shaped the caves of Gobustan. Early man held religious ceremonies here. The primitive pictures show human or animal silhouettes carved out by obsidian on soft limestone. The pictures in Gobustan are rich with many themes: they depict men and women, wild bulls, deer, wild horses, boar, and hunting scenes. The majority of the pictures show ceremonial scenes, prayers and daily life. There are interesting images of tribal dancing, a symbol of the unity of the tribe. Rowing boats are prominent among pictures from the Neolithic period, showing that the ancient inhabitants of Gobustan had access to the sea too. There is a sign of the Sun on the front of each boat. Fish and fishing nets can be seen among the drawings, too.

There are also schematic drawings. People are shown raising their hands in prayer with the Bronze Age signs of the Sun and Moon above them. There are drawings of horsemen holding weapons in their hands that date back to the Iron Age. About 6,000 pictograms have been found inside and near the caves in Gobustan.

One stone bears a Latin inscription from the 1st century AD, referring to the Emperor Domitian's XII legion. Drawings from the early Middle Ages depict symbols, while pictograms of caravans and Arabic inscriptions began to emerge later. An inscription from the 13th century reads "Imad Shaki was here, he prayed and went away".

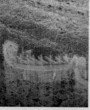

Stones with holes on each side, designed for tethering animals near the caves, are thought to have been left by pilgrims in medieval times. Many holes can be seen on the rocks designed to hold water or the blood of sacrificed animals. In Gobustan human graves have also been found. The oldest date to the Paleolithic era.

The pictograms and inscriptions at Gobustan show that the area was of religious and ceremonial importance from the Stone Age until the late Middle Ages.

74 What is the Maiden Tower?

The Maiden Tower is a Baku landmark, a much loved symbol of the city and of Azerbaijan. It looms dark and enigmatic, looking out to sea from the southern edge of Baku's old, walled city, the Ichari Shahar. The origins of the tower are shrouded in mystery - no-one knows for certain when it was built or what it was built for or even how it acquired its name Maiden Tower (*Qiz qalasi*). No written sources survive that record its construction or original function.

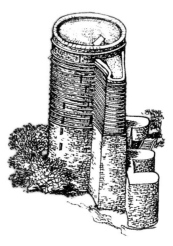

The tower was built in two periods. Most Azerbaijani scholars think the lower part of the monument, the first 13.7 metres, dates from the 7th-6th centuries BC.

The tower is 29.5 metres high and has a diameter of 16.5 metres. The walls are five metres thick at the base and four at the top. The tower is an eight-storied, cylindrical block of coastal rock. Each of the eight floors of the tower is crowned with a stone cupola with a round hole. The floors are connected by means of a stone staircase built into the walls. Daylight penetrates the tower through narrow windows, wider on the inside than the outside. From the first floor there are niches in the walls inside which was a clay pipe, 30 cm in diameter. A well 21 metres deep can be accessed from the second floor. In the southwest part of the tower are some inscriptions written in kufi (ancient Arabic) script, which translate as "The Tower of Masud, Davud's son". Because of the type of stone and its position, scholars think that the inscriptions may have been rebuilt into the walls of the Maiden Tower in the 12th century during reconstruction work.

The Maiden Tower may have been built by Davud oghlu Masud in the 12th century. Historians suggest that Davud oghlu Masud was a grandson of Sultan Mahmud, one of the Seljuk rulers. Davud oghlu Masud might also be the name of the architect who built the Maiden Tower.

The Maiden Tower, 12th century

The name Maiden Tower is a symbol of invincibility. Scholars from several Near Eastern countries, including Iran, have studied the tower, but have not formed a decisive argument to prove the real purpose of the building. Some researchers suggest that the tower was built for defence, but others think the Maiden Tower may have been a temple for fire-worshippers.

In 1960 restoration work was carried out. The unusual form and originality of the tower are always of great interest to Azerbaijani scholars.

Porcelain dishes, ceramics and glassware have been found in the Maiden Tower and nearby during excavations. These excavations prove that the Maiden Tower played an important role in the system of defence towers of Absheron (the towers of Ramana, Mardakan and Shagan).

Q&A

Tourist Information, Sites & Landmarks

The 22 hectares of the old walled city *(Ichari Shahar)* are the oldest part of Baku. This is why it is often known in English as the Old City, although the name *Ichari Shahar* literally means "inner city". Archeological excavations have revealed two cultural layers in the area; the first is from the 8th-13th centuries and the second from the 14th-17th centuries. Baku was the capital of the Shirvan shahs in the 12th century when the fortress walls were erected around the city. The Old City is a network of picturesque winding streets and medieval buildings, which makes it very popular with tourists. The Siniqqala minaret (1078), the Maiden Tower (12th century), the 15th century Shirvanshahs' Palace complex and later *caravanserais* (17th century), mosques, baths and market squares give the city a medieval aspect. The foundations of most of the buildings are built on rock.

Archaeological excavations have revealed the *Bayil Dashlari* or Bayil Stones that come from a castle now submerged in the Caspian Sea, some 300 metres from the Old City. Known as Sabayil Castle, the fortress was 180 metres long, 40 metres wide and surrounded with 15 towers. It was built on an island in the sea in the 15th century. Researchers think it was built for defensive purposes and possibly as a *caravanserai*.

Visitors to Old City can feel transported back in time to the Middle Ages. The complex has been included on UNESCO's World Heritage list and is now on the World Heritage in Danger list too.

Q&A

Information, Sites & Landmarks

76 Is the castle of Derbent still standing?

The city of Derbent, which is now in Dagestan, part of the Russian Federation, is an ancient Azerbaijani city. Greek and Roman sources refer to Derbent as the Caspian or Albanian passageway, Armenian and Georgian Albanian sources refer to it as the Gate of Chola, Byzantine sources as *Tzor* or Tair Walls, Iranian sources as *Darband*, the Closed Gates, and Arabic sources as *Bab-ul-Abvab*, the Gate of Gates. The Turkic peoples called the fortress *Demir qapi*, the Iron Gates and the Russians Derbent or *Iron Gates*. The city of Derbent is situated on a strategically important strip of land between the foothills of the Greater Caucasus Mountains and the Caspian Sea. The town was in the Chola region of Caucasian Albania (4th century BC to the 8th century AD) and was the residence of Iranian Sassanid rulers from the 5th century. As it was an important gateway north to south along the Caspian, Derbent was repeatedly attacked by Scythians, Sarmatians, Alans and Huns.

Two different views on the history of Derbent Castle have been in competition for a long time. Many medieval historians credited the Sassanid ruler Khosrov I Anushiravan (531-579) with construction of Derbent. Other sources show that the construction of the city dates much further back. One theory links the origins of Derbent with the mythical Iranian ruler Lekhars and another with Alexander the Great.

Only archaeological studies can determine the city's origins but throughout its history Derbent has been famous as a military fortress. Archaeological excavations have shown that before the Sassanids Derbent had huge fortress walls built around Narin-Gala hill. Even during the Sassanids' reign the layout of the walls did not change. Researchers think the first walls were built in Derbent in the the 8th-7th centuries BC.

In the 1st-3rd centuries AD, Derbent was famous not only as a defensive fortress but also as a centre of trade and handicrafts. In the 5th century Derbent was a Sassanid stronghold, key to repulsing the Huns' from the north. During the reign of Sassanid ruler Yezdekird II the castle was reconstructed and remained that way until the 6th century. The fortress was built of bricks of clay and then limestone. Researchers date the current walls of Derbent fortress to the first half of the 6th century and the Sassanid ruler Gubad.

The fortress, one of the most unassailable in history, is built on a hill, 350 meters above sea level. The fortress walls, 40 kilometres long, stretch down to the sea. The fortress has 14 gates to the north and south. The Derbent city walls were restored more than once in the 18th and 19th centuries.

Derbent was the centre of the Derbent Khanate, a medieval Azerbaijani state. It was occupied by Russia during the Russian-Persian war and is now part of the Russian Federation. Its history and and beauty make it very popular with tourists.

77 Where was the first Christian church in the Caucasus?

Christianity was officially recognized in Azerbaijan in the early 4th century AD, according to historical records. Christianity was widespread in Caucasian Albania, then a powerful state on the territory of Azerbaijan. However, the new religion began to spread here even earlier. A *History of Albania* by Albanian historian Moisey Kalankatuklu preserves precious records on the spread of Christianity and the construction of various churches. Historical records describe the Albanian church as an apostolic church. The apostle St Eliseus spread Christianity in Azerbaijan between 54 and 57 AD, earlier than in Georgia and Armenia. Only three centuries later, in 327 AD, did the Armenians adopt Chritianity, thanks to the missionary St Gregory.

A History of Albania records that the missionary activity of St Thaddeus, a disciple of Jesus, ended in failure in Armenia, since Sanatruk, the pagan Armenian king, had ordered the arrest and execution of the apostle. St Eliseus, a disciple of St Thaddeus, returned to Jerusalem and proclaimed that the apostle had fallen martyr. St Jacob, the religious brother of Jesus, sent St Eliseus to Caucasian Albania to preach Christianity there. St Eliseus headed for

The Church of St Eliseus (1st century AD), the village of Kish, Sheki District

Caucasian Albania (now Azerbaijan) through Persia and began to spread the faith. He went to the village of Kish in the region of Uti (now north-western Azerbaijan) and began to build a church. The church of Kish in Sheki District is the first Christian church built in Caucasian Albania and the South Caucasus as a whole. The church walls are of planed stones, about one metre thick. The cylindrical dome on the roof of the church is completed with a pointed, conical cover. The church has been repeatedly reconstructed, but remains well preserved. Although the church has no markings, it once had an inscription showing that it was the church of St Eliseus and had been reconstructed in 1244 by Seraphim, archdeacon of the Albanian Church. In 1836 after the Albanian Church was abolished by order of the Russian tsar, the inscription on the church was completely erased, as happened with other Albanian churches, too. Throughout the centuries this church has been an educational centre of the Albanian Church. Interestingly, the village where the church stands has been known as Kish, which means "religion, belief, and worship", for more than 2,000 years.

On 10 April 2003 the State Committee for Religious Affairs registered the Albanian-Udin Society of Azerbaijan. This marked the resurgence of the Albanian Church. Up to 130 monuments belonging to the Christian churches of Caucasian Albania have been registered throughout the territory of the Republic of Azerbaijan to date.

78 What is the history of the Shirvanshahs' Palace?

The Shirvanshahs' Palace complex is one of Azerbaijan's best preserved and most attractive historic monuments. It was built in Baku's Old City in 1420-60 by the order of the then Shirvan shah, Khalilullah I (1417-1462). The palace is situated on the highest point of one of the hills of the walled Old City or *Ichari Shahar*. Picturesquely spread over three ter-race-yards the ensemble can be seen from the sea and the heights surrounding the city. Its building is crowned with cupolas with proportioned portals and a minaret. It has fine, deep carvings of decorations and inscriptions and splendid masonry.

The ensemble contains a dwelling house, *Divankhana* or court room, the Shirvanshahs' tomb, a palace mosque with minaret, a bath-house, the mausoleum of court scientist Seyid Yahya Bakuvi and the later Eastern Gate. The dwelling house follows strict, concise forms. Its smooth walls have warm, sunny tones; the stately portal has deep niches and the upper windows and window slits on the ground floor are covered in stone tracery known as *shabaka*. The *Divankhana* was the place for official receptions and state meetings. The rotunda of the *Divankhana* is crowned with a cut-stone cupola with a pointed arch, surrounded by an arcade. The high, well-proportioned portal of the main entrance is decorated with ornaments and inscriptions of unusual polish and beauty. The *Turba*, the Shirvanshahs' family tomb, is the work of architect Muhammad Ali, whose name was skil-fully ciphered in the ornamental medallions on the portal, which is beautiful and rich like the portal of the *Divankhana*. The palace mosque is situated next to the tomb. The polished ornamentation of Arabic writing around the top of its minaret announces the date of the building, 1441. In the southern yard of the complex stands the octangular mausoleum of court scientist Seyid Yahya Bakuvi. The entrance cupola of the Bakuvi minaret at the Eastern Gate was built in 1585-86 by Ottoman Sultan Murad III.

Archeological excavations revealed a 26-room bathhouse, an underground water supply pipe 10 metres deep and a well containing 500 litres of water. It has been partially destroyed, but what remains shows the rational arrangement of the premises, surrounded by cupolas and arches, and the skilfully arranged sys-

tem of water-supply and water-heating. The Eastern Portal is the work of archi-tect Amirshah (1585) and is the only part of the palace built in the 16th century.

The government of Azerbaijan declared the ensemble a State Historical and Architectural Reserve and Museum, the Shirvanshahs' Palace Complex, in 1964. Baku's Old City, including the complex and Maiden Tower, is on UNESCO's World Heritage List.

79 What is Azerbaijan's connection to the Great Silk Road?

The international trading route, known as the Great Silk Road, operated from the 2nd century BC until the 16th century AD. The road, which actually followed a variety of routes, started in China, passed through Central Asia and the Near East and onto North Africa and Spain. Its varied routes linked most of the world's major powers of the time. The Silk Road connected people from different traditions and cultures. In Azerbaijan it stimulated the development of the silk industry in regions such as Shaki, Ganja, Nakhchivan, Tabriz and Derbent.

In medieval times Azeri silk taken to Europe was as popular as Chinese silk and was noted for its high quality. Silk worms are thought to have been brought from China to Azerbaijan. Arabic geographers of the Middle Ages (Ibn Hovqal and Al Mukkaddasi) noted that in the 9th and 10th centuries AD silk produced in towns such as Shamakhi, Barda and Ganja had been exported to other countries. Azerbaijani silk was very popular in Europe in the 13th-14th centuries where it was exported by traders from Venice and Florence. The Venetian ambassador, A. Kontarini, who travelled to Shamakhi in 1475, noted that different kinds of silks were produced there. Later the discovery of sea routes to India, China and elsewhere reduced the use and influence of the Silk Road.

At present Azerbaijan maintains good bilateral trading relations with up to 120 countries. Globalization, Azerbaijan's strengthening role in the world and its position at the crossroads of East and West put it on the map for the restoration of historical transit routes and networks. Analysis of the main trends of development of the world economy forecasts that major financial, commodity and information flows of the 21st century will be focused on the triangle USA-Europe-Asia.

The TRACECA project (Transport Corridor Europe-Caucasus-Asia, the restoration of the Silk Road) played a major role in the development of Azerbaijan's foreign policy in the 1990s. The Baku conference on the restoration of the Silk Road on 8-9 September 1998, in which 32 states and 13 international organizations participated, showed that Azerbaijan was a network hub and significant point for its restoration. Azerbaijan became an active participant in TRACECA. Azerbaijan benefits economically from the operation of this transport corridor, which links up to 30 European and Asian countries. Full operation of the corridor will also stimulate Azerbaijan's integration into the international economic system.

80 What is the *Atashgah*?

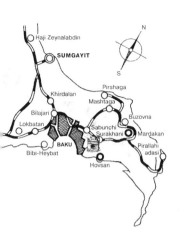

The *Atashgah* is a fire temple, 30 kilometres from Baku, in Surakhani on the Absheron peninsula. *Atashgah* or fire temples sprang up in the 17th-18th centuries at places where permanent fires burned. These fires had been honoured since the origins of the Zoroastrian religion in which fire is a sacred symbol. Throughout the 18th century prayer-rooms, monastic cells and *caravanserais* were built. At the beginning of the 19th century the *Atashgah* at Surakhani looked as it does now. The temple is a pentagonal building with an outer wall and portal entrance. A quadrangular rotunda marks the main temple altar in the middle of the yard. There is a guest-room in the traditional Absheron style, a *balakhana*, over the portal entrance. Built according to local architectural traditions, the *Atashgah* combines fire-temple features. The earliest building of the complex is the stable (1713), while the most recent are the central temple-altar, built with the funds of merchant Kanchagar in 1866 in the Indian system of chronology, or 1810, according to inscriptions.

There are many inscriptions, carved in Indian calligraphy, in the cells. Sixteen inscriptions, formulas, poems and phrases were carved in ancient Sanskrit. The temple was attended until 1880, when the last Indian died or left for home. As well as the temple there is a 15th century *caravanserai*.

The temple was restored in 1975. In 1998 it was included on UNESCO's World Heritage tentative list. The territory of the *Atashgah* was declared a historical and architectural reserve called Atashgah Temple by presidential decree in December 2007. The temple is open for visitors.

Q&A

Tourist Information, Sites & Landmarks

St Bartholomew

Azerbaijan is one of the first areas in the world where Christianity spread, although Muslims are now the majority here. According to historical sources, Christianity was brought to Azerbaijan by the Apostles Bartholomew and Thaddeus and Thaddeus's disciple Eliseus.

Holy legend says that St Bartholomew, who spread Christianity in India and Asia Minor, came to Azerbaijan, then Caucasian Albania. His preaching was successful - many people who witnessed the miracles performed by the apostle came to believe in Christ. But his teaching came up against serious resistance from many priests and magicians and their supporter

Astiag, brother of the ruler. Although the apostle cured the sick daughter of a local lord by christening her family, Astiag, stirred up by the priests, arrested Bartholomew and took him to Albania's ancient religious centre, the city of Baruk (now Baku), to punish him. Here, near the Maiden Tower, then a Zoroastrian temple, St Bartholomew was crucified. According to religious legend, this happened in 71 AD. The place where he was killed still stands near the Maiden Tower and bore a commemorative inscription until 1936.

During his visit to Azerbaijan in April 2003 Bartholomew I, the Ecumenical Patriarch, said prayers at the spot that a church might be built there.

Another church of St Bartholomew was built in 1903 in Bilajary, another part of Baku.

Apostle Bartholomew's chapel, erected on the spot where he was martyred near the Maiden Tower. The chapel is no longer standing

82 Is Azerbaijan mentioned in the Qur'an?

FROM THE QUR'AN:

*Did you think the Sleepers of the Cave and
Al-Raqim a wonder among our signs?*

Sura Al-Kahf (The Cave),
18.9 (as translated by N.J. Dawood)

The cave Ashab al-Kahf is mentioned in the 18th sura or chapter of the Holy Qur'an. Ashab al-Kahf is the name of a cave and place of pilgrimage in the Nakhchivan Autonomous Republic, 12 km north-east of the city of Nakhchivan, which is considered a magical, holy place. In translation from the Arabic Ashab-al-Kahf means "cave dwellers". The name *Ashab-al-Kahf* derives from a story called the "famous dreamers of Efes". The story tells the tale of young God-fearing men in a city of pagans who escaped from persecution by hiding in a cave facing north. God made them fall asleep together with their dog and they awoke 309 years later in the time of Roman Emperor Diocletian (284-305 AD). Waking from a long sleep, the cave dwellers sent one of their number to buy food. When he arrived at the bazaar with ancient money, people were intrigued. They fol-lowed the man to the cave, but the cave dwellers had disappeared. The people were amazed. Some time later a shrine was built at the cave. The same stories from the Qur'an are also in the Indian leg-end *Mahabharata*, the Jewish holy book the *Talmud* and in various Christian sources. The features described in verse 17 of the Cave *sura* as well as the other parameters mentioned in the holy book suggest that the cave is indeed situated in Nakhchivan. There is no other place in the world where the rays of the Sun fall on sleepers from left and right, as described in the Qur'an. Medieval authors wrote that the graves of the cave dwellers were near Efes and Amman or in various places in Central Asia, Syria and Spain.

Construction work was carried out in 1996 around Ashab al-Kahf on the initia-tive of President Heydar Aliyev. The place of pilgrimage is thought to have been built in the 7th century BC. Every year many tourists and pilgrims visit the cave.

The cave of Ashab al-Kahf, Nakhchivan

Tourist Information, Sites & Landmarks

Q&A

177

83 Where is the Burning Mountain?

The Absheron peninsula is home to the Burning Mountain *(Yanar Dagh)*, a rare geological site. Natural gas escaping from the ground burns constantly here. Travellers saw it thousands of years ago and wrote of natural flames that were never extinguished on land and at sea. Yanar Dagh is a historical and nature reserve, popular with visitors.

Azerbaijan has been known as the Land of Fire for millennia, because of the many places where gas coming out of the ground starts to burn. Nowadays there are 12 such fires throughout the republic. The Burning Mountain, the most famous of all, is 10-12 kilometres north of Baku just outside the village of Mahammadi, on the Absheron peninsula. This unique natural phenomenon was formed by the relief of the land and consists of mainly marsh-gas condensate which comes to the surface under strong pressure.

Other natural phenomena connected with gas eruptions include mud volcanoes or volcanoids. Azerbaijan has the largest number of mud volcanoes in the world. They mainly consist of marsh-gas, but also of other hydrocarbons and ineffective gases. There are some 300 mud volcanoes in Azerbaijan. The biggest are Galmas, Toragai and Boyuk Kanizdagh. Eight islands in the Baku archipelago have emerged as a result of mud volcano activity (Garasu, Gil, Zanbil and Zangi-Mughan).

84 How was the lake of Goygol formed?

Goygol (*goy* means blue and *gol* lake) is a picturesque lake, formed in 1139 when an earthquake caused part of Kapaz Mountain to fall into the Aghsu River and block it. Goygol is in northwest Azerbaijan and the surrounding area has been declared the Goygol Reserve. The reserve is home to rare species of deer, gazelle and other animals. There are more lakes nearby, formed as a result of earthquakes, including Maral Gol, Zali Gol and Agh Gol. The seven lakes in total are a symbol of Goygol District and the whole of Azerbaijan. Goygol is 1,556 metres above sea level and surrounded by breathtaking, dense mountain forest. Covering an area of 79 hectares, the lake is 2.5 km long and 93 metres at its deepest point. Its water is rich in calcium. The lake freezes until April. Its mysterious natural beauty makes Goygol the most popular ecotourism centre in Azerbaijan.

85 How old is Baku's underground railway?

In the early 1930s Baku was a densely populated industrial, cultural and scientific centre both for the Caucasus and USSR as a whole. After the metros in Moscow and Leningrad (St Petersburg) had been built, an underground system was pencilled into the development plan for Baku. It would relieve overground transport and clear the narrow streets of many vehicles.

But the Second World War hindered the realization of the plans. Only in 1947, two years after the destructive war, did the government decide to begin research into the project. In 1951 the blueprint for the first line was approved and construction of the 12.1 km underground railway line began. On 6 November, 1967 Baku's metro, the first underground railway in the Near East, was opened and Baku became the fifth city in the Soviet Union to have an underground. The initial stage of Baku's underground covered 10 kilometres and consisted of five stations, four of them very deep underground.

Baku's underground rail system is original in its construction. It has many 60-40 degree inclines and plenty of curved lines.

The architecture of the metro stations is distinctive. All the halls and stations are decorated with national Azerbaijani designs and motifs.

Baku's underground has two lines with an overall length of roughly 32 km. Trains with a maximum speed of 90 km/h travel at an average speed of 38-48 km/h. In the early days the underground carried fewer than 100,000 passengers, but now it carries more than 400,000. On the eve of the 40th anniversary of Baku's underground it carried its four billionth passenger. The metro now has 20 stations, 19 underground and one overground. The network is being extended to cover 52 km and have 32 stations.

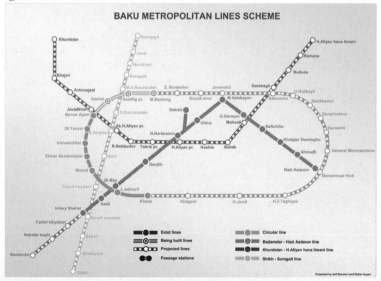

BAKU METROPOLITAN LINES SCHEME

Sport, Leisure, Food & Drink

The Azerbaijani people have long played the ancient games of *topaldiqach* (which literally means "ball kidnapping"), *surpapaq, yayliqqachirtdi* ("headscarf kidnapping"), *chovkan* (a variety of polo), *chilling-aghach, gulash* (wrestling), *nard* (backgammon), cock-fighting, Seven Beauties, *diradoyma* and others.

Chovkan is one of the best known national games. Its name derives from the wooden instrument used to play the game, similar to a hockey stick. *Chovkan* is mentioned in the *Dada Qorqud* epic (7th century AD) and in Nizami's poem *Khosrov and Shirin*. Players on horseback must hit the ball with a *chovkan*, a 120-130 cm long wooden stick curved at the end, through the rival's goal. The game is played on a pitch which is 120-130 metres long and 60-150 wide. The goal posts at both ends of the pitch are two metres high and five metres wide. The game lasts two hours, including a break, and is accompanied by music. All the players wear national costume (a hat, *arkhaliq* or tight-fitting jacket, pantaloons and a light *arkhaliq*). Three umpires manage the game.

Chiling-aghach is played with a stick and peg and is a popular children's game in Azerbaijan. The game is similar to British cricket and American baseball. But during the game a little wooden stick (10-12 cm long) is used instead of a ball.

Nard or backgammon is the oldest recorded game in human history. Backgammon is widely believed to have originated in Mesopotamia in the ancient Persian Empire. The game was played on wooden boards or stones, with numbered dice made from bone, stone, wood or pottery. Throughout the history of the game, backgammon has been associated with royals and nobles. Many artefacts show the popularity of the game amongst the aristocrats of Persia, Greece, Rome and the Far East. The Persians call backgammon *takhteh nard* which translates from Persian as "battle on wood" (*takhteh* is a wooden board and nard is battle). When the Persians invaded Egypt, they introduced the game and it

Kandirbaz - a tight-rope walker

became known as *tau*. The Greeks still call backgammon *tavli* while the Turks call it *tavla*.

Cock-fighting is the name of a game played in spring at *Novruz* (real cock-fighting with birds is also popular). There are two teams. One of them is named Night and the other Day. A circle is drawn on the ground with a radius of six to seven metres. Both teams are inside the circle and stand on one leg, keeping their hands on their waist. One of the teams stands on the left leg, the other on the right. When the game begins, members of one team try to take out the members of the other team. During the fight all the participants must keep their hands on their waists and one foot in the air.

Seven Beauties is a competition in which seven girls are given hooks and different coloured threads. At the appointed time they must crochet stockings. The girl who crochets the best quality stockings faster than the other girls will be the winner.

Diradoyma is a game for two teams of five players each. Four players from each team play while the fifth is a reserve. The game consists of two halves with two-minute breaks throughout. The aim of the game is to win over to one's side as many players as possible.

Cock-fighting

Nard

Chovkan - a type of polo

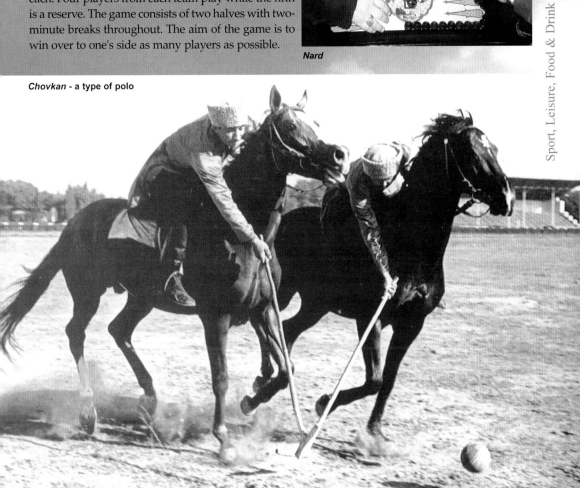

AZERBAIJAN

87 Does Azerbaijan compete in the Olympics?

Azerbaijani sportsmen competed in nine Olympic Games since 1952 as part of the USSR team, winning 10 gold, 11 silver and seven bronze medals. In 1992 five Azerbaijani sportsmen competed in the Olympic Games in Barcelona as part of the CIS team and two of them won gold medals. Azerbaijan joined the International Olympic Movement after the foundation of the National Olympic Committee on 14 January 1992. The NOC has been a member of the European Olympic Committee since 2 November 1992 and was officially recognized by the International Olympic Committee on 23 September 1993.

In 1996 a team of 23 athletes from the Azerbaijani Republic competed in the Atlanta Olympic Games independently for the first time. The team won one gold medal and came 61st out of 197 countries. An Azerbaijani team of 33 sportsmen and women competed in 10 disciplines in the 2000 Olympics in Sydney. They won two gold medals and one bronze, which put them in 34th place out of 199 states and 23rd in Europe. Azerbaijan was represented by 38 athletes at the 2004 Games in Athens who won one gold and four bronze medals. Azerbaijan came 50th in the medals table. In the Beijing Games in 2008 Azerbaijan won one gold medal in judo, two silver medals in wrestling and four bronze (two in wrestling, one in judo and one in boxing) coming in 39th in the medals table.

Rashid Mammadbayov (1897-1970)
Wrestler, Azerbaijan's first Olympic medal winner

In 2007 the International Olympic Committee accepted Baku's application to become a candidate city to host the 2016 Summer Olympics. In June 2008 Azerbaijan was eliminated when the candidate city short list was announced.

Q&A

Sport, Leisure, Food & Drink

Some sports are well developed in Azerbaijan. National teams have won tournaments in freestyle and Greco-Roman wrestling, boxing, equestrian sport, basketball, karate, swimming and chess. The year 2002 saw the highest records for national sport. In European and world championships Azerbaijani sportsmen won 175 medals of which 55 were gold, 43 silver and 77 bronze. Azerbaijan was represented by judo, track and field, freestyle and Greco-Roman wrestling, power lifting, swimming, volleyball (women) and field hockey (women) teams in the 2004 summer Olympics.

European championships in freestyle wrestling and bodybuilding have been held in Azerbaijan. The Azerrail women's volleyball team is one of the top eight teams in international tournaments. In 2005 Azerbaijan hosted a world championship for the first time in its history, the Rhythmic Gymnastics World Championship.

Great achievements have been made in chess in Azerbaijan. In Soviet times, the name of Baku - native Gary Kasparov was synonymous with the concept of chess. Since then new names have appeared, such as Aynur Sofiyeva, Firuza Valikhanli, Ilaha Qadimova, Teymur Rajabov, Shahriyar Mammadyarov, Eltaj Safarli and international umpire Faiq Hasanov are well-known national chess players.

The Association of Football Federations of Azerbaijan is a member of European football's governing body, UEFA, and the international governing body, FIFA. The Azerbaijani national team competes in the qualifying rounds for the European Championships and World Cup while Azerbaijani club sides take part in the Champions League and UEFA Cup competitions.

Q&A

Sport, Leisure, Food & Drink

89 How do Azerbaijanis spend their leisure time?

Azerbaijan's most common leisure activities are home-based or social. Watching television and videos and listening to the radio and music are by far the most popular pastimes. Since there are no local soap operas in Azerbaijan, Latin American and Turkish soaps are very popular, especially amongst housewives and young people. In the past few years reality TV shows and music competitions have hit the small screen and enjoy good audience figures. Listening to music is popular, both Azerbaijani and foreign music, jazz and pop.

The most widespread leisure activity outside the home for adults is to visit tea houses, cafes and restaurants. Strolling about the city with friends and relatives and going sightseeing are another popular way to relax. Azerbaijan has more than 100 cinemas and 27 theatres, most of them in Baku.

In summer city dwellers like to go to the country or the beach to relax. Men often play football whilst women generally prefer swimming and fitness classes.

Chaykhanas (tea-houses) are a very popular place for Azerbaijani men to spend their leisure time. They offer good company in friendly surroundings. Where else can a complete stranger appear and join a conversation with a diverse group of people? Every Azerbaijani village has at least one chaykhana. *Chaykhanas* are not only places to drink tea, but also public meeting places, for pensioners in particular. There is no need for television and radio, as the *chaykhana* can supply whatever information you need. *Chaykhanas* are also a place where the latest events of the day are debated, in other words a talking shop or parliament.

Traditionally, tea is served in a pear-shaped glass, often with other flavours (lemon, flower juice). It is not compulsory to drink tea in a chaykhana and every *chaykhana* landlord will say that the tea business remains very profitable and enjoyable. Many *chaykhanas* serve food, from snacks to full meals. Games such as backgammon and dominoes are usually played in the tea houses, especially in the villages. Modern *chaykhanas* have a variety of games.

187

90 What are Azerbaijan's most popular dishes?

Azerbaijan's rich cooking can be considered a culinary gem. The country's resources and location at the crossroads of East and West have led to a very varied national cuisine. Azerbaijan has long been famed for its cookery amongst travellers and historians. The abundance of vegetables, fruit, fragrant herbs and spices has inspired Azerbaijani cooks to invent new national dishes, which are truly distinctive. Even the most sophisticated gourmets from all over the world appreciate the exquisite taste and subtle aroma of these Azerbaijani dishes.

Azerbaijan is also known as the home of centenarians. Researchers say that this is due, first, to Azerbaijan's salubrious climate, second, to the healthy way of life of its people and, last but not least, to the wholesome food and eating habits.

Azerbaijani soups are prepared from very concentrated meat stock, more concentrated and thicker than European soups. Lavishly used spices and a special cooking technique lend them a special aroma. Some Azerbaijani dishes can be served as both first and second courses. These include *piti* and *kufta-bozbash*. When they are served as two courses, the meat stock is served separately from the other ingredients (meat, peas, and potatoes) which are treated as a second course although they have been cooked in the stock.

A favourite Azerbaijani dish is a rice dish, *plov or pilau*, with meat, fish, fruit or other ingredients. Popular types of pilau include lamb *pilau (kourma pilau)*, chicken *pilau (toyuq pilau)*, sweet pilau made with dried fruit *(shirin pilau)* and *sudlu pilau*, rice pudding with milk. There are some 40 varieties of *pilau*.

Azerbaijani cuisine has a range of kebabs. Beef and lamb kebabs are made from pieces of meat, while *lula* and tava kebab are made from minced lamb with added rump fat. These dishes are popular across the country.

The Azerbaijani people also have many fish dishes. The most popular specialties are sturgeon kebab, *kutum*, stuffed fish, fish *pilau*, *lavangi* (fish stuffed with minced walnut and fried onion), sturgeon *pilau* and *baliq-chikhirtma*.

In Azerbaijan, tea is served before dessert. All sorts of herbs, fresh tomatoes and cucumbers (salted or pickled in winter) are always served at the start of banquets and celebratory meals. Dovgha, a soup made from yoghurt and herbs, is often served after the second course (especially *pilau*), as *dovgha* aids digestion. Dinner often ends with sherbet, a favourite drink in Azerbaijan, or with pastries.

Fragrant Azerbaijani tea is a symbol of heart-felt hospitality. It is served with quince, fig, water-melon rind, apricot, cherry, peach, plum, cornelian cherry, walnut, strawberry, dewberry, grape or mulberry jam.

Below are some recipes for classic Azerbaijani dishes. The quantities are sufficient for one portion. We hope that you and your family will enjoy these recipes. Bon appetit!

Sport, Leisure, Food & Drink

Dushbara

Lamb - 108 g; wheat flour - 40 g; egg - 1/4; onions - 18 g; coriander leaves - 25 g or dried mint - 1 g; grape vinegar, pepper and salt to taste.

Dushbara are small, Azerbaijani dumplings served in broth. The stock is prepared from bones while the meat is minced together with the onions and spices to make the filling. Mix the flour with water into a dough, roll it out 1 mm thick and cut into uniform squares. Put 2-3 g of the filling in the middle of each square. Fold the squares lengthwise or diagonally. Bend back the ears. Boil in the stock for five minutes until the dumplings rise to the surface. At home dushbara dumplings are usually made very small so that you can scoop four or five of them with a tablespoon at a time. Grape vinegar with garlic is served separately to be added to the soup and the dumplings are seasoned with coriander leaves or dried mint.

Kufta-Bozbash

Mutton -163 g; rump fat - 20 g; rice - 15 g; fresh cherry plum - 30 g or dried - 10 g; chickpeas - 25 g; potatoes - 150 g; onions - 18 g; saffron - 0.1 g; dried mint - 0.1 g; pepper and salt to taste.

Soak the chickpeas. Make meat stock from the bones and put the chickpeas into the boiling stock. Mince the meat and onions. Add rice, salt and pepper, mix thoroughly and make meat balls; one to two balls for one helping. Put two to three rinsed dried cherry plums inside each ball. When the chickpeas are cooked, put the balls, potatoes and finely chopped browned onions into the stock. Simmer until cooked. Add pepper, a saffron infusion and salt 10-12 minutes before the dish is ready. To serve, sprinkle with fresh coriander leaves in summer and dried mint in winter.

Piti

The ingredients are the same as for kufta-bozbash. In summer saffron is replaced by fresh tomatoes.

Soak the chickpeas in water for four to five hours. Boil the meat and chickpeas in a saucepan on a slow fire. Add potatoes, coarsely chopped onions, rinsed cherry plums, salt and saffron infusion 30 minutes before the dish is ready and simmer until cooked. As a rule, piti is served in the pan in which it was cooked and poured out onto plates. Peeled onions and sumakh (barberry powder) are served with piti.

Sturgeon Kebab

Sturgeon - 347 g; vegetable oil - 5 g or sour cream - 10 g; onions - 24 g; spring onions - 32 g; lemon - 1/5; narsharab (pomegranate sauce) - 5 g; sumakh - 1 g; pepper 0.1 g; salt to taste.

Clean the sturgeon as usual, cut into 40-50 g pieces, sprinkle with salt and pepper, brush with sour cream and roast on a charcoal fire for 7-10 minutes. Lay the cooked fish out on the dish, garnish with fresh tomatoes and shredded onions. Serve narsharab and sumakh separately.

Lula Kebab

Lamb - 330 g; rump fat - 20 g; onions - 20 g; spring onions - 40 g; parsley and basil - 15 g; wheat flour - 45 g; sumakh - 3 g; salt and pepper to taste.

Mince the lamb, onions and fat together, add pepper and salt and mix thoroughly. Cool the minced meat in the refrigerator for 20 minutes. Shape short sausages from the minced meat and mould around a spit which should be a little thicker than a shashlik spit. Roast over burning charcoals. Wrap in lavash to serve. Lula-kebab is served with raw onions cut in rings, sumakh, chopped fresh herbs and onion or tomatoes roasted on a spit.

Lamb Kebab or Shashlik

Lamb - 330 g; onions - 60 g; spring onions - 40 g; parsley and basil - 10 g; sumakh - 3 g or narsharab - 5 g; salt and pepper to taste.

Take the meat from the loin or hind leg, cut into 35-40 g pieces, sprinkle with pepper and salt, put on a spit and roast over a charcoal fire. Serve the shashlik as soon as it is cooked. Season with onions cut in rings or spring onions. Sumakh or narsharab, salt and pepper are served separately. In summer, serve 100 g of tomatoes roasted on a spit or fresh tomatoes.

Sabza-Qovurma Pilau

Lamb - 221 g; rice - 150 g; melted butter - 50 g; onions - 50 g; fresh herbs (kavar, coriander, spinach, sorrel) - 150 g; abqora (juice of unripe grapes) - 5 g or citric acid - 0.1 g; saffron - 0.1 g; pepper -0.2 g; salt to taste.

Cut the lamb into 35-40 g pieces, sprinkle with pepper and salt and brown. Add the abqora, softened onions and coarsely chopped greens and stew until cooked. Cook rice separately and colour part of it with a saffron infusion. Lay the rice out on a plate and the cooked *sabza-qovurma* next to it. Pour melted butter over the dish.

Toyuq-Pilau

Chicken - 207 g; rice - 100 g; onions - 20 g; shelled almonds - 10 g; melted butter - 50 g; lavashana (rolled thin tablets of dried cherry plums) or cornelian cherries - 10 g; raisins - 50 g; caraway seeds - 0.1 g; saffron - 0.1 g; pepper -0.1 g; salt to taste.

Boil the chicken in water until it's cooked. Simmer the fruit in oil separately, add softened onions and caraway. Put the cooked rice on a plate, place a piece of chicken and cooked fruit and *qazmaq* on top of it and pour melted butter over the dish.

Qiyma-Pilau

Lamb - 221 g; rice - 100 g; melted butter - 50 g; raisins - 30 g; dried cornelian cherries -20 g; onions - 40 g; chestnuts - 30 g; saffron - 0.1 g; wheat flour - 6 g; egg - 1/8 ; cinnamon - 0.2 g; pepper - 0.1 g; salt to taste.

Make dough with the wheat flour and egg. Mince the lamb and fry in oil. Brown the washed cornelian cherries and raisins and cooked and peeled chestnuts in oil separately and add to the minced meat. Cook the mixture *(qiyma)* until ready. Put the cooked rice on a plate, garnish with the *qiyma*, add the *qazmaq* from the bottom of the rice pan, pour melted butter over the dish and sprinkle with cinnamon.

Kalam Dolmasi (Stuffed Cabbage Leaves)

Lamb -163 g; rice - 20 g; peas - 10 g; onions - 15 g; cabbage - 220 g; chestnuts - 50 g; coriander - 15 g; tomatoes - 50 g; grape vinegar - 10 g or citric acid - 2 g; sugar - 5 g.

Mince the lamb with the onions, add the rice, peeled and finely cut chestnuts steeped in cold water, shelled peas, tomatoes, greens, pepper and salt and mix thoroughly. Parboil the cabbage and separate the leaves. Put the filling on the leaves and wrap them into parcels, three for one helping. Place the rolled up leaf parcels in a saucepan, pour meat stock in and simmer until the parcels are cooked.

Add sauce made from sugar and grape vinegar 20 minutes before the dish is ready. To serve, pour over the *dolma* the juice in which they have been cooked, and sprinkle with cinnamon.

Yarpaq Dolmasi (Stuffed Vine Leaves)

Lamb - 108 g; rice - 30 g; onions - 20 g; coriander, dill and mint leaves - 15 g; vine leaves - 40 g; plain yoghurt - 20 g; melted butter - 10 g; salt, pepper and cinnamon to taste.

Mince the lamb and onions. Add the rice, chopped greens (coriander, dill and mint), salt, pepper and, optionally, shelled chickpeas steeped in cold water. Parboil the fresh grape leaves. Mix the filling thoroughly and wrap in the leaves, 25 g of filling to each piece. Put the *dolma* into a thick-bottomed saucepan, half-cover in water and simmer for one hour until cooked. Serve with yoghurt.

Meat Qutab (Meat Pancake)

Lamb - 108 g; onions - 20 g; lavashana (rolled thin tablets of dried cherry plums) - 15 g or pomegranates - 20 g; wheat flour - 110 g; melted butter - 30 g; sumakh - 3 g; pepper - 0.1 g; salt to taste.

Take the wheat flour, add salt and make a dough. Roll out the dough 0.5-1 mm thick and cut into round pieces the size of a pie plate. Mince the lamb and onions, add pepper, salt, *lavashana* and pomegranate. Mix thoroughly. Wrap the filling in pieces of dough in the shape of a crescent and fry in oil in a frying pan. Sprinkle with *sumakh* to serve.

Qutab with Greens (Herb Pancake)

Greens (spinach - 150 g, sorrel - 150 g, spring onions - 50 g, coriander and dill - 15 g); wheat flour - 140 g; melted butter - 20 g; butter - 20 g; lavashana - 10 g; egg - 1/5; yoghurt - 50 g; pepper - 0.1 g; salt to taste.

Wash the herbs, chop coarsely and stew with the softened onions. Add salt, pepper and *lavashana* and mix thoroughly. Make dough with the flour, water, egg and salt. Roll the dough out thinly and cut out into pieces the size of a plate. Fold the filling in the rolled out dough in the shape of a crescent and fry both sides on a skillet.

To serve, pour melted butter over the *qutabi*. Serve the yoghurt separately.

Shakarbura

Top grade wheat flour - 240 g; melted butter - 60 g; whole milk - 80 g; egg - 1; yeast - 8 g; shelled almonds or other nuts - 200 g; sugar - 200 g; cardamom - 0.4 g; salt to taste.

Heat the milk to 30-35°C, add the yeast, salt, egg, butter oil and sieved flour and make a dough. Leave the dough to stand for 1-1.5 hours, divide into 30 g balls and roll into small round pieces 2 cm thick. Put the filling in the middle of each round piece, fold up and plait the edges. Decorate by pricking the dough and bake for 25-30 minutes at a temperature of 160-180°C.

To make the filling, grate shelled roasted almonds or walnuts and mix with sugar in equal proportions.

Pakhlava

Top grade wheat flour - 240 g; melted butter - 60 g; whole milk - 80 g; egg - 1; yeast - 8 g; shelled almonds or other nuts - 200 g; sugar - 200 g; vanilla - 0.2 g; saffron - 0.4 g; honey - 20 g.

Prepare the dough and filling as for shakarbura. Roll the dough 0.5 mm thick. Put one sheet of dough on a greased tray, spread a 3-4 mm layer of filling over it and cover with another sheet of dough, grease the dough and spread a layer of filling. Continue in this way until you have 8-10 layers.

Cut the pakhlava into diamond-shaped pieces of 10x4 cm and brush with egg yolk mixed with saffron. Place half a walnut kernel or pistachio nut in the middle of each lozenge and bake for 35-40 minutes at a temperature of 180-200°C. Glaze the *pakhlava* with syrup or honey 15 minutes before it is ready.

191

91 Why do Azerbaijanis like drinking tea?

Tea-drinking emerged in the East so it is no surprise that tea is the most popular drink in Azerbaijan. No-one knows when tea was first drunk in Azerbaijan, but the first tea bush was grown in 1896 in the village of Seyidaturba, Lankaran. Tea has been cultivated in Azerbaijan since 1912 and from the 1920s it was done on a broader, more commercial scale. Tea-plantations were established in the south, in Lankaran, Astara and Masalli districts, and the northwest, in Zaqatala, Balakan and Qakh districts. Later, tea factories began to process local varieties of tea. During the Soviet period Azerbaijani brands of tea (Azerbaijani Wreath, Extra) were exported to Germany, Yugoslavia, Hungary and France.

To make tea, water is boiled in a kettle or samovar. The boiled water is poured onto tea leaves (usually two to three teaspoons of tea leaves) in a teapot and left on the stove to brew for a minute. Care must be taken lest the tea brews for too long and loses its taste. Once the tea has brewed, it is poured into cups or glasses and boiled water is added according to taste. Tea is traditionally served with sugar, jam or other sweets. Tea is often drunk through sugar lumps or jam, held in the mouth.

Tea parties are very popular in every Azerbaijani family. Tea is an essential component of Azerbaijani hospitality and guests are usually greeted on arrival with a cup of fine-flavoured tea.

92 What is Azerbaijani humour like?

Azerbaijanis, like other nations, have their own specific sense of humour. Azerbaijani humour is rooted in folklore and everyday life. Three characters - Molla Nasraddin, Haji Dayi (Uncle Haji) and Bahlul Dananda - are popular in jokes and funny stories in Azerbaijan and throughout the Near East. Some literary critics think that Molla Nasraddin was a real person who has yet to be identified. The molla is a hero who criticizes and mocks backwardness, illiteracy, unfairness in the matrimonial relationship, failings in bringing up children, greed, ignorance, theft and particularly religious superstition. Through their hero Molla Nasraddin the people are criticizing all the failings of daily life in these stories.

Jalil Mammadquluzada, a prominent Azerbaijani writer and literary critic of the late 19th and early 20th century, took the pen-name *Molla Nasraddin.* He also published the journal *Molla Nasraddin* (1906), the first satirical magazine in Azerbaijan and the Near East. (For more about Jalil Mammadquluzada and *Molla Nasraddin* journal, see page).

Over the centuries people have invented anecdotes, funny stories, satirical verses, puzzles and funny proverbs concerning *Molla Nasraddin.* They have been compiled under the title *Anecdotes of Molla Nasraddin* and other titles and repeatedly reprinted. Today you cannot find any Azerbaijani who doesn't know at least one of the stories or anecdotes of the molla. Scenes from everyday life are the most frequent. Here are some examples:

> *One day a neighbour called on Molla.*
> *"Molla, I want to borrow your donkey."*
> *"I'm sorry," Molla said, "but I have already lent it out."*
> *No sooner had he spoken, than the braying of a donkey could be heard coming from Molla's stable.*
> *"But Molla, I can hear your donkey in there."*
> *"Shame on you," Molla said indignantly, "that you would take the word of a donkey over my word."*

One day the King invited Molla to his palace for dinner. The royal chef prepared, among others, a cabbage recipe for the occasion. After the dinner, the King asked, "How did you like the cabbage?"

"It was delicious," Molla complimented him

"I thought it tasted awful," said the King.

"You are right," added Molla, "it was very bland."

"But you just said it tasted delicious," the King exclaimed.

"Yes, but I am a servant of His Majesty, not of the cabbage," he replied.

The Tale of the Cat

One day Molla bought three okes (an oke is 2.8 pounds) of meat and took it home to his wife. Then he returned to work. Immediately, his wife called her friends and prepared a superb dinner. In the evening, Molla returned for supper, and his wife offered him nothing but bread and onions.

He turned to her and said, "But why haven't you cooked something with the meat?"

"I rinsed the meat and was going to put it on the stove when this damned cat came up and took it away," she said.

Molla at once ran to get the scales. Then he found the cat and weighed it. It was exactly three okes!

Then he turned to his wife and said, "Look here! If what I have just weighed is the cat, then where's the meat? But if this is the meat, then where's the cat?"

questions

93

to

94

Etiquette

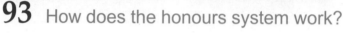

93 How does the honours system work?

Honours in Azerbaijan are awarded by decision of the president of the Azerbaijani Republic. The first and highest honour is National Hero of Azerbaijan, with a special honour Martyr of 20 January. Prominent scholars and cultural figures and those who have made great achievements in their profession are granted the awards People's Poet, People's Writer, People's Artist, People's Architect and so on, while there is a secondary award, Honoured Poet, Honoured Writer, Honoured Architect etc. Specialists in different fields are awarded particular honours, orders and medals by the head of state. These include *the Order of Heydar Aliyev, the Order of Independence, the Order of Glory, the Order of Prosperity, the orders For Bravery* and *For the Sake of the Motherland, the Shah Ismail Order, the Order of the Azerbaijani Flag, the Order of Honour, the Order of Friendship, the Medal of Honour for Public Service and the Medal of Honour for Military Service.* Talented young people and students and Olympic medal winners receive special awards.

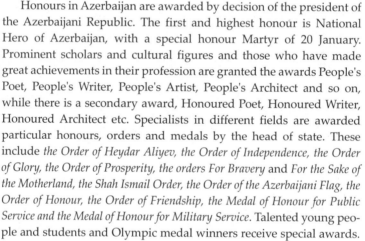

94 How is the president addressed?

Your Excellency or *Zati-alilari* is the form of address used for the president. Another form of address, *janab* (Mister), is very common - for example, *Janab President* (Mr President). The full title appears as *Zati-alilari Janab President* (Your/His Excellency Mr President). As a rule all cabinet ministers are addressed as *janab*.

Traditionally the most common form of address for Azerbaijani men is *muallim*, which means teacher. *Bay/Bey* (literally a noble man) is also a male form of address, showing respect and dignity. Adult men, regardless of their profession, are usually addressed as *muallim*.

Women are traditionally addressed as *khanim* (madam).

Making Contacts

95 How can I trace my relatives and friends in Azerbaijan?

One way to trace people is to place an advertisement in the personal column of local newspapers in the area where your relatives or friends were last known to be living. The addresses of local newspapers in Azerbaijan can be obtained from local annual directories. Visitors to Azerbaijan can trace their relatives and friends through local authorities or current telephone directories, which can be obtained from local libraries.

Birth, marriage and death certificates feature the individuals' addresses and copies of the certificates may be viewed at local authority offices (the Marriage Registry Office). Further advice can be found from the National Archives:

The Republic of Azerbaijan, Baku, AZ 1106
3, Z. Bunyadov Ave.
The National Board of Archives
Tel: +99412 462 96 36
Fax: +99412 462 96 53

Descendants of people who have played an important part in the history of Azerbaijan can contact the Genealogy Society about their family tree.
Baku 28, Bul-Bul Ave., Flat 43
The Azerbaijani Historic Genealogy Society
Tel: +99412 498 22 24 (Academician Chingiz Qajar)
E-mail: kamrangajar@hotmail.com

96 Where can I get birth, marriage and death certificates and divorce records?

To obtain certificates of birth, marriage and death in Azerbaijan since 1890, contact the appropriate offices, including the local marriage registry offices.

AZ1073, Baku
1, Inshaatchilar Ave.
Ministry of Justice of the Republic of Azerbaijan
The Department of Notary and Citizen's Status Offices
Tel: +99412 430 09 77
Fax: +99 412 430 09 81
E-mail: incus@azdata.net
Web-site: www.justice.gov.az

97 How can I keep business links with Azerbaijan?

Azerbaijan is a country rich in natural and human resources. Apart from abundant reserves of oil, gas and minerals, it has untapped potential in a number of sectors for the development of new business. The workforce is well educated and the labour costs are highly competitive. The country's strategic location at the gateway of east and west gives it access to the large markets of the former Soviet republics, Iran, Turkey and the European Union (EU).

Political Stability

Azerbaijan's political environment is remarkably stable. There has been continuity of leadership and government in recent years. Domestically, the country has made steady progress in the arena of political and social reforms. Internationally, Azerbaijan has maintained harmonious relations with Russia as well as with the United States, the EU, Turkey and Iran, strengthening not only political but commercial ties to these countries.

Economic Growth

The country has achieved impressive macroeconomic stabilization since independence in October 1991. The government has taken effective measures to ensure price stability and currency convertibility. Gross domestic product, which was $30 billion in 2007, has grown approximately 100 per cent since 2004. The country is also making noteworthy progress towards a market economy.

Government Committed to Foreign Direct Investment

The Azerbaijani government welcomes foreign direct investment (FDI) in Azerbaijan. In the relatively short period since independence, it has made continuous efforts to open up the economy and establish laws and regulations that are favourable to foreign investors. The foreign exchange regime and currency transfer policies are liberal and there are no major constraints on commercial activity. The law permits foreigners to wholly own companies. Special efforts are currently being made to improve the transparency of the regulatory system, further reduce bureaucracy and corruption, and develop additional incentives for attracting foreign investors.

Developing the Non-Oil Sectors

Having secured investment in the oil and gas sector, the Azerbaijani government is turning attention to developing the non-oil sectors of the economy. Promising sectors are agribusiness (food processing and packaging), textiles, manufacturing, infrastructure (telecommunications, utilities, transportation) and services (financial). Investment opportunities are available through the privatization or acquisition of liquidated assets, such as land, buildings and machinery belonging to state-owned companies. In addition, there is significant potential for new ventures and greenfield investments in several sectors. While foreign investment is not without challenges, a number of foreign companies are successfully investing in the country. The facts show that committed and capable foreign investors can do profitable business in Azerbaijan.

Azerbaijan, Baku AZ 1066
23, Niyazi St.
Ministry of Economic Development of the Republic of Azerbaijan
Tel: +99 412 492 41 10
Fax: +99 412 492 58 95
E-mail: office@economy.gov.az
Web-site: www.economy.gov.az

Azerbaijan, Baku AZ 1110,
57, Acad. Hasan Aliyev St., 3rd Floor
Azerbaijan National Entrepreneurs' Confederation
Tel: +99 465 72 42/ 465 72 43
Fax: +99 465 72 43
E-mail: azerenterprise@artel.net.com
Web-site: www.ASK.org.az

CBS POLYGRAPHIC PRODUCTION

We have the experience and equipment for all your print requirements:

COMPETITIVE PRICING & RELIABILITY FOR

COMPLETE PRINTING SERVICE

Magazines ▪ High-coloured newspapers ▪ Books ▪ Booklets ▪ Bookmarks ▪ Brochures ▪ Business cards ▪ Flyers ▪ Folders ▪ Leaflets ▪ Invitations ▪ Postcards ▪ Posters

Full spectrum of printing products: High-coloured products 70 x 100 mm; printing of magazines, catalogues, booklets and books of world standards level; high-quality printing of high-coloured newspapers; forms and documents of any size; all types of other-printing productions: (heated binding, fillister, cold lamination, packing, thread sewed and clip sewed binding); colour separation size 810 x 1120 mm; digital print with 3 metres width (for external advertisement).

Adress: 3 Sharifzade street, Az1000, Baku, Azerbaijan
Phone: (+99412)447 75 05, 447 75 04, 434 98 17
Fax: (+99412) 447 75 04
E-mail: cbs_pp@list.ru

Questions

98
to
100

**Practical Advice &
Useful Addresses**

98 Whom should I contact in an emergency?

Emergencies are tackled by the Ministry of Emergency Situations of the Azerbaijani Republic. The ministry ensures civil defence, fire safety and protection from natural disasters (earthquakes, floods, avalanches, wild fires, landslides, floods, etc.) and man-made accidents (fires and explosions, chemical and radiation leaks, serious transport accidents, building collapse, etc.). The ministry provides a flexible response to potential emergencies and organizes the protection of strategically important establishments that are vulnerable to natural, man-made or terrorist threat. The ministry has at its disposal professionally trained Civil Defence Forces, fire prevention teams, divers, rescue crews and special facilities and equipment.

The Ministry of Emergency Situations has a telephone hot line 112. This is the number to dial to report an emergency or ask for help. Information reported via the hot line is immediately transmitted to the relevant structures (for example, in case of a fire to the local branch of the State Fire Prevention Service or in case of an air accident to the Aviation Rescue Detachments and Civil Defence Forces) and a rescue team is sent to the scene at once. The hot line can be dialled from any mobile operator across the country round the clock, without limit and free of charge.

As well as the general hot line, the following telephone services also operate in the country 24 hours a day:

101 - Fire Service
102 - Police
103 - Ambulance
These services are free of charge.
For more detailed information, go to www.fhn.gov.az

99 Where can I find out about postage rates?

Any Post Office in Azerbaijan can advise on postage rates within Azerbaijan or overseas. There are two postage rates - rapid and standard. For further information or details of charges, contact the following:

Azerbaijan, Baku AZ 1000
33, Azerbaijan Ave.
Ministry of Communication and Information Technology of the Azerbaijani Republic
Tel: +99412 498 58 38
Fax: +99412 498 79 12/498 80 19
E-mail: mincom@mincom.gov.az
Web-site: www.mincom.gov.az

Azerbaijan, Baku AZ 1000,
36, U. Hajibayov St.
Azarpocht State Enterprise
Tel: +99412 493 05 06
Fax: +99412 493 00 37
E-mail: azerpost@azerpost.rabita.az
Web-site: www.azerpost.rabita.az

A postage stamp issued by the Azerbaijani Post Office to honour Azerbaijani football referee Tofiq Bahramov, who was awarded the Golden Whistle at the 1966 World Cup in England

100 Where can I find useful addresses?

The Tourism Head Office

To find out about travel opportunities, hotels and resorts contact:
AZ 1007, Baku
65, Neftchilar Ave.
The Tourism Head Office of the Ministry of Culture and Tourism of the Republic of Azerbaijan
Tel: +99 412 492 87 13
Fax: +99 412 492 43 15
E-mail: info@turizm.az
Web-site: www.turizm.az

Embassies and Consulates

Information about Azerbaijan's embassies and representatives abroad can be obtained from:
AZ 1009, Baku
4, S.Qurbanov St.
The Ministry of Foreign Affairs of the Republic of Azerbaijan
Tel: +994 12 492 96 92
Fax: +994 12 498 84 80
E-mail: secretariat@mfa.gov.az
Web-site: www.mfa.gov.az/eng/dipser/missions_abroad_eng.shtml
To find out about embassies in Azerbaijan visit:
Web-site: www.mfa.gov.az/eng/diplomatic_corps/embassies.shtml

Members of the Milli Majlis

Members of the Milli Majlis, Azerbaijan' s supreme legislative body, can be contacted at:
AZ 1152, Baku
1 Parliament Ave.
The Milli Majlis of the Republic of Azerbaijan
Tel: +994 12 498 97 48 / 439 86 64
Fax: +994 12 498 97 22
E-mail: azmm@meclis.qov.az
Web-site: www.meclis.gov.az

National Press

To find out about newspapers and magazines published in Azerbaijan contact:
AZ 1130, Baku
60, Ilhampasha Dadashov
The Press Council of Azerbaijan
Tel/Fax: +99 412 498 27 48
Web-site: www.presscouncil.az

Non-Governmental Organizations

For details of National NGOs, see the Azerbaijan National Non-Governmental Organizations Forum:
Web-site: www.ngoforum.az

Practical Advice & Useful Addresses

Youth Exchange

Anyone wishing to organize youth exchanges with Azerbaijani organizations and youth unions should contact:
AZ1072, Baku
4, Olympic St.
The Ministry of Youth and Sport of the Republic of Azerbaijan
Tel: +99 412 465 64 42
Fax: +99 412 465 64 38
E-mail: myst@myst.gov.az
Web-site: www.myst.gov.az

Television Companies

To find out about TV and radio companies in Azerbaijan contact:
AZ 1000, Baku
105, Nizami St.
The Television and Radio Broadcasting Council
Tel: +994 12 498 36 59
Fax: +994 12 498 76 68
Web-site: www.ntrc.gov.az

Universities

The State Students Admission Commission (SSAC) is the central agency which acts on behalf of all state registered universities and colleges.
AZ 1078 Baku
17, Hasan Aliyev St.
The State Students Admission Commission of the Azerbaijani Republic
Tel/Fax: +994 12 440 30 09/498 76 12/498 80 19
E-mail: office@az.in-baku.com
Web-site: www.tqdk.gov.az

Taxes and customs regulations

For information about taxes and customs regulations contact:
AZ 1073, Baku,
16, Landau Street
The Ministry of Taxes of the Republic of Azerbaijan
Tel: +994 12 403 89 70
Fax: +994 12 403 89 71
E-mail: info@taxes.gov.az
Web-site: www.taxes.gov.az

AZ 1073, Baku,
2 Inshaatchilar Ave.
The State Customs Committee of the Republic of Azerbaijan
Tel: +994 12 438 80 80
Fax: +994 12 498 18 36
E-mail: external@customs.gov.az
Web-site: www.az-customs.net

Bibliography

Azərbaycan Sovet Ensiklopediyası. I cild. Bakı, 1976
Azərbaycan Sovet Ensiklopediyası. II cild. Bakı, 1978
Azərbaycan Sovet Ensiklopediyası. III cild. Bakı, 1979
Azərbaycan Sovet Ensiklopediyası. IV cild. Bakı, 1980
Azərbaycan Sovet Ensiklopediyası. V cild. Bakı, 1981
Azərbaycan Sovet Ensiklopediyası. VI cild. Bakı, 1982
Azərbaycan Sovet Ensiklopediyası. VII cild. Bakı, 1983
Azərbaycan Sovet Ensiklopediyası. VIII cild. Bakı, 1984
Azərbaycan Sovet Ensiklopediyası. IX cild. Bakı, 1986
Azərbaycan Sovet Ensiklopediyası. X cild. Bakı, 1987
Azərbaycan tarixi. Bakı,1993
Azərbaycan tarixi. Bakı,1994
Azərbaycan tarixi. Bakı,1996
Azərbaycan tarixi. I cilddə. I cild. Bakı,1998
Azərbaycan ədəbiyyatı tarixi . I cild. Bakı, 1960-1967
Azərbaycanın regionları 2004. Bakı, 2004
Azərbaycanda sahibkarlıq-2003. Statistik məcmuə. Bakı, 2003
Azərbaycanın Statistik Göstəriciləri 2001. Bakı, 2001
Ticarət və Xidmət. Statistik Məcmuə. Bakı, 2004
Azərbaycan Dövlət Akademik Opera və Balet Teatrı.
(broşura). Bakı, 2000
Azərbaycan Respublikası Konstitusiya Məhkəməsi.
(broşura). Bakı, 2003
Azərbaycan. Bakı, 1998
Azərbaycanın Bəxtiyarı. Bakı,1995
Azərbaycan Dövlət Kitabı. Bakı, 2001
Azərbaycan Elmlər Akademiyası-50. Bakı, 1995
Azərbaycan kulinariyası. /Tərtibçi: Əhməd Cabir-Əhmədov.
Bakı 1990
Azərbaycan mətbəxi. /Tərtibçilər: Qəhrəman Bünyadov,
Qəşəm İsabəyli. Bakı 1993.
Azərbaycan Respublikasının Konstitusiyası Bakı, 2002
Azərbaycan tarixi sənədlər və nəşrlər üzrə. Bakı, 1990
Azərbaycan Tarixi Xəritələri. Bakı, 1994
Azərbaycan xalq lətifələri. Bakı, 1978
Azərbaycan xalq musiqisi. Bakı, 1981
Azərbaycan xalq rəqsləri. Bakı, 1959
Bakı metropoliteni 35 il. Bakı, 2002
Qarabağnamələr. II kitab. Bakı, 1991
Bəhlul Danəndə lətifələri. / Toplayanaı Nurəddin Seyidov.
Bakı, 2001
Qayıdış (1990-1993). Bakı, 1996
Kitabi Dədə Qurqud. Bakı 1988
Qur'an./ərəb dilindən tərcümə edənlər: Z. Bünyadov və V.
Məmmədəliyev Bakı, 1992
DEPORTASİYA. Azərbaycanlıların Ermənistan ərazisindən
tarixi-etnik torpaqlarından deportasiyası. Bakı, 1998
Bünyadov Z.M. Azərbaycan Atabəyləri dövləti (1136-1225-
ci illər). Bakı, 1985
Cavid H. Seçilmiş əsərləri. 4 cilddə. Bakı, 1982-1984

Cəfərzadə İ.M. Qobustan. Qayaüstü rəsmlər. Bakı, 1999
Cəfərov Ə. İnsanlığın səhəri. Bakı, 1994
Cəfərov C.H. Azərbaycan teatrı (1873-1973). Bakı, 1974
Cəfərov N. Azərbaycanşünaslığa giriş. Bakı, 2001
Əfəndiyev P. Azərbaycanın şifahi xalq ədəbiyyatı. Bakı,
1992
Əhədov A.F. Azərbaycanda din və dini təsisatlar. Bakı, 1991
Ələkbərli Ə.Y. Qədim türk-oğuz yurdu - "Ermənistan".
Bakı, 1994
Əliyev C., Budaqov B. Türklər, azərbaycanlılar, ermənilər:
TARİXİ HƏQİQƏTİN "GENOSİDİ". Moskva, 2003
Əliyev İ. Azərbaycanda Olimpiya Hərəkatı. Bakı, 2002
"Əsrin Müqaviləsi" 10 il". Bakı, 2004
Əsrlərə bərabər illər 1969-1999 Faktlar və Rəqəmlər.
Hacıyev A. Tiflis Azərbaycan Teatrı. Bakı, 1984
Hacıyev C. XX əsr Azərbaycan ədəbiyyatı tarixi. Bakı, 1955
Heyət C. Azərbaycanın şifahi xalq ədəbiyyatı. Bakı, 1990
Hüseynzadə Ç., Rəhmanov C., Əliyev A. Heydər Əliyev və
Azərbaycanda Olimpiya Hərəkatı. Bakı, 2002
Hüseynov M.M. Uzaq Daş dövrü. Bakı, 1973
Hüseynov H. Vətənpərvər şair Səməd Vurğun. Bakı, 1942
Hüseynov M.M. Azərbaycan arxeologiyası. (Daş dövrü).
Bakı, 1975
Xudiyev. N. Azərbaycan ədəbi dili tarixi. Bakı, 1955
Göyüşov R. Qarabağın keçmişinə səyahət. Bakı., 1993
Göyüşöv R.B. Azərbaycan arxeologiyası. Bakı, 1986
Hacıyev A.N. Qars və Araz-Türk respublikalarının
tarixindən. Bakı, 1994
Hüseynov F. "Molla Nəsrəddin və Molla Nəsrəddinçilər".
Bakı-1986
Hacıyev A.H. Qars və Araz-Türk respublikalarının
tarixindən. Bakı, 1994
Həsənov C.P. Azərbaycan beynəlxalq münasibətlər
sistemində (1918-1920-ci illər). Bakı, 1993
Hüseynova H.K. Azərbaycan Avropa inteqrasiya prosesləri
sistemində (1991-1997-ci illər). Bakı, 1998
İsgəndərov A.C. 1918-ci il mart qırğınının tarixşünaslığı.
Bakı, 1997
İsmayılov M. Azərbaycan musiqisinin janrları. Bakı, 1960
Kərimov K. Opera haqqında söhbət. Bakı, 1996
Kərimov K.C., Əfəndiyev R.S., Rzayev N.İ., Həbibov N.D.
Azərbaycan incəsənəti. Monoqrafiya. Bakı, 1992
Kərimov M.. Azərbaycan musiqi alətləri. Bakı, 2003
Qasımzadə F.S. XIX əsr Azərbaycan ədəbiyyatı tarixi.
Bakı, 1974
Qurbanov A. Azərpbaycan dilçiliyinin müasir məsələləri.
Bakı, 2002
Quliyev H. Məhəmməd Əsəd bəy. Həyat və yaradıcılığı.
Bakı 2005
Mahmudov Y.M. Azərbaycan diplomatiyası. Bakı, 1996

Mahmudov Y. Şükürov K. Qarabağ. Real tarix, faktlar, sənədlər. Bakı 2005

Məhərrəmov A. Bakı Dövlət Universiteti. Bakı, 2000

Məmmədbəyli H. Nəsirəddin Tusi. Bakı, 1980

Məmmədova F.C. Azərbaycanın (Albaniyanın) siyasi tarixi və tarixi coğrafiyası. Bakı,1993

Məmmədov İ. Əsədov S. Ermənistan azərbaycanlıları və onların acı taleyi. Bakı, 1992

Məmmədov V. "Əkinçi" qəzeti. Bakı, 1976

Mirzəyev R.Ş. Heydər Əliyev və müstəqil Azərbaycan dövlətinin yeni neft strategiyası. Bakı, 1999

Nəbiyev A.M. İlaxır çərşənbələr. Bakı, 1992

Nəğmələr, İnanclar, Alqışlar. Toplayanı, tərtib edəni və nəşrə hazırlayanı prof. A. Nəbiyev. Bakı, 1986

Şəhrili Hacı Ə., Nağıyev R., Ağayev Hacı A., Yaqubov Ş. On ikinci şeyxülislam. Bakı, 2000

Paşayev A.Ə. Açılmamış səhifələrin izi ilə. Bakı, 2001

Rəhimova A. Azərbaycan musiqisində meyxana janrı. Bakı, 2002

Rəhmətov Ə. Azərbaycanın xalq çalğı alətləri Bakı, 1975

Rüstəmov C.N. Qobustan-Azərbaycanın qədim mədəniyyət ocağı. Bakı, 2000

Sabir M.Ə. Hophopnamə. I-III Cild. B., 1962-1965

Sadıxov N. Azərbaycanın kino rejissorları: Portretlər. Bakı, 1988

Səfərli Ə. Yusifov X., Qədim və orta əsrlər Azərbaycan ədəbiyyatı. Bakı, 1982

Seyidzadə D.B. Azərbaycan XX əsrin əvvəllərində: müstəqilliyə aparan yollar. Bakı, 2004

Süleymanov M. Oxuduqlarım, eşitdiklərim, gördüklərim, Bakı, 1987

Şahverdiyev A. Azərbaycan mətbuat tarixi. Bakı, 2006

Şahbazlı F. Azərbaycan dilçiliyi və professor Ə.M.Dəmirçizadə. Bakı, 2000

Vahabzadə B. M. Seçilmiş əsərləri. 2 cilddə. Bakı, 1974-1975

Vəkilov R.Ə. Azərbaycan Respublikasının yaranma tarixi. Bakı, 1998

Vəliyev V. Azərbaycanın şifahi xalq ədəbiyyatı. Bakı, 1970

Zeynalov N. Azərbaycan mətbuat tarixi. Bakı, 1973

Zöhrabov R. Muğam. Bakı, 1991

Zəkuyev Ə. Bəhmənyarın fəlsəfi görüşləri. Bakı, 1958

"Azərbaycan" qəzeti, 4 mart, 1993

"Azərbaycan" qəzeti, 18 oktyabr, 1994

"Azərbaycan" qəzeti, 16 dekabr, 1995

"Azərbaycan" qəzeti, 1 aprel, 1998

"Azərbaycan" qəzeti, 26 oktyabr, 1999

"Azərbaycan" qəzeti, 12 may. 2001

"Azərbaycan" qəzeti, 27 iyul, 2002

"Azərbaycan" qəzeti, 24 noyabr, 2002

"Azərbaycan" qəzeti, 30 noyabr, 2003

"Azərbaycan" qəzeti, 20 mart, 2003

"Azərbaycan" qəzeti, 8 aprel, 2003

"Azərbaycan" qəzeti, 25 aprel, 2003

"Azərbaycan" qəzeti, 10 iyun, 2003

"Azərbaycan" qəzeti, 17 iyun, 2003

"Azərbaycan" qəzeti, 6 iyul, 2003

"Azərbaycan" qəzeti, 9 fevral, 2005

"Kaspi", 4-6 avqust, 2001

"Olimpiya dünyası" qəzeti, 11-14 oktyabr, 2002

"Xalq" qəzeti, 14 sentyabr, 1997

"Xalq" qəzeti, 1 iyun, 2002

"Xalq" qəzeti, 11 oktyabr, 2002

"Xalq" qəzeti, 13 may, 2003

"Azərbaycan-İRS" jurnalı, 2003, №14-15.

"Diaspora" jurnalı 2003, №2-3

"Olimpiya" jurnalı, 1998, №1.

"Olimpiya" jurnalı, 1999, №1.

"Olimpiya" jurnalı, 2004, №3.

Azərbaycan Milli Olimpiya Komitəsi 10 il ("Olimpiya" jurnalının xüsusi buraxılışı). Bakı, 2002.

XXVIII Yay Olimpiya Oyunları. AFİNA-2004 ("Olimpiya" jurnalının xüsusi buraxılışı). Bakı, 2002.

"Qobustan" incəsənət toplusu, 1990, №5

"Qobustan" incəsənət toplusu,1972, №2

Azərbaycan Respublikası Ali Sovetinin Məlumatı. 1991, № 24 (853)

Azərbaycan Respublikası Ali Sovetinin Məlumatı. 1992, № 11 (864)

Azərbaycan Respublikası Ali Sovetinin Məlumatı. 1992, № 13 (866)

Azərbaycan Respublikası Ali Sovetinin Məlumatı. 1992, № 13 (866)

Azərbaycan Respublikası Ali Sovetinin Məlumatı. 1992, № 21 (874)

Анекдоты "Мола Насреддин"а. Баку, 1975

Конфликт в Нагорном Карабахе (Сборник статей). Баку, 1990

Народы Кавказа. т.I.Москва, 1960

Народы Кавказа. т.II.Москва, 1962

Яазыки Народов СССР. т.I. Москва, 1966

Языки Азии и Африки. кн. II. Москва, 1978

Алиев К.Г. Писатели античности об Азербайджане. Баку, 2001

Ашурбейли С.Б. История города Баку. (Период средневековья). Баку 1992

Гусейнов Г.Н. Из истории общественной и философской мысли в Азербайджане XIX века. Баку, 1958

Ефендиев И. Народный поет Самед Вургун. Баку, 1956

Жузе П.К. К выяснению значения слова "тат". Баку, 1930

Ибрагимов М.Дж. Предпринимательская деятельность Г.З.Тагиева. Баку, 1990

Миллер Б.В. Талышский язык. Москва, 1953

Мамедова.Ф. Кавказская Албания и албаны. Баку, 2005

Каджар Ч. Старая Шуша. Баку, 2007
Тревер К.В. Очерки по истории и культуре Кавказской
Албании. М-Л., 1959
Фархадов Р. Вагиф Мустафазаде. Баку, 1986
Фатуллаев Ш.С. Градостроительство и архитектура
Азербайджана XIX-начала XX века. Ленинград, 1986
"Бакинский рабочий", 30 декабря 1998

Azeri-British News.1.2. November-December 2001
(Newsletter of the Azerbaijan-Great Britain Youth Society)
"Azerbaijan International", 1997, Winter
"Azerbaijan International", 1998, Autumn.
"Azerbaijan International", 1998, Winter
"Azerbaijan International", 1999, Autumn
"Azerbaijan Review". November/December, 2002
"Azerbaijan Review".March/April, 2003
 Nakhichevan, 2004, March (01)
Silk Road. № 3 (5) 1998. Baku. Azerbaijan University 1998
Investor's Handbook, Baku, 2003
Genocide Khojaly./Project by: Azerbaijan-Great Britain
Youth Society. Baku, 2002
Azerbaijan and Great Britain: Co-operation & Partnership.
1991-2001.
Publisher: Azerbaijan-Great Britain Youth Society Baku,
2002
Azerbaijan. Edited by Tamara Dragadze. London, 2000
Azerbaijan, Baki. Centers of History and Culture, concise
illustrated Reference Book&Guide. By Ismayil Mammadov.
Baku, 2002
Mark Elliot. Azerbaijan with excursions to Georgia.
Trailblazer publications, 2004
Mirzayev R. Road starting from Contract of Century. Baku,
2000
Rasim Efendi. Art of Azerbaijan. Baku, 2004
Qajar Chingiz. The Famous Sons of Ancient and Medieval
Azerbaijan
Swietochowski T. Russia and Azerbaijan. A Borderland in
Transition. New York, 1995
Trading with Azerbaijan. An official publication of the
Azerbaijan Ministry of Trade.
Tagiyeva R. Azerbaijani carpet. Baku, 1999
USACC Investment Guide to Azerbaijan 2000.
Washington, 2000

www.azerbaijan.az
www.karabakh.co.uk
www.heydar-aliyev.org
www.constcourt.gov.az
www.science.az
www. baku-media.ru